Passing By

Passing By

Gender and Public Harassment

Carol Brooks Gardner

UNIVERSITY OF CALIFORNIA PRESS

Berkeley   Los Angeles   London

University of California Press
Berkeley and Los Angeles, California

University of California Press, Ltd.
London, England

Library of Congress Cataloging-in-Publication Data

Gardner, Carol Brooks.
    Passing by: gender and public harassment / Carol Brooks Gardner.
       p.   cm.
    Includes bibliographical references (p. 241) and index.
    ISBN 0-520-20215-5 (pbk; alk. paper)
       1. Sexual harassment of women—Indiana—Indianapolis.
    2. Invective—Indiana—Indianapolis.   3. Etiquette—Indiana—
    Indianapolis.   4. Women—Crimes against—Indiana—Indianapolis.
    I. Title.
    HQ1237.5U6G37   1995
    305.42—dc20   95-3208
                                                          CIP

    2   3   4   5   6   7   8   9

To Abby and Bill
To my mother and my father

Where women walk in public processions in the streets the
    same as the men,
Where they enter the public assembly and take places the
    same as the men;
Where the city of the faithfullest friends stands,
Where the city of the cleanliness of the sexes stands,
Where the city of the healthiest fathers stands,
Where the city of the best-bodied mothers stands,
There the great city stands.

                Walt Whitman, Song of the Broad Axe

CONTENTS

PREFACE

Because our society's sensitivity to public harassment is only beginning, I envision this book as of importance to women and men equally. Because I know that other social groups besides women are targets of public harassment, I intend this book for the general reader. I know, however, that I sometimes use methods and terms with which some readers may be unfamiliar. I have explained these as well as need be, I think. What may be less apparent is the validity and reliability of my sampling approach, that of ethnography, the intensive study of some aspects of a culture. Many anthropologists have written more faithfully and certainly more extensively than I on ethnography as a method. What the general, even the academic, reader needs to recall is that an ethnography concentrates on process and on characterization, not on sophisticated statistics that seem to tell us much but can be pseudo-scientific mystification. Ethnography can also elucidate the out-of-awareness "achievement" of social categories, and this understanding of what we ordinarily accept as seamless and "individualistic" expression as—for the moment—self-conscious attainment is inherent in my approach.

So, although my sample *is* a sizable one, I often speak here in "quasi-numericals" like *frequently* or *most individuals.* As should also be clear from a careful reading, however, I have recorded quite detailed numbers, which are available for any interested reader, as is my open-ended interview schedule.

Another point: I often write as if I alone have discovered public harassment. It *is* true that I have named it. Many colleagues have written about the phenomenon of marked incivility in the street and about streets and public places as sites for more brutal behavior. I am grateful, then, to such authors as Bell (1993), Blauner (1989), Feagin (1991), Feagin and Feagin (1978), and Stanko (1985, 1990). Thus, many academics realize the ramifications of ordinary, taken-for-granted civility. The cost of its loss tells us its importance and the power of its abrogation. Women have not yet had their Stonewalls, but some day they may.

ACKNOWLEDGMENTS

I must thank many who helped me complete this book. First, I owe an intellectual debt to those who have helped me develop my ideas: Elijah Anderson, Nancy S. Blum, Jon Ende, Robert Emerson, Erving Goffman, James A. Holstein, Dell Hymes, Gale Miller, Thaddeus Müller, Melvin Pollner, Dr. Wolfram Rieger, Elizabeth Stanko, Gregory W. H. Smith, Barrie Thorne, Linda Van Leuven, Candace West, and Don Zimmerman. Of course, no one (save Jim Holstein) is responsible for errors I have made. Douglas Maynard, Judith Stacey, and Carol A. B. Warren helped me reorganize an unruly first draft. Cynthia G. Bowman and Gregory Fehribach advised me on the law. Some colleagues were particularly stalwart intellectual beacons and unremitting consciences: I refer to Bob Emerson, Candace West, and Greg Smith. I was guided by the wisdom of my editors, Stanley Holwitz and Rebecca Frazier, and my conscientious copy editor, J. D. Brown. All these academic colleagues were invaluable. In these days of skittish social interpretations and "correctnesses," political and otherwise, conscientious spiritual advice is as invaluable as editorial advice, and even more difficult to come by. Therefore, last, *not* least, I thank Rabbi Sandy Eisenberg Sasso.

Foremost among those who helped with research were my interviewers. Not all have chosen to be identified, since sometimes the
sensitive subject matter of these interviews undeservedly stigmatizes
those who ask as well as those who tell. Those whom I may identify
are: Philip Bryant, John P. Downey, Tanya Gower, Bridget Grimes,
Elise Hertz, Jackie Montrie, Keith Parrish, Susan Petty-Joyce, Marc
Schecter, Melody Owen Stiles, and Brian Withem. Without these interviewers, I could not have covered so extensive a selection of opinion. I am also grateful to students at Indianapolis universities and
Indianapolis residents who allowed me to quote from their written
work: Ouise Berger, Cathy Clark, Elaine Davis, "Mary Doe," John P.
Downey, Almia (Jo) Ferree, Lynda Fox, Donna H., Shannon H.,
Stephanie Mohsenzadeh, Kudzai Mumbiro, Michael Q., "Mary Roe,"
"John Smith," Mary Ellen Ton, and Kelly Wong. Alice Wong was my
conscience concerning women with disabilities. Without Cathy Clark's
aid, the index would never have progressed from A to B.

At Indiana University, Dean John D. Barlow was supportive of
my research with release, time, and funds, as were Deans Barbara
Jackson, Erwin Boschmann, and, foremost, William Plater. Support
from the Indiana University's Center of Philanthropy helped me to
develop the materials for chapter 2's discussion of public aid. At the
Center, I thank in particular Dwight Burlingame and Anita Plotin-
sky. I am very grateful to Alice Brooks Abbott and Morris Dembo for
financial help—the informal, interest-free, family variety.

Research, clerical, and computer assistance from many helped make
the book a reality: Penny Bodenhamer, Wendy Hancock Becher, An-
drea Campoli, Beryl Cohen, Jerry Cummins, Lori Siler, Suzy Sulami,
William Stuckey, and, again, Brian Withem. For hospitality, I am
grateful to Nancy Blum, Marcus Bird, and Ginger Emerson.

Finally, I am grateful to my friends and family, who believed in this
book as much as I did. My mother, Alice Abbott, has always been a
model, even if I've not always been dutiful in profiting from her example. My friends Nancy Blum, Mary Schroeder, and Jesse and Elliott

Berger may be surprised to see their names here: with natures so supportive as theirs, they may not realize how much they have done for me. I thank my husband Bill, who helped in more ways than I can name (and for more months than he probably cares to name). My daughter Abigail helped in many ways, from bringing me dinner, to helping me find a reference buried in a pile of papers, to relating her own observations and experiences. Not for nothing does her Hebrew name mean "service." As I've explained to her, today's children function as did the helpful academic wives of the past: much work, much help, little credit. Undoubtedly these children note—as academic wives must have done—the completion of a book with a sigh of relief. Probably a propitiatory sushi dinner won't suffice for repayment. Perhaps this will: I promise, Abby, to be as helpful when you write your first book as you have been for mine.

CHAPTER ONE

Introduction

Women and Public Places

> I was out bicycling once and I saw a woman who wore a hot-
> pink Spandex body suit, riding a hot-pink ten-speed bike. I assumed
> she wanted to be noticed, so I said hello. She sprinted away from me.
> I have no idea what was on that woman's mind.
>
> *Marty Westerman,* How to Flirt: A Practical Guide *(1992)*

In 1990 I drove from Indianapolis to Washington with my husband and my nine-year-old daughter. We stopped in a small town near the Indiana-Ohio border to refuel the car. As usual, I pumped the gas, then went, by myself, into the station to pay for it. Behind the counter was a young man half my age, hugely fat and grinning broadly. I placed my charge card on the neutral ground of the rubber mat between us, smiled briefly, and stated the amount the pump showed.

The young man completed the electronic transaction. I thanked him politely, and he replied "you're welcome" and moved as if to hand the credit card back. I found myself smiling again as I reached for the card, and as I did so, the young cashier playfully retracted the card and waved it at me, out of my reach.

"Say 'please,'" he said. "Ask for it nicely!"

I smiled again—I could not help myself—but managed to say

nothing, and shaking his head and laughing ruefully the young man at last returned my charge card.

It was a game I recognized from my own experience as a woman in public places and from my interviews with hundreds of women and men in the Midwest and throughout the country. It was not news to me that age and social class—I was at least two decades older than the young cashier and dressed, if not for success, at least professionally— were things that might have counted between two men, yet counted for nothing for me. Nevertheless, being treated as the juvenile or merely playworthy object of someone else's enjoyment will probably always take me by surprise. Like many other women to whom I have spoken in the course of the Indiana interviews reported in this book, in public places, at least, I want to think of myself more as a citizen than as a source for gender games. That fact alone probably accounts for my fascination with public places, where rituals—sometimes argued by women and men alike to be innocuous, even flattering, or explained away as the province only of the lower classes or the youthful—can be transformed into full-fledged verbal abuse or can escalate into unambiguous physical assault, even rape. And although this book focuses on the routine troubles of women, I could also write about some of the routine pleasures of public places. For women and those in other social categories who are disadvantaged in public places, even these routine pleasures will be experienced with knowledge of what *can* occur. A counterpoint to the opening epigraph is this informant's narrative:

> About a year ago, I was aerobic-walking near a mall, for exercise. It wasn't very late, just past dusk. It was the summertime. It was nice out. As I went by one of the stores, a man standing outside said hello to me, and just to be polite, I smiled and said hello back. Then he started to follow me, keeping talking to me. I was only a few blocks away from home, so I started to run. The man started to run too, and he caught me and raped me. At gunpoint. They never caught him.

Such possibilities affect the experience of civility that all citizens feel.

In my work on this book, I discovered I was not the only woman (or indeed the only person of either sex) to be intrigued and troubled by everyday life in public places. Simply put, most of the women I spoke with shared my concerns for the particular ease and even physical safety women feel in public places today. By *public places,* I mean *those sites and contexts that our society understands to be open to all; our characteristic behavior and appearance for public places do and are meant to vary from those for private dwellings.* Communication in public places is characteristically appearance dependent; that is, the individual relies on her or his estimation of another's discernible, visible form as a clue to what is, for the context, significant identity, and the individual understands that others will judge her or him in the same way. In chapter 2, "Contexts," I expand this basic definition to include semipublic venues such as stores and restaurants, public festivals and celebrations, parks and recreational areas, and places of entertainment like movie houses and concert halls. Slightly different and characteristic rules will apply for all of these sites, with all segments of society aiming for civility. But the everyday courtesies we believe to comprise civility can mean more than we ordinarily think.

Both liberals and conservatives now embrace civility as a good, simply because what is evident in our public places is often so horrifying that some call to arms seems needed (see Coser 1988 on the political identification of civility). Formerly, civility was seen as a straitjacket. Now crime is taken to be a reality. Our desire for authenticity as defined by our own social categories produces effects that are in some ways opposite to what we mean by civility: We value whatever the person does if it is an authentic representation of the category we momentarily consider essential to the individual's being *and* is defensible. Thus, we also value the individual's loyalties to the social categories with which we believe she or he should identify—a modern-to-postmodern trouble, since if individuals have ten or twenty selves, any one such self might well be argued to be authentic (Goffman 1959; Tuan

1982). Civility and authenticity can clash when we are among strangers: Often, once civility lapses when authenticity is expressed, as I noted while observing a group of young African-American men. Every passing white stranger, especially the middle-aged and old, was a target for hoots and hollers that referred to their alleged ugliness, yet African-Americans who passed by were conspicuously ignored. This example features public harassment by African-American men to whites of both sexes; but troubles among strangers can be instigated by a member of any group against a member of any group.

These young men's hoots and hollers are among a general set of troubles to which all citizens are subject. I call these actions *public harassment,* that is, *that group of abuses, harryings, and annoyances characteristic of public places and uniquely facilitated by communication in public.* Public harassment includes pinching, slapping, hitting, shouted remarks, vulgarity, insults, sly innuendo, ogling, and stalking. Public harassment is on a continuum of possible events, beginning when customary civility among strangers is abrogated and ending with the transition to violent crime: assault, rape, or murder. Women, upon whose experiences I focus in this book, can currently experience shouted insults, determined trailing, and pinches and grabs by strange men and be fairly certain that no one—not the perpetrator and probably no official—will think anything of note has happened. Thus, public harassment is a sort of civic denial, the study of how, why, and with what effects this harassment exists for women and men.

STUDYING PUBLIC HARASSMENT

In order to represent the views of as many women and men as possible, I observed and interviewed in one city, Indianapolis, Indiana. I do not chronicle what happens across the nation with regard to public harassment; I do provide a detailed description of what happens in one large Midwestern city. I examined public places in Indianapolis both systematically and fortuitously for five years, from 1988 through

1993. I took care in these observations to cover all sections of the city and to be present at varied times of the day in all sections. I also observed at a representative selection of mundane and notable or spectacular events in several public spaces: movie theaters, grocery stores, and dry cleaners, the opera and the symphony, and graduation ceremonies. I took notes on site whenever possible; when it was not, I recorded interactions as soon afterward as I could.

My interviewers scheduled their interviews, and so, for the most part, did I. Some of my interviews were requested on the spot—that is, I sometimes asked an individual if I could interview her or him at the time of the incident. Most were happy to talk, although some were not interested in answering all of the questions I put to them. I have included some partial interviews in my analysis, specifically those that provide interesting insights.

Of the 506 interviews, I did nearly 400, or about 80 percent. I also used fourteen other interviewers, whom I trained for the task myself. These men and women often interviewed informants whose specialized experience in public places, they felt, would match their own. Five of these interviewers were, like myself, white women who identified themselves as heterosexual. Also among my other interviewers were two African-American women, two Asian-American women, and five men. Two interviewers had contacts with gays, lesbians, or bisexuals.

The interviews themselves were free-form and in depth. Interview questions included ones that solicited the person's feelings and opinions about public places, the range of their "good" and "bad" experiences there, and their strategies for managing a situation deemed a "trouble" or a "problem." Informants defined what good and bad experiences were. I also asked whether they had publicly harassed others and, if so, I asked them to give an interpretation for this conduct.

Often, women informants needed little in the way of a formal interview or prepared questions. My interviewers and I were often able to ask informants to talk about their concerns; we discovered that they would neatly cover many or most of our questions without prompting. This was a tribute, perhaps, to how much an informant was troubled by public abuse. A typical interview lasted an hour, although the range was thirty minutes to three hours. Men's interviews tended to be briefer and less detailed than women's, but this was not always the case. Many men had reasons of their own to have experienced public harassment. Premier among men with more experience than they would have liked were gay or bisexual men, men who were members of an ethnic or racial minority like African-, Jewish, or Asian-Americans, and men with disabilities. One of the foremost results of my research was to identify which groups of men did, and which did not, feel that they shared the troubles of public harassment with women.[1]

My interviewers and I spoke with 506 citizens of Indianapolis and the surrounding area: 293 were women and 213 were men. About half of these 506 informants identified themselves as white; 21 of these identified themselves as Jews. About half of the 506 identified themselves as people of color or as racially mixed. Indianapolis is about 20 percent nonwhite, so I overrepresented nonwhites in my group of informants to get a satisfactory sample of Asian-Americans, African-Americans, and those who identified themselves as "mixed race." There were 259 white informants, 114 African-Americans, 58 Asian-Americans, and 75 informants who identified themselves as racially mixed. All groups were divided approximately evenly between women and men.

All social classes were represented by the respondents. I evaluated socioeconomic status by occupation, speech, and income, judging 116 informants to be upper class, 285 to be middle class, and 105 to be working or lower class. Informants were relatively young: 100 were between fifteen and twenty years of age, 299 were between twenty-one and thirty-five, 75 were between thirty-six and sixty-five, and 32 between sixty-six and eighty-five. Forty informants mentioned they had a disability that they felt was a difficulty in public places; these disabil-

1. See the discussion in chapter 5, "Interpretations."

ities ranged from stuttering, to hearing loss, to epilepsy, to diabetes, to using a wheelchair. Thus, 466 informants allowed themselves to be identified as able-bodied.

About 10 percent of informants identified themselves as gay, lesbian, or bisexual. I did not specifically ask informants for their sexual preference, but some disclosed this to me. A total of 454 informants either identified themselves as heterosexual or expressed no sexual preference to me or to other interviewers (I presume there were gays, lesbians, and bisexuals among the 454). Of the 52 informants who identified themselves as gay, lesbian, or bisexual, 29 were lesbian or bisexual women and 23 were gay or bisexual men.

Sixty-six of the women interviewed had had experience with violence or near-violence by men in public places: 12 had been stranger-raped; 22 had been in a situation that they thought was likely to turn into stranger-rape but had not; and 32 had experienced serious physical harassment from a stranger—one woman was knocked off her bicycle into a ditch when a man playfully patted her buttocks, other women were simply and casually punched by passing strangers. I neither particularly selected nor rejected women who identified themselves as having experienced violence in public places. I did not ask women directly if they had been stranger-raped, so that the 34 who chose to reveal a rape or near-rape were probably only a portion of the women in the sample who had had these experiences.

In general, I ask the reader to accept Indianapolis as representative not in any statistical sense but as representative of the range, diversity, and tenor of public harassment and women's reactions to it. Although there are certainly ways in which the Indianapolis area may be typical of the state or the Midwest, I have not distinguished what is distinct about Indianapolis, or Indiana, or the Midwest from what is typical of the United States as a whole. My interviews elsewhere in the country suggest that there are more patterns that are nationally typical than there are patterns that can be ascribed to regional color. My purpose is to outline the basic situation of public harassment.

Although my observations continued for five years and although my interviews run into the hundreds, it is not a statistical portrayal I give. Instead, I suggest that Indianapolis is a microcosm that represents the public harassment of women by men throughout the United States. I do present some data and suggest some correlations, but I am not interested in numbers of incidents *per se*. My primary interest is how women manage public places—and what these tactics have to say about women's situation in society in general. I am also interested in what men have to say about their public harassment of women and how both sexes interpret public harassment: We live in a time of competing paradigms for events like public harassment, and in a time of voluble interpreters, both generous and mean-spirited on all positions. Women's and men's interpretations limn the present relationship between the sexes as much as they do public harassment.

This is not, however, a story of one situation in which women are besieged by men. Instead, it is a story of women contending with difficult circumstances for which they receive little sympathy from popular belief, advice, or legal and medical practice. Perhaps this book will provide some of that guidance to women, and to men as well.

The ways in which the women I interviewed coped with individual circumstances will not always please readers. Having lectured on this research in different venues and for different audiences, I know that what some of my informants say and what some have done will amuse or outrage some readers. Yet part of the reader's task is to feel the situation of a woman experiencing harassment: to feel her fright, to understand what she has been taught and read, to think—as she thinks at the moment—of what might happen to her, and to remember—as she remembers—what has happened to her among strangers.

GENDER AND THE IMPACT OF PUBLIC HARASSMENT

Public places can engender a characteristic set of incivilities that can injure an individual's self-esteem either fleetingly or, since the occurrence of these incivilities is repetitive and recursive, more momentously and even permanently. Women often see the dilemma and dissatisfaction of public harassment as evocative of larger issues in their relations with men—as men often see them as evoking their own perceived gender dilemmas. Few women have practiced gender-specific public harassment toward strange men with anything like the same sense of freedom, entitlement, and righteousness that men exhibit, aside from the breach that teen or young adult women sometimes accomplish in groups.

Yet women do publicly harass. Often female harassment is milder; sometimes gender is the focus, but more often it is race or ethnicity, sexual preference, or disability. Many have documented women's fear of stranger-rape (Brownmiller 1974; Stanko 1985). It is disturbing that, as much as fear of rape restrains women in public places, women *do* muster sufficient racism or homophobia to overcome these fears and to harass members of "other" ethnicities or sexual preference groups.

We as a society have neglected public harassment, especially the heterosexually romanticized public harassment that women experience from men: the vulgar slur that pretends to be flattery, the act of caressing a breast or buttock that a man might explain was compelled because the woman was so alluring, the screams and blows from playful men who harry women because men believe them lovely—or because they believe them to be no better than dogs. Instead of examining the breached rules of public places *per se,* society prefers to examine tangential issues—architecture, city life, etiquette, and civility—that reflect some, although customarily few, of these public harassment abuses.

This neglect is regrettable. In women's lives, public harassment abuses are frequent reminders of the ever-present relevance of their gender. In the history-less present of public places, gender norms need to be constantly established and are being constantly accomplished. Public harassment reinforces the basic division between the sexes and prescribes the conduct or mere presence of some while punishing others. In the same way, African-American citizens of Indianapolis consistently report that white merchants and clerks sometimes doubt their ability to pay for even quite small purchases or purchases the white person believes are luxuries (Gardner 1994). As a result, for African-Americans in general, every normal act of paying becomes imbued with proof of financial stability.

Likewise, gender among strangers must constantly be "proven," even though this is out of awareness, never presumed to be achieved once and for all. Women can come to understand tacitly or explicitly that their claims as members of the category "women" are something that they need to work constantly at achieving, with the hope that this achievement will prove satisfactory to their current audience—and that audience in the public realm may rapidly shift and thus change its standards, making it hard to know how to please reliably. It is not simply a "good" appearance that will make a woman immune (she may hope) to public harassment or even public notice, since each judge evaluates one woman differently. Neither is "good behavior," even when understood as proper traditional feminine behavior, any guarantee of escape from public harassment, since the extremes of "flattering" public attention are sometimes as troublesome as disapprobation.

In the course of mounting this proof, women sometimes modify their lives and attitudes, their opinions about themselves, their appearance—even their bodies by, for example, plastic surgery. A government lawyer in her thirties told me she had changed her pattern of travel to work to avoid the summertime clutter of male workers near her downtown Indianapolis office building who shouted their appraisals of every entering woman:

> I now take the long way to work. That is to say, I go about three blocks out of my way, so I can enter inconspicuously at the back of the building. I don't want to go all through that, the hassling and the grief from guys. I don't want to be reminded how they, men, have power over me, as a woman. I just want to concentrate on my job and think about being a good public servant. I want that to be most important.

For this woman, the workers symbolized greater issues, to be sure. But is her case unusual, or is her discomfort atypical? My observations and interviews say that neither is true.

INTERPRETING PUBLIC HARASSMENT

In chapter 4, "Behavior," I elaborate on some forms of public harassment often encountered by women and others. For now, it will be enough to point out that public harassment can result in an alienation of the individual in public places from fellow citizens both female and male, undermine the trust and civility that many analysts now hold up as the cure for urban ills, and create both a gulf between private and public realms and a gulf between the individual's private and public selves.

Forced dependence on the private realm is often counseled as a remedy for troubles in public places: Women are, and have traditionally been, advised to forsake success outside the home for contented containment within it. (When one encounters a front-page article in the travel section of the Sunday *New York Times* on the attractions of "travel in the home"—armchair travel—it is somehow natural that a woman is the author [Berne 1993].) Thus, when speaking of incidents of public harassment that women have traditionally regarded as trivial or on which women are reminded to "refuse to dwell," some women informants suggested that public harassment is another method of "segregation," a force for relegation to the home. Some women, in more dramatic comparisons, likened their experiences to the Holocaust, to the rape of women and girls in former Yugoslavia, to the experience of being in a pornographic movie, and to Asian-American internment during World War II. Further, white women often compared their situation to that of African-Americans in general; some African-American women discovered through public harassment that they lived in a sexist as well as a racist society.

In short, the public harassment of women is pertinent to feminist concerns with the reification of the public/private split. Public harassment also suggests ways in which a different environment has affected women's sense of self in society. Public harassment suggests that a woman's unchallenged female self is still located in the home: It is at home, less so in the workplace, that a woman is still an authority on her own experience, without the clutter of etiquette and popular advice, medicalized and legalized labels, and socialization to cloud what she knows to be true. In public places, the harassment of women can still be romanticized, eroticized, or erased.

Incidents like the one I experienced in the Indiana gas station are, I know, at the innocuous end of a spectrum of public harassment that affects women. Many women informants—and more men—actively supported these acts with traditional depoliticized interpretations. Yet almost every woman who supported them was also disturbed by many public harassment abuses; almost no men counted themselves upset by any form of public harassment.

Part of the message of this book is that romanticized accounts of public harassment and unsatisfactory strategies for managing public harassment are not necessarily linked. Women informants who expressed traditional romanticized definitions of public harassment did not invariably feel that they were unable to handle harassment; conversely, women with highly developed politicized feminist consciousness were not always satisfied with their methods of handling harassment. In fact, chapters 5 and 6, on interpretations of and strategies for handling public harassment, tell a more complicated story. Public harassment is, paradoxically, a situation in which even self-identified feminists said they fell back on what they counted as "traditional" strategies for sound and self-protective reasons I will detail later. More than this, women who specifically said they were "not feminists" sometimes acted more actively than did their feminist sisters.

Our current attention to public places is characterized by media attention to the homeless, the deinstitutionalized chronically mentally ill, the affronts to those perceived as lesbian and gay, drive-by shootings, and the victims of startling acts of violence such as the Central

Park Jogger, Rodney King, and Reginald Denny. I am afraid that these subjects will haunt us for some time. Media attention has also been focused on the power of racial conflict, discrimination, and harassment to burst from private places and workplaces into the public realm. Although I concentrate on more mundane and often verbal interactions or minor physical altercations, all these recent media topics underline the price women, gay men and lesbians, and people of color can pay for their trust in and civility toward strangers. These stories also highlight the sound reasons informants sometimes had for suspicion of strangers. These extreme possibilities always coexist with the civility-based etiquette of public places—an uneasy pairing in the consciousness of many citizens who venture into public. Public harassment has long existed, but for some groups it is now beginning to be a more widespread or legitimized cause for complaint and action.

Another part of the message of this book, then, is that although public harassment like gay-baiting and -bashing and racial tension and hostility are realities in public places, we have no excuse to ignore the sexual discrimination and harassment that also occur there. Our attention to these other forms of conflict forbids us to take gender-based public harassment for granted any longer or to write it off as a signifier of little more than momentary inconvenience. Instead, we need to see public harassment as on a continuum of incivility that we can manage by informal strategies or by invoking existing laws or creating new ones.

Most of the sociological and feminist research on the position of women in contemporary American society has focused on either the home or the workplace. With several notable exceptions, such as the work of Mary Jo Deegan (1987), Lyn Lofland (1973), and Elizabeth Stanko (1985), the situation of women in public places has been neglected. In part this neglect reflects popular notions of the irrelevance or triviality of public place behaviors and situations that suggest public places are merely irrelevant transitways for citizens engaged in work, leisure, or travel. But incidents of public harassment are not irrelevant and are sometimes deeply felt and significant to the individual. To ignore public harassment robs us of understanding of a context, the public realm, in which we all spend an appreciable portion of our lives and which, indeed, most of us could not for long avoid. Worse, to ignore public harassment blinds us to the active discrimination that we still tolerate and that we ourselves—women as well as men, Jews as well as Gentiles, people of color as well as whites—commit in public places. For, paradoxically, public places are contexts that also allow the disadvantaged to avenge themselves against the advantaged or, in the contextual pecking order, against the even more disadvantaged.

WOMEN AND MEN, TARGETS AND OFFENDERS

Public harassment affects men as well as women, and women are sometimes responsible for acts of public harassment. If public harassment cannot be understood as a situation in which men are inevitably vile offenders and women are inevitably innocent gulls, then public places are perhaps the most complex of all contexts to analyze. Women sometimes publicly harass members of social categories different from their own or social categories that they think merit disapproval. I once saw an Indianapolis woman, passing by a gay bar, momentarily drop the hand of her toddler to scream at, then shove, a man who was attempting to enter. She thereby provided passing members of the public with as neat a lesson in virulent homophobia as the lessons in virulent sexism provided by any group of foul-mouthed construction workers who touch and scream at passing women. She also furnished her child with a vibrant lesson about the disdain to which gay men can be freely subjected and the violence with which they may be treated. Onlookers learn from public harassment, too: Here, they may have learned about their fellow citizens' fear- or hatred-induced inaction in coming to the defense of, even rebuking, someone categorized as gay. I have also observed women insult members of a race different from their own or, as service personnel, subject someone of a different race to heavily communicated inattention, plodding service, recalcitrant help, humiliating scrutiny, or condescending and intrusive banter that played to the customer's race. Women as well as men also practice public harassment against people with disabilities.

Public harassment can be practiced by and on anyone. It is one weapon in the armamentarium for indicating contempt, displeasure, and veiled loathing and hostility. Although I concentrate on women as targets in this book, plainly there are other books to be written about the public harassment of lesbians, bisexuals, and gay men or the public harassment of African-Americans or other ethnic groups.

By practicing public harassment, women contribute to the continual sustenance of a social order, namely the public order, that is capable of repressing and demeaning others. Thus, women often sustain the character of the very order that victimizes them. This is so because of their behavior and attitudes toward public harassment in which gender seems to be the point, as well as toward public harassment directed at a victim's ethnicity or disability. Some women refuse to criticize men offenders; some women fault women victims. Those women who practice public harassment on members of another social category give themselves a stake in the traditional apologetics their own harassers will use. This leads to another conundrum, that of choosing strategies for response and philosophies to match those strategies. The call is for civility, but what is needed are practical solutions that can achieve civility where it is lacking and preserve it where it exists.

In the chapters that follow, I elaborate the public harassment of women by men as pervading all contexts, involving all types of men, and encompassing many kinds of behavior and degrees of offense and harm. I also describe how women and men account for public harassment, and how women choose strategies for dealing with it. To begin, I describe how targets of public harassment interact with, modify the actions of, and potentially change places with their harassers. Involved in this groundwork is to make the basis of my work explicit.

I emphasize certain public places among those generally recognized as such by Americans. Of course I am limited by the character of Indianapolis, which lets me report (for example) citizens' behavior in the carnival atmosphere that overtakes the city during the Indianapolis 500, but prevents me from writing about a city that allows same-sex citizens to kiss or hold hands in public places (as I might if I were writing about parts of Manhattan) or ensures that access to public transportation enables people with mobility impairment to be more faithfully represented in public places (as I might if I were writing about Berkeley, California). My focus on Indianapolis constrains my discussion, for the most part, to the public places of cities rather than small towns. My methodology also limits me to a discussion of public places of the present time without much attention to their development. In addition, my discussion is based of course on the public places of American society as distinct from other cultures.

TARGETS OF PUBLIC HARASSMENT

I write especially about the ways in which the various manifestations of public (dis)order to which women are regularly subjected are part of a more general pattern of the communication through which public order can and does operate. More specifically, I explore the characteristic form of social control that we find with regard to these breaches of public order and speculate on the ways in which this social control is related to the experiences of women. I suggest, first of all, that it is useful to think of women—as well as some other groups—as habitually *situationally disadvantaged* in public places: Whatever their status or advantage in other contexts, in public places they are subject to public harassment.

Targets of public harassment are often, although not always, the traditional targets of discrimination elsewhere. These are women, ethnic and racial minorities, gays, people with disabilities, the fat, the old, the disordered—even the inappropriately or unattractively dressed and their complement, those who stand out winningly in appearance. Celebrities and the notorious will sometimes be disadvantaged in public places by autograph hounds, gawkers, *paparazzi,* stalkers, or aficionados who seek the most modest of souvenirs: just to behold the famous. If the famous receive treatment akin to public harassment, there is something different at stake when a curious fan lingers, leers, goggles, stalks, or unendingly snaps pictures of a favorite star. In gender-based harassment, the impression left on an anonymous woman in public (and, arguably, on the harasser and all who witness the act as well) is that the victim is equal to and can be compared with all other women; what the individual who intrudes on a celebrity seeks is tied to her or his singularity. Strange men on the street certainly stalk women, importune them, and stare, but none ever asks a passing anonymous woman for her autograph.

The distinctive public treatment of women in America is influenced by tradition and custom, law, and even medical and psychiatric labels. These areas share underpinnings that support and sustain the social order of public places with regard to gender and the expectations for and practices of public harassment. The prescriptions to women in public places that are supported by etiquette, crime prevention, law, and medicine contain one general theme: The competence of women is presumed to be limited when compared to that of men. Traditional rules of etiquette support this limited competence by denying women certain activities such as smoking in public, by requiring that women be accompanied in public, and by instructing women to mute their presence by wearing drab or unremarkable clothing or by keeping their voices low and their carriage dainty and graceful. Even when women are advised to take up certain strategies to "prevent crime" in public, these strategies too often involve symbolic dependency and incompetence.[2] Our culture also names and labels mental illnesses of public places, the foremost of them agoraphobia (pp. 35–40).

2. These strategies are discussed in chapter 6.

These illnesses are also understood as affecting women and men differently, that is, as being "gendered"; thus they exaggerate, recapitulate, and sustain women's fear and men's aggression in public. Ironically, agoraphobia effectively removes women (or reinforces their removal) from the public order; it helps segregate public places in terms of gender and may reinforce for men the notion that the public is their realm, in which women are welcomed principally as decorative and insecure.

POPULAR ETIQUETTE AND ADVICE: ROMANTICIZING THE PUBLIC ORDER

Traditional American etiquette of public places is the expression of a shared set of norms for presentation and conduct—in short, etiquette tells us how society thinks individuals should relate to the public order. Gender is often a central consideration in this relational behavior.

Overall, our civility-based etiquette for public places both assumes equal rights for all and attempts to ensure fulfillment of special needs, such as those of the elderly or people with disabilities; it both guarantees the individual at least some degree of self-expression and curtails the impact her or his self-expression could have on others. When conflicts between individuals arise, there is an etiquette for defenders and critics alike, even when the issue has special moral loading, as does smoking (Ford 1988:35). Gender differences are presently downplayed as factors in public life, however; indeed, to do so is part of the new "egalitarian" etiquette of equal responsibility in public (Hochschild 1991).

Inasmuch as the requirements of etiquette demand that women demonstrate their gender in public places in ways that have connotations of, for example, frailty, incompetence, and subordination, the individual who complies implies (or is willing for the moment to seem to imply) a larger belief in the present system of gender relations as well. Part of our assumptions about behavior in public places is that, overall, this behavior serves as reliable evidence for, or a clue to, private identity and behavior. Public harassment attempts to suggest there is a congruence between public and private selves. Traditional etiquette—with which women are typically acquainted, even if they choose not to meet its expectations—provides just this type of schooling. Some women choose to ignore traditional etiquette in favor of the more egalitarian model, and some men do so too, but traditional expectations in places like streets and restaurants remain an uneasy presence nonetheless. Such gender expectations, although they may not be chosen, are still part of what women (and men) know is available as acceptable behavior, one of a variety of paths of action to recognize, evaluate, choose, take, and support.

There are four different general dimensions along which etiquette and sometimes "prudent" advice on crime prevention for women suggest women's presence be marked in public places: (1) in some situations, women should be absent from public places; (2) women should adopt distinctive behavior when in public and especially so when with men in a public courtship situation; (3) companions can provide a woman with the solution to many of the discomforts of public places; and (4) women should behave as unremarkably as possible when in public, customarily damping appearance and activity. These recommendations constitute part of folk wisdom and appear in advice manuals, and have done so consistently from the 1860s. Etiquette and crime-prevention advisers tell women to avoid public places at night, state that a "true lady" does not walk in certain neighborhoods, or observe that proper women avoid bars and other environments that connote moral laxity. Etiquette also suggests that women in public places practice an abridged agenda of activities. For example, women should not engage in traditionally "masculine" activities: They should not smoke while walking on city or town streets (although women may smoke if they wish on country roads, where they are less likely to be observed by many people [Vanderbilt 1972:317]). Women were once specifically enjoined to maintain a modest, graceful, and measured gait—certainly not a purposeful "masculine" stride—when in public and to avoid looking at people, happenings, or the offerings of shop windows. To look seemed "an invitation to the impertinent" (Aresty 1970:206, analyzing nineteenth-century etiquette manuals). To accept this advice could result in a population of women who put at least some of their energy when in public into looking demonstrably, if silently, "like women," rather than, for instance, enjoying a walk or the passing pedestrian parade. Then too, in the service of crime prevention, women are often contradictorily advised to limit the ways in which they can be identified as women, the better to discourage attack. In short, a woman has always been obligated to try to appear to be someone whom a discerning heterosexual man would be eager to know. At the same time, she must make it clear that to secure her acquaintance would be a taxing act, one not to be accomplished by a stranger or, at least, not just any stranger.

As etiquette suggests, a woman should take a companion with her as a solution to the prohibition on appearing alone. Erving Goffman wrote of the appearance of a woman in public places as an "incomplete participation unit": observers always expect to see her presence ratified by another individual, preferably a man, and she herself may feel awkward when alone (Goffman 1971). In fact, a shrewd "solution" for the woman prohibited from engaging in some public activities—such as dining out, or simply being present in public at certain hours or in certain areas—is to have someone else engage in them for her. Chaperons and escorts were recommended in the nineteenth and early twentieth centuries for women making even modest forays outside the home. A woman taking a short trip, for instance, could expect an escort to accompany her to the depot, check her baggage, procure her ticket, scout out her seat, stow her packages or luggage, and "make her seat and surroundings as agreeable as possible, taking a seat near her, or by the side of her if she requests it, and do all he can to make her journey a pleasant one" (Aresty 1970:206, quoting an 1850 book).

Today, some women etiquette writers see the advantage of a companion to buffer a woman from men with less-than-courteous behavior: "I admit I do not mind the protection of a man on those occasions when I am about to be accosted by someone a little more crazed or dangerous . . . as often occurs on the streets of our larger cities" (Stewart 1987:393). Companions both solve and bring about what women perceive as problems of public places: Once a woman has secured a companion, she is, she might say, protected from strangers, but she is still faced with any problems posed by the companion's presence.

Advice also counsels a woman to adapt herself to the public sphere by calling as little attention to herself as possible—she should mute individuality but not gender. Such requirements emphasize that the public realm is a man's realm, not a woman's. There have been and continue to be a number of methods for accomplishing this public blandness. In the nineteenth century, for example, etiquette writers advised women to encroach as little as possible on the public by speaking as little and as quietly as they could (Farrar 1849:238). One authority of the day noted that a woman who was expressive—even visible—in public places might have her conduct open to the worst possible interpretation: In public, "let your conduct be modest and quiet" (Hartley 1860:113; see also "Censor" c. 1899:109). Women were advised to select clothing that was visually "quiet" for public wear, so as not to attract the eye of others or suggest unseemly pride in appearance, and were sometimes told in manuals that it was "never good form to be elaborately dressed in a public place" (Manning c. 1880: 328; see also Dale 1891:139). A dress for the street should be "quiet in color," the bonnet or hat "quiet and inexpressive" (Manning c. 1880: 239). A proper woman's clothing spoke in genteel and dulcet tones: she need not.

One way to avoid distinguishing oneself in public is to make sure that the public self cannot be traced to the private one; that is, it remains anonymous. Etiquette manuals specify that, although a woman in public will be noted by men and possibly even appreciated, she is not to be identified. She is expected to restrict information that will allow others, men especially, to initiate or further acquaintance with her. For example, she is not to freely give out her name or any information that connotes she will be available or accessible in the future.

In addition to these four recommendations for communicating gender in public places, codified etiquette suggests what a woman should do when etiquette fails to protect her in public, especially from mild harassment. Some advice of the last thirty years tells the offended woman to do whatever she likes as long as she continues to feel "in control" (see, for example, *Glamour* 1969:41). Recent writing is not typically so open-minded: It frequently reinforces a woman's sense that public harassment is her fault by removing the offense from the public context and making it seem harmless, calling a woman's attention to only a small set of public abuses, and suggesting few, if any, satisfactory plans to counter harassment. Traditional advice and etiquette counsel women gratefully to accept or purposefully to ignore verbal and nonverbal harassment in general.

Women are also inhibited from assertively reacting to men who offend them by the canon of popular and psychiatric advice about such men, a canon that simultaneously warns women that offenders like *frotteurs,* exhibitionists, and voyeurs are generally harmless, yet all the same can be lethal. A newspaper column in the early 1960s provided one interpretation when it asked women, "Do You Like to Be Whistled At?" and received, for example, such positive answers as these: Whistles are expressions of approval, compliments, and "a perk-me-up to a girl" (quoted in Goffman 1963:144–145*n*). Women can be offered a set of "right" and "wrong" responses, as in a *Glamour* magazine test—titled "Do You Act Like a Beauty?"—that gave its readers lessons in how to act as responsibly beautiful women:

> You're walking along the street and a workman whistles appreciatively at you. You:
> a. Ignore him.
> b. Tell him he's being pretty fresh.

    c. Call a cop.

    d. Smile in friendly acknowledgment and keep walking.

  (*Glamour* 1969:138–139)

Glamour's correct answer is "d."

    In the beginning of the second wave of the women's movement, feminist advice occasionally appeared (see, for example, Feminist Intervention Group 1974), as did academic analyses of the sometimes explosive changes in public etiquette even among the unacquainted (Walum 1974 is one example). The tide seems to have turned, however. In response to various forms of nonverbal and verbal harassment in public, a woman in the otherwise more egalitarian 1980s (and 1990s) is brusquely advised to "learn to walk with your nose in the air without falling off the curb" (Martin 1982:105). Such curt advice, echoed by women's memories of their family's socialization about how a woman should act in public, makes it easy to see why evaluative public harassment pervades all public contexts—a woman's appearance is a sturdy standard by which to judge and a sturdy staff on which to lean should a man want to manufacture an occasion to harass.

    A woman's appearance is, of course, a different entity from a man's. It is a part of every situation in which she finds herself; there are, in some sense, no dinners for which she does not have to dress. More, a woman's appearance is public information, addressed, as Goffman said in conversation, "to whom it may concern." It is understandable that there is often an asymmetry of attractiveness between the man who utters an evaluative remark and the woman who receives it. Women informants noted that men delivering evaluative street remarks, even if the comments were positive, often fell far below middle-class standards of dress tidiness and hygiene themselves.

    Cases where the usual standards of appearance, class, health, or race are mixed are especially striking and clarify how much more closely defined in public women are when compared to men. I once saw a stylish woman dressed in a fashionably short-skirted suit and silk blouse that I recognized as a designer ensemble costing more than $500. As she exited a downtown skyscraper, attaché case in one hand and a co-ordinating $200 purse in the other, a shabbily dressed, filth-caked man surveyed her critically. He tried to grab her arm and missed, but nevertheless got off a salvo bespeaking his fashion expertise: "*That* skirt's too short for a suit. Looks silly. Why don't you dress decent? Looks funny." Her shoulders stiffened, then slumped, as she walked away. Undoubtedly, something spurs the lower classes to jeer at the upper; their usual point is the greater pretense and posturing of the upper classes. Women often said they could more easily construe a comment, touch, or other instance of public harassment as "complimentary" if it came from a well-dressed, attractive man of their own or a higher so-cial class. In these reversals, a woman could be revealed as an unthink-ing classist or racist: Harassment, she might imply, is the act of a social inferior.

Thus, the usual stance of the writers of etiquette books is to advise a woman to ignore public harassment or put the best face on a harass-ing incident. In this way, the woman who has been positively evalu-ated by a passing strange man might read in an etiquette manual that the man was helping correct her appearance flaws, bolstering her con-fidence, or actually had enabled her "to project the aura of beauty to the men who are really in your life and not just passing by" (Geng 1979:76). But these explanations are often labored, and etiquette by definition deals only with those offenses decent enough to be men-tioned at all. No etiquette book advises a woman if, how, or how hard she should slap the man who has just covertly stroked her breast as she stands in a queue at a ticket counter. It is little wonder that a woman who reported such an incident said she spent most of her five or so minutes in line debating what she should do. By the time she de-cided, her harasser had skulked away. In short, etiquette and advice books often dispense scant advice after all; they suggest few options to ensure safety whether in any given incident or in the future and fail to inform women of legal options.

Other etiquette writers advise men to intrude on a strange woman's privacy in public in the spirit of courtship and appreciation. With this in mind, a manual for teenage boys suggests that "wolf whistles are a harmless pastime and a big compliment to a girl" (Corinth and Sargent 1970:69). Trailing strange women can be advised as a proper step to secure attention and acquaintance, as when a young man who fancies a young woman is counseled to watch the woman from the window to ascertain her schedule, then follow her to strike up an acquaintance (Corinth and Sargent 1970:68).

In part, I suggest, the current discrepancy between etiquette rules for women and those for men exists because the role that women already play in public subjects them to other strategies of limited competence. The public order supplies women with a self that is regularly profaned, especially when women are young, by catcalls, vulgarity, and other street remarks, by differential and usually poorer treatment in shops and restaurants, by varying expectations of what items of information a woman is obliged to disclose. But women have more tasks in public places than to project a pleasing appearance: They are also expected to appear and to act in ways that are actively "crime-preventive." In this, women in public have responsibility distinguished from that of men.

SAFE CONDUCT: ADVICE TO WOMEN ON PREVENTING CRIME

In addition to providing constant evidence that they are women interested in the attention of men—that is, interested in heterosexual courtship—and are women of traditional mold, women are also obliged to be conscious of their sex's duty to "prevent crime." For women in public, crime prevention does not mean to refrain from pulling a bank heist or turning a mean penny as a pickpocket: For women, crime prevention is, essentially, evading the role of target for men criminals by muting personal attractiveness. That there is such a volume of this "crime-preventive" literature directed toward women victims, not men perpetrators, is significant.

A woman is to seem identifiably a woman in public places, but not an easily available one. This combination of tasks is one that can ruin life in public places for any woman, especially the young, adventurous, and intelligent, as this journal entry written by Sylvia Plath at the age of nineteen suggests:

> Being born a woman is my awful tragedy. . . . Yes, my consuming desire to mingle with road crews, sailors and soldiers, barroom regulars—to be part of a scene, anonymous, listening, recording—all is spoiled by the fact that I am a girl, a female always in danger of assault and battery. My consuming interest in men and their lives is often misconstructed as a desire to seduce them, or as an invitation to intimacy. Yes, God, I want to talk to everybody I can as deeply as I can. I want to be able to sleep in an open field, to travel west, to walk freely at night. (Plath 1982:77–78)

There are, and for some time have been, a plethora of books and articles directed to women in the name of street crime prevention. Men have been the authors of most of these books for the last twenty-five years. Often these books have titles like *How to Protect Yourself Today* or *Lady Beware!* There is no complementary literature for men: When books are specifically written for men, they are overwhelmingly on self-defense skills. Available in addition is a general, non-gender-specific literature on crime prevention, and to a lesser degree on self-defense, now that every large city and many small cities envision urban territory as a battleground and the well-secured house as the only haven.

The subset of literature directed at women, however, stands apart in the extremity of measures advised and the amount of fear engendered. Perhaps this asymmetry is a sound one: Crimes may be more psychologically traumatic for women, and there is certainly no equivalent of rape for men by women. Regardless, this literature is notable for the near-paranoia and discomfort that would result if women applied their recommended course of action faithfully. The point, then, is not to stress that these measures are or are not wise, but to contemplate the type of public existence that they foster in women. Sometimes advice books for women are explicitly directed to the men who, a book assumes, will actually instruct women in self-defense (see Tegner 1965).

I am of course discussing mainly advice articles and books that advise women to take up strategies other than fighting or battling back. In the last ten years, a small but increasing number of articles recommends "self-defense" fighting instead of the "self-defense" skill of evasion. Other articles engage in a debate between the merits of fight versus flight, typically leaving the reader in a quandary.

Not only do women understand crime to be an integral possibility in public places, but they are also presented folklore and advice that contains its own dilemmas, one of which is the tension between a woman's obligation to be attractive *and* to prevent crime. For example, women can read that while conducting themselves with circumspection they must nevertheless project a feminine appearance. Often, a woman reads, the most valuable safety technique is that which allows her to combine traditional appearance with safety—to "still be aggressive in certain appropriate areas and at the same time maintain [her] own self-defined degree of femininity" (Burg 1979:12), to look "feminine but not vulnerable" (Lomack 1966:iii). Crime-prevention writing tells a woman that she must not slouch down the street in army fatigues with a grenade in her belt, looking over her shoulder at every footfall. She should be safe, but approachable. She should be safe, but well-turned-out. She should be safe, but skillful with the latest practices of makeup application. She should be safe, but always prepared to smile in friendly self-confidence. For a time, every media report on women's crime prevention alluded to Guardian Angel Lisa Sliwa, a model *and* an effective crime-fighter. So could we be, too, these reports implied. An article in *Vogue,* no doubt meant to quiet women's fears about danger in public places, showed a photo of Sliwa in well-tailored camouflage, slick hairdo, and full makeup and noted that she "does modeling to pay bills" for her crime-prevention training program (Schefer 1985:496).

Researchers state that, although men experience crime in higher numbers, women report a higher fear of crime (Balkin 1979:343–358; Clemente and Kleiman 1977). In public, fear of rape is a cardinal fear for women (Riger and Gordon 1981:71–92; Warr 1985), since public places are the most common sites for stranger rape (Ledray 1986). Yet thoughtful researchers such as Zauberman have pointed out that social science has sometimes conflated women's fear of rape with women's fear of public harassment: Acts that swell the statistics are in some cases, then, acts of public harassment (1982).

Sometimes etiquette and popular wisdom combine to suggest that there is another reason for keeping to a home that comes to seem like a bastion: If women are harshly judged in public, the home can appear the only shelter from such criticism. All women, moreover, are advised to prevent crime by making their homes even greater prisons. One recommendation is that women simply stay home at night; another exhorts women to erect barricades. Sometimes the barricades involve only the prudent acquisition of artifacts such as locks, curtains that do not admit light or allow shadow, window grilles, and other means to baffle peeping and entry. In other cases these strategies involve constant self-monitoring and much preparation, even aid by a man who plays the part of the evildoer in order to judge the efficacy of the precautions: A woman is told to have a boyfriend, husband, or ex-husband scrutinize her home to make sure there is no chink through which entry, either physical or visual, might be gained. Women are sometimes encouraged to think of their homes as minor Maginot lines and strange men as slavering opportunists:

> With regard to windows, there is another important word on prevention: A woman should never be visible to persons on the outside, particularly if she is alone. Everyone from Peeping Toms to rapists

and sadistic killers, let alone normal males, will be attracted if he spots a nude, semi-dressed, or even a fully but enticingly dressed woman through an uncurtained window. (Barthol 1979:42–43)

When fortifications are adopted, a woman at home may find herself as preoccupied with crime as she is when outside.

Women themselves report that they take great pains to avoid crime when in public places. Yet because women are fearful of crime and because this fear ends at no predictable age and can be avoided by no reliable means, women can never be sure that their precautions will be effective. Likewise, women can never be sure what activities on a man's part are precursors to battery, rape, or other violent crime, so that women commonly classify any public harassment as abuse preceding rape or violent crime (Grahame 1985). Too, folk knowledge and popular prescriptive advice can have significant repercussions on women's interaction in public places, on the way in which women are perceived, and on the way in which women perceive themselves (Heath 1984). Women's perceived responsibility for victimization has led them to define part of their task as "becoming streetwise," "taking necessary precautions," and "preventing crime" (Edwards 1987; Radford 1987).

Women often dutifully say they feel that they should follow folk wisdom and recommendations found in the media as well. Prescriptions about prudent behavior when on the streets and even near the home are part of the folk wisdom of the young urban woman and often ostensibly offer women solutions for avoiding harm. Yet prescriptions also advise women to adopt behavior that results in a formal profanation of the self, that is, in the presentation of a self with unworthy, contemptible, even repulsive qualities, qualities that may in no way reflect what the woman feels is or should be her "real" self or the self she is advised to project in other facets of her life. The self that is situated appropriately to "preventing crime" in public places can come to seem ridiculous to the woman, and the presentation process can seem at times also impractical.

Other crime-prevention strategies project limited competence and dependence, much as do the prescriptions of etiquette: (1) the woman's adoption of an "apparent escort," either real or manufactured, which suggests that she is unable to cope with appearing in public places without at least the pretense of male companionship; (2) the woman's presentation of a formally "profaned self," which requires her to debase her "situated self" through actions that would normally hold her up to ridicule and which requires additionally that she present her profaned self with the speed and competence of a skilled actor; (3) "anticipated peril," recommended preventive measures that sometimes occupy, even overwhelm, a woman's time when she is *not* in public.

The Apparent Escort

One key precaution for public behavior simply counsels the woman alone in public not to be alone or, at least, not to seem alone: women themselves say they feel they should effect or simulate a man escort, since attackers will presumably shy away from this strengthened front. The advice literature also often recommends engineering the escort by, for instance, having "a male fellow employee escort you to your car and see you safely started—you might even drive him back to the office" (Barthol 1979:102), or even managing to be near a man by, for example, standing near the occupied ticket booth in a subway station (Field 1980:112). Walking close to a group of people, if they look safe and are not, of course, all men, is also recommended (Barthol 1979:99). Even when there is no special danger, companionship is not to be discarded lightly. A woman, when at the movies, may be told to go with a companion (preferably a man) who, for example, "decides to venture into the lobby to buy popcorn," since tagging along "might turn out to be fun, and it's certainly safer" (Burg 1979:114).

A background assumption is that if a woman cannot manage to secure a man's company she will simply not go out—she will employ the strategy of avoidance. She will not attend the opera, she will not go to the store for a carton of milk past dusk, she will not venture into "dangerous" neighborhoods. And, indeed, many women said that they took their firm rules of avoidance for public places so much for granted that to ask about them was laughable: *Of course* a woman does not go out at night alone, *of course* she does not drive through such-and-such a neighborhood even in the daytime, *of course* she uses dates and friends—even those she considers tiresome or uncongenial—to attend events that she is afraid to attend alone. (One informant told me she had ended up by marrying an habitual escort she originally considered dull, but who was impressively protective.) So taken for granted are women's precautions that they make even the extreme recommendations of the advice literature seem plausible measures.

Adhering to this advice emphasizes that, in public places, a woman's sole "true" or "real" self must be considered insufficient protection since it is of insufficient strength for her own safety. At the least she must create a shadow, a tissue of a man, which can be suggested by the merest hints and evidence. There are products on the market that sham male companionship by providing a woman with, for example, the inflatable torso of a man for her front car seat. Ironically, even an artificial man can confer more protection than can a woman's own reality.

Women sometimes invent another shadow presence, that of the imagined harasser or attacker. Crime-prevention advice collaborates by exhorting a woman actively and extensively to role-play her relationship with the criminal, thereby reinforcing a woman's construction of her ideal enemy through crime-preventive exercises. She is told to "role-play," to ask herself what the street harasser wants from her and how she would break into her home (Monkerud and Heiny 1980:14) or to sham an attack on her own home, "with the help of a coat, a hanger, and a hook" (Griffith 1978:165). She is advised to practice memorizing the faces of men in magazines, the better to handle mug shots when actual crime occurs (Griffith 1978:172–173). Just as her imaginings of an apparent escort eat at the strength of the self she presents in public, so her hypothesis of a criminal builds the strength imputed to others as compared to the strength she can award herself.

Profaning the Self in the Name of Safety

Women can come to feel constrained to present themselves in an out-of-role fashion, one belying their knowledge of how they should properly express gender through their public behavior, in the process of behaving in a crime-conscious manner. For instance, a woman can read that to deter crime she should inform a man that she has AIDS or a venereal disease or should—presuming she is an adequate actor—"act crazy." A new commercial product in the 1980s consisted of a capsule of "real skunk essence that you pin to your clothes and then crush and douse yourself with" in case of danger; its smell will, of course, "repulse your assailant" (Mosedale 1986:105). This advice informs us what categories women and men find reliably loathsome: AIDS, STDs, or body odor seem safe bets to advice writers.

Imagine how strange comparable advice would be to a man threatened with street violence. Would a man be told to smear himself with skunk essence to discourage a robber, or to inform a batterer that the blood he will shed on the attacker will be tainted with a disease transmitted by bodily fluids? It is now a commonplace that an attractively dressed woman does not "cause" a man to rape her any more than a well-dressed man causes a man to rob him, yet it is not so commonly noted that men are *not* advised to fake insanity or to sham morally impugning disease with the alacrity that women are so advised. Of course, the discrepancy results in part from the fact that women, not men, are threatened with rape, a crime more injurious to women than simple robbery can be for a man (Burgess and Holstrom 1974; Neiderbach 1985), and society does not commonly prepare women to be as capable of physical retaliation as men.[3] But men threatened with violent muggings might be in dire need of measures of avoidance as well; certainly the surprise or disgust element in a man "acting crazy" or claiming he has AIDS would currently be as effective. Society assumes that the man's self-esteem needs and prestige warrants public pretense of competence and purity, while a woman's self-esteem and prestige can easily be sacrificed.

There is another grave contingency for the woman's sense of self. This results from the common thread of advice in these warnings to the woman either to act deliberately ridiculous in hopes of disarming her attacker or to perform actions that are normally considered ridiculous when performed in public. Thus, if a woman is cornered or threatened, informants said that they understood the following behaviors to be effective: to tell an attacker that she was pregnant or menstruating or that she carried disease, or to act crudely or surprisingly or to try to appear to be "crazy." In the literature, too, women are frequently counseled to adopt "non-aggressive—but disgusting—behavior" (Wilson 1977:151); to act by "ingenuity born of desperation" and claim "to be pregnant or epileptic or the carrier of a venereal disease" (Duckett 1982:68); to have "herpes or even AIDS" (Kaye 1985:74); to "pretend to have an epileptic seizure, or fainting spell" (Berman 1980); to "faint or go limp; urinate, drool or even throw up" (Schraub 1979:153); to "quack like a duck" (Scribner 1988:129); or make sounds like a cow and flap her arms like an airplane (Pickering 1983:129). She is told not to be afraid to "make a scene [or] do anything to attract attention to yourself. That's exactly what you want" (Field 1980:120). However, attracting attention to herself is not among the normal woman's desiderata in public places, nor is behaving "sexually aggressively," another recommended pose (Scribner 1988:129). A threatened woman should "act insane; eat grass, jump around, etc." (Krupp

3. The men discussed in advice books are envisioned as strong, competent, crafty, and unrapable.

1978); she should "sing out loud. . . . Make a fool of yourself" (Kaye 1985:72). Some of this advice also is intended to disgust the potential criminal, as when women are advised to tell rapists that they have venereal disease (Schraub 1979:153) and to perhaps carry an old penicillin bottle to bolster such claims (Pickering 1983:121).

Again, men are not counseled to act purposefully odd or disgusting in the pursuit of crime prevention. Their dignity is to be respected, as evidenced by the lack of advice books written for their benefit. (In fact, most behavior and etiquette books do not seem written for men's benefit: fulfilling rules of etiquette is thought of as a woman's concern.) Likewise, men are not counseled to act as if the attacker has had more effect on them than he has in fact had, which is what advice to act as if the approach triggers an epileptic fit, vomiting, or uncontrollable micturition amounts to.

In yet other instances, a woman is told plainly to anticipate peril—to perform actions before she is sure there is a danger. These actions will make her appear to be out-of-role in public; they will seem silly because they are overcautious or unfathomable to others—and perhaps to herself as well.

Anticipating Peril

Some practices are intended to prepare the woman for the worst that might happen; moreover, they are practices that she is to keep in mind at all times: "Don't let down. Ever!" (Kaye 1985:74). In addition to a recommended general mental vigilance, a woman learns that there are certain precautions she can take to ward off or lessen the likelihood that she will become involved in danger. She should, for instance, know the bus schedule so that she will not have to wait longer than necessary, and she should carry a purse purposefully close to the body, hugging it "like a football" for the duration of her journey, under her coat or jacket or tightly by its straps or tucking it between the feet when it must be put down, for example, at a grocery counter (Barthol

1979:102). Sometimes the literature informs a woman that she should plan considerably ahead, as when she is told to choose her home with an eye to security or to get acquainted with her neighbors with a view toward enlisting them in case of danger (Bertram 1975). Such advice amounts to an honorable, not to say prudent, ulterior motive for making friends. Another measure is to walk through the physical territory of the street in advance. Phenomenologically, events are thereby divided into "trial" ones and "real" ones; in public places this division is foreign to most men. Few men feel called upon to test-drive their pathways home and back, as they would test-drive a car. By making practice runs the woman decides to engage in mental mapping of common routes, with an eye to potential help in case of danger.

Women who attempt to be crime conscious—who are attempting to give the appearance of attractive and casual self-contained noninvolvement in public—understandably find it a strain simultaneously to prime themselves to run, scream, enter the nearest building, stand in a carefully considered "safe" spot, walk in the middle of the street with dignity, and refuse apparently innocent (and perhaps actually innocent) requests for aid and information. Did she remember to pack skunk essence? Is that male mannikin propped in a lifelike pose in her passenger seat? The artifacts of crime prevention can also weigh on her.

Not only does a woman receive advice that fosters paranoid thought (albeit she is repeatedly told that nothing is wrong with paranoia when in public), whatever activities she carves out for herself when in public are spoiled by the imperative to think of crime—not window shopping or a place to eat, not the next article she must write or her child's progress in school. Crime prevention becomes the background against which other involvements are experienced.

Current psychology adds another dimension when it describes a population of overwhelmingly men authors of women's troubles in public places and a population of sufferers of agoraphobia as overwhelmingly female. Interestingly, popular media attention has recently focused on agoraphobia, encouraging an increasingly loose definition for women agoraphobics, whereas the plight of the few men agora-phobics has been slighted (it is often noted they have "problems" with masculinity).

PSYCHOLOGICAL DISORDER IN PUBLIC: (MEN) AGGRESSORS AND (WOMEN) VICTIMS

Psychological labeling for troubles that occur in public places is dis-concertingly gender stereotypic. These labels describe men who rule and misuse the public realm and women who shrink from it. The labels—and the arguments for them—contrast with the ease often presumed by etiquette.

Men and Disorder in Public

Men's psychologically described problems in public places are primar-ily those that refer to the actions they practice on women. Public ha-rassment can be fondling or touching a stranger, but psychiatrists only note it when it is done for sexual gratification; it is treated as a sexual disorder or perversion called *frottage*. Both popular and psychiatric advice tell women that men who pinch or grab, trail, or ogle are not deeply disturbed (Ellis and Abarbanel 1973; Gebhard 1965). In fact, they are portrayed as rather ordinary, and women victims are advised that they should shrug off offenses. Such advice suggests that the of-fense is nugatory—and this can inhibit a woman's determination to retaliate.

Yet, somewhat contrarily, etiquette books and psychiatrists' advice also counsel women that, of these offenders, the more deeply dis-turbed may be touched off like firecrackers by women who mock them or become angry. Thus, this advice also inhibits a woman's reac-tion for fear of possible retaliation. One thread of advice may down-play the level of mental disturbance of those who touch women for sexual gratification, *frotteurs,* by stating that *"frotteurs* are only truly perverted when they avoid coitus and other sex acts" (Ellis and Abarbanel 1973:807). The *DSM-IIIR* emphasizes that the *frotteur* has a traditionally romantic fantasy about his victim: The *frotteur* idealizes an attractive, unsuspecting, and nonconsenting partner, then "rubs his genitals against the victim's thighs and buttocks or fondles her genitalia or breasts with his hands. While doing this he fantasizes an exclusive, caring relationship with his victim" (American Psychiatric Association 1987:283)—all told, quite a romance.

Men who become sexually aroused while scrutinizing strange women are labeled voyeurs or peepers; voyeurism or peeping was defined legally as a male-only offense until sexual equality legislation (Gebhard 1965:358–379). There are also men who compel women's scrutiny. These men, who force the witnessing of their genitalia, are called exhibitionists, and exhibitionism was also legally defined as an offense that only men could commit (Gebhard 1965:380–399).

Psychology, then, suggests that the use of gaze, touch, and pursuit vis-à-vis a member of the opposite sex was portrayed as premierly a man's, not a woman's, prerogative and that, in fact, these acts were offensive and illegal solely when men did them. One sexologist noted: "If a man stands naked in a window and a woman watches from the street, he can be arrested as an exhibitionist. If the situation is reversed, and a man in the street watches a woman undressing, he can be arrested for voyeurism" (Francoeur 1991:536). Defining voyeurism, exhibitionism, and frottage as male-only crimes reinforces men's power in public places, as it devalues women's use of these acts in retaliation. Often, even criminologists and psychiatrists mention that these offenses are on a disconcerting continuum with much noncriminal and nonpathological behavior. As analysts of sexual types rightly point out, offensive visual scrutiny in public is in some respects "normal" and certainly it is currently "legal," since "a lounger on the street watching passing girls, or a person watching a strip-tease act could qualify as a voyeur" (Gebhard 1965:358). Perhaps the ultimate territorial control, however, may be said to be that which is believed to come from within the individual's psyche. For women and public places, that control can best be exercised by the pathological fear of public places that is termed agoraphobia.

Agoraphobia

Women, along with other situationally disadvantaged groups in public, sometimes feel that public places hold potential danger or discomfort: Public harassment engraves such a feeling into the sensibilities of many women. Agoraphobia, or the debilitating fear of being in the open or in public places, is overwhelmingly a woman's phobia: Some estimates say as many as 80 percent to 95 percent of agoraphobics are women (Marks and Herst 1970). The high prevalence of agoraphobia for Anglo-American women is an internally generated equivalent to public harassment: It closes off public places for women too neurotically frightened to enter them. But agoraphobia often appears at points when all women experience changed attention in public, such as pregnancy and adolescence, for instance. Physical changes in appearance may well trigger different responses in public that are actual events, not fancies of neurosis, for the woman. Thus, the commencement of agoraphobia may be traced to real changes in reactions on the part of others in public places.

Agoraphobia delineates the ways in which women and men are disposed to understand public places, and it emphasizes that women's distrust of public places is both something for which there is ample warrant and something which the culture sustains by supplying a psychologically stigmatizing label for those who have this extreme fear. Moreover, by displaying or being known to possess an "irrational" phobia of public places, all nonagoraphobic women's fears about public places are by extension suggested to be baseless. Paradoxically, media attention to agoraphobia often therefore does a disservice to nonagoraphobic women.

Interestingly enough, agoraphobic and nonagoraphobic women use similar advice and sometimes strategies for managing their fear in public places and for handling public harassment. Agoraphobic women manage fear by absenting themselves from the public realm, as women have often been advised to do and many women still say they strategically do. Agoraphobic women use another person, even an inanimate object, as a protective companion when in public, just as nonphobic women have been encouraged to take with them chaperons or escorts and just as some nonphobic women say they strategically do in order to calm their fear or prevent harassment (Gardner 1983). Agoraphobia erects for a woman a steadfast psychic barrier against the threats posed by streets and places of business, but this barrier, as well as the strategies used to manage it, parallel the barriers and strategies of routine and everyday public harassment.

Agoraphobic women are in dire need of strategies to limit, defuse, or modify presence in public. Their need would be hard to argue with: One woman shook with tremors whenever she went out of the house. She said that she was forced to crawl along a pavement that seemed to waver; that she spent her days in the back bedroom of her home, since that was the place farthest from the street; that she passed her days in trepidation, thinking obsessively about the horrors that awaited her if she dared to go out in public; that she had further reduced her sphere by transforming her bedroom (and sometimes her bed) into the only safe zone, with occasional dashes to the kitchen for food or to the bathroom; and that she blacked out windows facing the street.

Indeed, the agoraphobic's home often becomes an antithesis of public places. As one agoraphobic woman said, "I spend most of my days in the bedroom of my house, thinking about how awful it would be if I went outside." Yet a nonphobic woman said: "Nowhere in this city is safe. I spend more time than I'd care to deciding where I can go safely and what I should do to insure my own safety. It's enough to drive you crazy." Thus, typical agoraphobic patterns of participation in public places can highlight nonphobic ones. Both agoraphobic and nonagoraphobic women must be concerned with how constraints on presentation and involvement will cause them to appear when in public contexts (Goffman 1963). Agoraphobics thus develop intense fears of those regions where they believe they will be judged by unknown others, whose judgments they are sure will be negative. Although agoraphobic women are the most clearly defined and most extremely affected class of female sufferers who find attendance in public places to be a profound problem, even women *not* labeled agoraphobic sometimes avoid public space in favor of private. That the tactics taken up by and advised for nonphobic women are also used by the phobic demonstrates a sisterhood between the two classes of women and suggests that both respond to similar difficulties of presentation in public places and both respond in similar ways. Agoraphobic women occupy a place on the same continuum as nonagoraphobic women: they too have the same presentational concerns, use the same strategies, and take, in some measure, the same risks. It is not so much, then, that there is a set of women who are unbalanced with regard to public places, but that the reasonable and the phobic share a plight.

Public order emphasizes gender in diverse ways, some of which I have treated in this first chapter and some of which I treat in chapters to follow. The public order can highlight gender by: etiquette and popular belief that hold women to be incomplete when alone in public; suggesting that women alone in public are morally lax, linking them with sex workers, who are outside of traditional middle-class mores; demanding that women prepare a different, and more carefully attended to, appearance for public places; and recasting women's fear of public places as a mental disorder known as agoraphobia. By emphasizing gender in all these ways, public order sustains, iterates, and constantly reiterates gender as a fundamental division of society.

Finally, when the individual in public presents a "gendered" public self, she or he reinforces the gender she or he does *not* display. To be a perfect lady as one flounces down the street bolsters the notion and the existence of perfect gentlemen, even if they are not in evidence. Similarly, to be identifiable as a gay or lesbian citizen in a heterosexual area of public places calls into question the heterosexuality of all citizens, making their heterosexuality something to be achieved, not taken for granted.

It will become clear that public harassment has the power to reinforce gender divisions, even to drive a wedge between women and men—not just between women and strange men, but in families as well. More than a few female informants noted that an incident of public harassment had the effect of an epiphany upon them: they began to question the motives of all men, including husbands, fathers, and brothers.

Public harassment is a regular and lifelong occurrence for women, not merely the province of young and attractive women for whom harassment is the price paid for the many perquisites of youth and beauty. Public harassment has happened forever and is forever happening as a feature of women's lives. (As I wrote these pages, I spoke to my ninety-one-year-old mother, who related that while walking to get her morning paper, a "young man in his forties" grabbed her, kissed her, and "wouldn't let go." Whatever old age holds for women, it does not hold public respect.) In fact, although a woman's appearance is often the subject of talk and the unexpressed topic of non-verbal harassment patterns, a woman can as easily be faulted for failing to have her accomplishments noted. And when her appearance is judged to fall below the standards of the moment, as it inevitably will as she ages, criticisms are harsh indeed and compliments are said ironically.

The situation of women in public places is especially significant because it is here that women have confronted and continue to confront a variety of contradictorily oppressive behavioral requirements. I talk about these requirements as common conundrums, marks of harassment that women can share with those in other social categories.

I choose to examine this unpleasant side of cross-gender relations in public places for two reasons. First, public place encounters, despite their brevity and their often stereotyped character, can have deep, lasting impact. Public place interaction is frequent, recurrent, and pervasive, and, as the next chapter will show, harassment that occurs in public, particularly for women who face other disadvantages in public places like disability or minority race, can have a significant additive impact, just because of this frequency. Such experiences can be lasting, stimulating fear. A white Jewish paralegal in her twenties, who cited fear of anti-Semitism as among her concerns, said that after one memorable incident she left the house accompanied as often as possible:

> One time some redneck construction workers formed two lines and cheered me on as I was walking to work, and they followed me into the building and everything. I've never really felt the same since that incident. I've changed since that happened. For one thing, I now make it a point to go out with someone else as much as I can; I find I don't get hassled as much. [I go out accompanied by] my Mom, my husband, my [six- and eighteen-month-old] babies. Sometimes people hassle me because of my [physically disabled] son, but I can handle that better than what those men did to me.

This book deals with women in public places and, more particularly, the troubles women experience there in interactions with men. My aim is to set out the character of public harassment abuses and the strategies women use to manage them and to point out that women's problems are, in some measure, the problems of certain other groups who share their circumstances. However, an immediate caveat is this: It is not that women have no pleasant encounters with men in public places, or that woman-woman encounters are free of judgment and strife, or that men, even white, heterosexual, able-bodied middle-class men of hegemonic repute, suffer no public harassment abuses or dilemmas of their own. Simply, I concentrate on the troubles of women because our society has not dealt as elaborately with the experiences of those who routinely experience problems in public places as it has with those who navigate their waters smoothly. For women, a group that has a set of problems and a set of contingencies for which they must plan, the authors of many of these problems and the focus of much of this contingency planning is, and must be, men.

CHAPTER TWO

Contexts

I've been pretty and young, then old and not so pretty. I've had
the money to dress well, then not. I've been skinny, then I've been
fat. I've been married with children, I've been a gay woman out on
the town with my girlfriend. I tell you, after sixty years: It happens
everywhere, all the time, sexual terrorism by men in the streets. It
shouldn't.

Middle-aged white lawyer, Indianapolis

Since every student of public places defines public places in a slightly
different way, I discuss what comprises public places for this work.
Because my work is rooted in a feminist consciousness, I discuss in
particular the ways in which the division into private and public is one
that gender belies: As public harassment shows, gender is a category
that needs to be achieved even when among strangers, and the public
as well as the private realm has sets of dangers for those who comply
with traditional definitions of gender as well as for those who deviate.

Throughout, I hypothesize that public harassment toward women
is neither new nor simple, that varieties of public harassment are not
limited to our culture but, rather, that they present a manipulation of
the common symbols of many times and societies, and that women's
troubles in public places in our own culture are many-faceted, with
moral, legal, political, and psychological connotations and implications.

Finally, I elaborate a useful concept, *situational disadvantage,* with regard to the case of women in public places.

Public places are those regions that are simultaneously everyone's and no one's, to which all are theoretically allowed access, even given the symbolic welcome of civility. Yet public places are also sites for mockery and downright humiliation, the threat or the reality of interpersonal violence, verbal insults and injuries, avoidances and shunnings, and the mere withholding of the rituals of civility, an act that communicates to the individual that she or he is not entitled to the small courtesies of everyday life due every stranger. At the same time, the accessibility of public places offers the victim of public harassment clear evidence that others receive better treatment.

Recent feminist scholarship has been especially intrigued by the so-called "public/private split" that, scholars argue, has existed in society as a rationale for sequestering women in the home and forbidding them to participate in the public sphere (Allen 1988; Smith 1991). For the most part, the public realm has been understood by feminists to be "public life"—the worlds of work and political participation, for example—and the private realm has been the home. A basic tenet of this feminist thought, then, is to support the move of women from their traditional private realm to the public realm that has been traditionally reserved for men. However, in most studies, one important characteristic of the public realm is neglected: the highly gendered nature of public places. Invasive public harassment can be of many forms, experienced as a contrast to competence elsewhere, as for this African-American nurse:

> One example of being put in my place by men I didn't even know was when I was doing the big shopping for the month, last month this was. First off, the male grocery clerk made some comment to the bag boy about all the help I'd need lifting all these supposedly big heavy bags. It took me a while to persuade them to let me get out of store alone. But when I dropped a jar going out of the store, nobody would help me, including the men who made a point of

how fragilistic [*sic*] I was. I had refused them nicely, not meanly, so I felt they at least might have helped.

Next, I wheeled my cart out to my car, and somebody pinched my butt as I was going.

Then finally I got the car loaded—turned out I was parked near a construction site and the guys were having lunch. You can guess the rest. [They hooted at her, and one threw a rock while doing so.] All the men were brothers—they weren't white men. By the time I got into my car I was exhausted, and it wasn't from lifting no big bags of groceries, neither.

Men—you can't live with 'em, you can't live without 'em, you can't get 'em to leave you alone.

Another deficit is that although feminist scholarship rightly portrays the worlds of private and public as more finely shaded and more sensitive to context than previously thought, we have as yet seen no typology that delineates those shades and defines those contexts with regard to the everyday world of the individual.

By definition, public places are quintessentially social but only in a limited sense. First, they heighten perceptions of gender, sexual preference, health status, race, and class, and reinforce our conviction that these traits are faithful indices of the characteristics, motives, intents, and activities of the particular members of the category observed, with the interests of "our group" foremost. The traits we note are those we find most significant in our society. Members of any group can find they wear group-provided blinders with regard to public harassment practiced by their group's members. This selective vision is a tribute to how little we discuss these public occurrences, which we do see and do commit, daily—and have for all our lives. Yet we typically believe that public places are democratic arenas where all are engaged in parallel pursuits, and we believe that all citizens deserve the trust and civility of all others.[1]

1. Public places are circumscribedly social in that an individual has least recourse to the goods, shelters, and defense of others to support and structure

Second, public places momentarily mute individual characteristics, and they often damp our attention to individual pleas and plights. Thus it is common for a woman to be taken and treated "only" as a beautiful woman or "only" as a mother; it is uncommon for the individual in public places to be appreciated as a working mother, college student, or tired physician, even when membership in these categories could be amply evident from appearance. The shorthand we use in public places features a small vocabulary indeed, a social reductionism to make any theorist tremble. No matter that we feel we have conquered job discrimination and have "other"-category friends. On the street we all are unrepentant recidivists.

Thus public places involve a basic set of categories for understanding and responding to strangers. This set is an algorithm that can be brutally or happily blunt, for we sometimes trust and help those we have little reason to favor, as well as distrusting or harassing those we see as easy victims but who may also be undeserving ones.

American public places encompass a diverse range of sites and situations, including businesses such as shops, service stations, and restaurants. Of course, this type of public place might not exist at all in other economic systems or smaller societies where individuals produce more goods and answer more needs in their own homes. In smaller, more interdependent communities such as indigenous cultures or subsistence farming communities, such an economic enterprise would be considered as the business of all members of the community. Likewise, in some tribal cultures, the individual who ventures away from a small village or encampment does so rarely and is likely to encounter so few strangers that public places in other areas have a radically different, deeply threatening aspect (Redfield 1953). It is difficult to think of

---

status elsewhere. In public we are all stereotypes, but fragile ones. It often seems, then, that it is among strangers in public places that general status counts least: that it is in public, on a street in Bedford–Stuyvesant or the Crenshaw, that an individual is, for example, least protected by his status as a middle-class white man.

primitive and provincial public sites in the same breath as we do urban sites, but I have no doubt that the potential for salience exists for both, as one case in particular shows.

A CASE IN POINT: SALLY'S DIARY

While interviewing women and men for this book, I also interviewed for another project, one that will document the experiences of gay, lesbian, and bisexual citizens in public places in Indianapolis. Two local gay community newspapers printed stories about this project and suggested informants call me. More widely noticed was an article about this project in a mainstream paper, the *Indianapolis Star*. In it, I described public harassment. Although the three articles asked only for gay male, bisexual, and lesbian informants, I also received calls from four women who identified themselves as heterosexual and asked me to interview them. They had received the same sort of harassment, they said, and believed it was just because they were women. Would I take down their experiences, too? I would, and did.

Sally was one of these four women. A bright, energetic student at a college outside Indiana, she was home for the summer when I interviewed her. With her long ash-blond hair and habit of wearing a jogging suit or sweatshirt and sweatpants with athletic-product labels, Sally looks very much like everyone's idea of a healthy young white Midwesterner. She had already decided to write a paper for an English class on her feelings about women's treatment in public places. She was surprised and happy to discover that I was also interested in something she found pervasive, troublesome, and troubling.

Sally had started a diary of all the events she considered troublesome that happened to her in public, and she offered to read one day's entries to me. We did not get much beyond the first hour recorded in the diary. Here is my summary of what happened to Sally between nine and ten o'clock on a weekday, as she did errands downtown:

9:05–9:10 Two young white men walking in the opposite direction "rake their eyes" over Sally's body. About 30 seconds later, another man walking in the opposite direction looks long and hard into her eyes and lasciviously licks his lips as she passes. After another minute or so, a middle-aged man and woman pass her: The man gazes with interest at her breasts, trying to peer down her sweatshirt (not possible), while the woman who accompanies him studiously looks away, as if to signal no-contest with Sally or to avoid witnessing her companion's assessment of Sally. After another minute, two men in business suits and briefcases come toward Sally. One, a white man, smiles and informs her she looks "good enough to eat," and his African-American companion nods sagely, specifying that Sally is "a vanilla shake."

9:15 Sally enters a department store. The clerk from whom she buys a scarf for her mother's birthday asks Sally to model it for him. She says she really doesn't have time today, thanks him politely, and leaves. The clerk says, "Well, maybe another time." Sally neither agrees nor disagrees.

9:20 Sally stops in a food court in search of coffee. In order to buy the coffee, she finds she must banter with the two young white servers, both of whom she estimates are younger than she is. Sally asks for extra sugar, which leads to a lengthy discussion of sweetness, Sally's general sweetness, and what Sally might taste like (sweet). Sally thinks she was polite but firm: "I told them I really needed the coffee soon in order to wake up. But that didn't work either, because they began talking about what I'd been doing last night that might have tired me out." Specifically, they speculate about Sally's sexual activities. As she walks away with her coffee, she hears one of the men mutter that she is "stuck on herself," while the other laughs loudly. Sally wrote: "I can feel that laugh etched in my back." Sally decides not to drink her coffee inside the food court, but to walk to Monument Circle, a central city drive with a monument and fountain surrounded by a stone bench.

9:25 Sally buys a newspaper "to give myself something to do" when she is drinking her coffee. The newsagent, a weary-looking middle-aged white man, silently takes Sally's money, but tosses her change on the stack of papers. Sally feels "relieved, but offended at the same time."

9:30 Sally is sitting at Monument Circle, drinking her coffee and reading, when she feels someone watching her and considers moving "to avoid trouble." She has put on sunglasses so that her reactions will not be easy to gauge and so that she can covertly look around her. The man watching Sally is well-dressed, white, middle-aged and, Sally thinks, taking an abnormally long time to dispose of a paper in a trashcan. In fact, his real purpose probably is to watch her, Sally decides; she also decides to make sure she keeps him in view.

9:35 The middle-aged man leaves and Sally "feels relieved again, since nothing bad happened." She suspects herself wrong about his attention; she asks herself if she is, after all, conceited. Almost as soon as he is gone, a casually dressed young African-American man bicycling around the Circle pulls up next to Sally, although there are plenty of other places to sit. He leans his bike against the bench, stretches, laughs to himself and mumbles something about what a nice day it is, all the while darting glances at Sally, who is by this time watching him covertly, too. She says nothing, pretending to be immersed in her paper. The young man finally snorts derisively, and reboards his bike, conspicuously turning his head away from Sally. As he pedals away, he mumbles something to himself: Sally cannot hear exactly what (she thinks she hears either the word "haughty" or "hoity-toity"), but she takes in an "angry intonation." She assumes he is speaking about her, so she makes sure she watches him until he is gone and keeps an eye out for him during the rest of the time she sits. Sally wonders if she has acted in a prejudiced way; decides she has not, and cites evidence to herself (her boyfriend at school is African-American). She still worries that the young man might have thought she did not speak because "he was Black instead of because I was afraid."

9:45 Sally reads the paper, drinks her coffee, but feels inside as if she is waiting for something else to happen. Nothing does, but Sally decides she will finish her errands another time and, further, that she will splurge for a cab ride home, since she does not want to risk anything more happening on the bus: A man had repeatedly changed his seat in order to get closer to Sally on her trip down. She writes, "I decided I was having a bad day."

In fact, Sally was only having a bad hour, at the most. Yet this was not an atypical entry in her diary, and Sally's is not an atypical story. Public harassment occurs in every context (and, as the next chapter shows, public harassment can also be expected from every sort of man).

In this chapter I want to explore a variety of contexts—by no means all of them—to suggest how public harassment exists and operates in different environments and under different circumstances. I have chosen three contexts: First, I explore the most "public" of these contexts, the street itself; next, I explore semipublic places where there is some talk or points of similarity between strangers, such as shops and stores; third, I examine in detail public aid encounters—helping behavior between strangers—as one instance of "ratified talk," an exchange between strangers on an allowable topic that can happen in any site.

PUBLIC HARASSMENT ON THE STREET

For women, the most public contexts—the street, parks, recreation spots, byways and alleys—are often the most frightening, for there women will be least protected from ill-meaning strangers. Yet on the street the individual believes herself to be freest to practice "turnabouts"—to fight fire with, if need be, even more fire. In sum, in public places, the same weapons are theoretically available to all.

Public place contexts are embedded. If one were to diagram these contexts, they might look something (but only something) like a series of concentric circles, with smaller and semipublic circles enclosed by larger and more public ones.[2] Perhaps the individual inhabits a large city whose public order is not monolithic: it shifts in character and pattern from neighborhood to neighborhood. Thus, the individual can expect to alter the self she or he presents to the public, depending on the other sites to which she or he goes. This rapid change may make it more likely that she or he will compare the treatment received by the public self with that received by the private self. Typical of the public harassment reported by female informants was to note that private triumphs came to feel, especially on the street, like nothing at all. A white lawyer in her mid-thirties remarked:

> No sooner had I left [my place of work] when some guy seemed to, well, come after me. He was saying things, you know, under his breath, I don't remember what, and laughing dirty at me, and I just couldn't seem to get away from him. It was awful. And it was just such a contrast: I'd just headed a board meeting and done a great job—I could tell people liked how I'd handled the case. So many good feelings—then to come outside, and poof! it's all gone.

Yet it is crucial to see that a model of concentric circles, or shifting roles, or identities defined by neighborhoods is not wholly accurate. In truth, one of the features of interaction in public is to make the potential harasser of one moment the next moment's potentially harassed. Features like gender are constantly to be accomplished.

To control unpredictable contexts, a woman can decide to choose certain streets, certain times, and certain companions, the better to ensure that she escapes public harassment. A particular woman may

2. This embeddedness enables reversals of harasser and harassed. Thus, there exist within public places some semipublic and protected semipublic nodules—a woman who has just been ogled by a strange man on the street can then ogle other men strangers in the safety of her health club.

remain within her own neighborhood, where she is and seems to others comfortable. On a trip downtown, she may be accompanied by a small child—a child who happens, for that excursion, to seem to guarantee her safety and to assure the approval of men strangers. She herself may decide to engage in other situationally advantaged behaviors entitled by her membership in some social categories: If she does not have a disability, she may choose to initiate relatively personal conversation with the stranger who uses a wheelchair; if white, perhaps she locks her car doors when she enters an African-American neighborhood; if heterosexual, perhaps she scowls at a pair of casually embracing women whom she categorizes as lesbian. In short, one instant's disadvantage can be another's advantage—one instant's harassed the next instant's harasser.

An unfriendly atmosphere can also become a warm welcome. Shouted at on the streets, a woman may find that her destination—a store where she is known, a cherished workplace, a woman-identified and friendly atmosphere like a particular bookstore or beauty salon—presents her with a distinct advantage. Not only can her identity and behavior shift between disadvantaged and advantaged, but the microclimates she passes through can likewise flicker from ones that definitely disadvantage her, to ones where she has a distinct advantage, to ones where she seems required to make or break her own advantage, perhaps even relax and complain to sympathetic others about what she has endured.

Many features of public places in general are most true of streets and other "public public" places. Thus, communication in public is heavily *appearance dependent,* that is, it relies on appraisal of the physical look, manner, nonverbal communication, and dress of the other. It is understood that, all other things being equal, the citizen will attempt to give the best possible appearance in public. (This is true barring some general fear for theft of valuable goods displayed.) With only appearance to rely on, however, both display and stereotypy are inevitable in any public setting, two sides of the coin of mutual easy judgment that public places encourage. Display occurs when the appearance that people present in public places is calculated for the effects, sometimes undeserved, that others will experience. Stereotypy occurs when the individual, presented with such a wealth of diverse symbols and little else by which to judge, begins to form facile judgments based on the tag-ends and wisps of appearance that are available to her or him. Inasmuch as wealth and capital can encourage display, perhaps stereotypy of this sort flourishes in industrialized and class-conscious atmospheres. Such an atmosphere enables some citizens to possess the means to mount careful and varying material displays, other citizens to try to emulate such displays, and all citizens to become connoisseurs in appreciating displays. For women, reliance on appearance can proliferate the measures they take to prepare for public places, as was true for informants, and stimulate a precise vocabulary of what "look" or "outfit" is suited to what street situation. In this way, women mentioned "my downtown outfit," "clothes for within-three-blocks-of-home," and "dresses to drive by" (see Rickey 1986:74 on "the errand outfit"). In just the same way, women seeking to spark acquaintance with strange men on the street will sometimes spend laborious hours in deciding how to erect a personal appearance fitting this goal (see O'Connor and Silverman 1989).[3] We evaluate the objects that a person carries or displays in order to arrive at clues to her or his identity; thus advice books on meeting opposite-sex strangers in public places routinely advise the individual to "use a prop" to "telegraph" interest and snag the attention of strangers (Westerman 1992:8off.).

3. Of course, the inescapable stereotypy that results will as easily splinter less privileged classes as it will alienate one class from another, as when a Korean-American in an African-American neighborhood is the object of catcalls that recapitulate stereotypes of Asian-Americans (Navarro 1990) or an African-American who enters a Korean-American business is accused of failures or moral lapses stereotypical of African-Americans (Sims 1990). These stereotypes and stereotyped accusations are a side effect of this display feature of public interaction in general.

Sometimes the citizen feels that strangers fix reliably on blatant symbols of a status peripheral to her or his "real" self, as when a woman using an electric wheelchair says strangers bypass usual greetings to offer remarks on her chair (Gardner 1992), or when a woman out with her four children says she is tired of strangers cheerfully chatting her up "as a mother, which I happen to feel I am only secondarily," or when catcalls target a tall woman as tall and "ignore the rest of me." In semipublic places, a citizen can flesh out and counteract stereotypes; on the street, where talk is tabu, that is much harder.

There are also oddments of personality or appearance that render citizens out of the pale of the pale, and these too are most salient in the street rather than the shop or when talk is legitimate. If these oddments are behavioral, they stem from personality, not social category; if physical, they are too minor or too quixotic to be considered disabilities. Strangers note a peripheral but noticeable trait, such as hair color, weight, or height, on which to comment. Here are members of minority groups so circumscribed in the discrimination they receive that their self-help groups (modern-day Red-Headed Leagues, for example, or clubs for "women of size") are often considered amusing clubs rather than serious congeries. Thus, the true outcasts are those who belong to no articulable disadvantaged group at all—that is, they belong to no social category that resonates with current sentiments about hard times in either private or public places, yet they are definitely picked out and disadvantaged. Among these, for example, are those whose constitution or personality seems to others to be so unreasonably nervous, vague, or belligerent that they can mount no satisfactorily composed public presentation—no public dogface. It would be an eloquent book indeed that could persuade the reader that the habitually jumpy merit the same label of "situationally disadvantaged" as do the members of groups such as women, those with disabilities, and minorities. Yet in public places these people can experience some of the same situational disadvantages.

Clearly, dependence on appearance favors those whose appearance connotes statuses that are held in high regard. To use crime as one example, appearance dependence favors those taken stereotypically to be no easy victims or those who can manipulate appearance to suggest strength or imperviousness to assault. Women, if strangers employ traditional stereotypes, will be taken as less capable of retaliation than men; again, the street will disadvantage women, semipublic places can protect them. As aspiring criminals depend on judgments of appearance to select prospective victims, so those who seek to escape victimization depend on assessment of strangers' appearance (and manipulation of their own) to avoid crime.

PUBLIC HARASSMENT IN SEMIPUBLIC PLACES: STORES, SCHOOLS, AND PURPOSEFUL PRESENCE

Men not only freely judge women and institute stagecrafted parodies with women as the butts of their jokes, they also attempt to alter the situation of many semipublic places in which they find themselves—places that arguably have a firm definition already. Moreover, in these sites and contexts, unlike the quintessentially public venue of the street, the person seems to be present with a purpose and an orientation. She is there to be served and to buy (as in a store or restaurant); she is there to serve a clientele (as at a job); she is there to receive the wisdom of professionals and the stimulation of a learning cohort (as in a school). Yet some semipublic sites, such as restaurants, stores, newsstands, and other service establishments, seem only to provide more opportunities for tailor-made incursions that trade on whatever added information a man gleans from the woman's relationship to the establishment. Others provide ironic counterdefinitions of the situation, as when a young woman of thirteen is "*potched* and smacked" in a gauntlet as she proceeds down the school hallway by "some younger boys I'd never seen before," or as when a woman finds higher learning disrupted by "seven or eight men, not in my class, who came into the room before the class [where she studied alone] and said embarrassing, dirty things to me."

Often protected by semipublic context—by those around her that she knows as well as by the contextual definition of the situation—a woman can also discover that the male performer exhibits greater rights to shift the definition of the situation to (typically) an eroticized or romanticized one of his own choosing. Perhaps the woman is a fellow customer, perhaps she is a server and thus the subject of remarks that come under the formal definition of workplace harassment from customers.[4] Of course, puns and innuendos are a staple of the woman's experience here, too. A young single white waitress from the Midwest, who was obliged to wear her first name on a tag, reported "male customers asking if I was on the menu. Another guy once asked, 'Has anyone ever told you that Candy is sweet to eat?' I felt *very* uncomfortable." Women customers are also freely available for intrusive comments, as in the case of a student who was "peacefully dining out," and "as the waiter was putting our food out on the table this 'gentleman' walked up to our table and directly looked at me and made the statement, 'Hey, I bet you taste better than that food on your plate!'"

One woman distinguished between the street, where she felt genuinely ill-at-ease, and places like stores and school, where she noted that men engage in "funny business, which sometimes is truly funny to me." In these semipublic contexts, she felt better able to deal with even hostile or vulgar comments or conduct, since there might be someone present with authority over the harasser and others around her who could be "sort of friends I can count on to defend me." Her stated opinion was the opinion of many—although many also offered cases of workplace harassment by customers in which their livelihoods were

---

4. Overall, I have not discussed those semipublic situations that are the main province of sexual harassment laws, such as employer/employee harassment. Discussion of the dynamics and legality of such cases is found, among other places, in Abramson (1993), Berger (1986), and MacKinnon (1979).

on the line. A final point: More than the strange male harasser in the street, the harasser in semipublic places opens himself up to criticism, possibly by partisans of his woman victim or by a set of people he will see again.

Because of the other possible definitions of semipublic situations—namely, those that involve the business or school—there is also the chance that a man will attempt what he hopes will be taken as a flattering remark, then use it as a stepping-stone to secure better service or some other perquisite. In this vein, an African-American college student who also worked as a waitress reported that some men who appended a flattering remark to a service request wanted to special-order a dish not on the menu or to ask for some substitution in a special that would not ordinarily be allowed. Plainly utilitarian remarks or contexts sometimes caused little suspicion, even when ambiguously housed in the rhetoric of heterosexual romance. Of course, if a woman entered a site or an event traditionally likely to cast doubt on her moral worth in the first place, she was even more likely to feel discomfort at the harassment of, for example, scrutiny, as for the woman awaiting her boyfriend at a wet T-shirt contest: "I left before he came. All the men there were staring at me. God, it was awful. I absolutely couldn't make my feet stay in that room one second longer. I put my head down and I walked out of there and I went home."

Interestingly, women unlikely to be taken as shameful participants were readily defined so by men in these contexts, once again showing that the men had the rights of definition and that the faintest deviant context readily bled onto any women nearby. Thus, a woman seated at a table in a strip joint with her husband was hooted and hassled by other men, in full view of her husband and much to her husband's chagrin as well as her own; a woman eating at a pricy restaurant seated under one of the few photos of scantily clad women got comments from men; a female clerk in a women's lingerie department was often lewdly scrutinized and rudely slurred "by men who seem to think I've got no more clothes on than one of the dummies." Context is thus a powerful definer that works to women's disadvantage at men's behest.

Although semipublic contexts have advantages over public, the possibility of a continuing contact can mean that a woman will have to strategize again and again with the same harasser for the length of her stay or with repeat customers who are also repeat harassers. An African-American manager noted the traditions and customs that supported her own harassment while in school:

> It started in junior high at [a private school]. Boys slapping your butt when you walked down the hall, elbowing your breasts when you're in a crowd or at your locker, the teachers making remarks. One time a boy I didn't know tripped me on purpose in the cafeteria and my tray fell all over, and he did it on purpose. His pals laughed at me. My counselor and teacher saw and no one did a thing and I was too frightened to. *Not* normally am I a frightened person.
>
> Then it continues in high school, even [an expensive private school]. There are lots of Blacks there, so it's not race. Same things go on. By the time you're ready for the world of work and going out in public places, you been socialized. The man who slapped my butt on the Circle probably wasn't the same man who slapped my butt when we were both eleven years old in junior high. He could've been, and that's my point.

There were about thirty women whose arguments about the etiology of public harassment virtually reproduced this woman's: All noted harassment by young men they did not know beginning in grade school or junior high; all said that school was, for them, the beginning of a career of being harassed in all contexts, from street to store to college classroom. A school in particular provides a setting where women are, in one woman's words, "a captive audience for harassment."

At the same time, the male teacher, or shop clerk, or physician has a different understanding of what takes place. Often he falls back on an understanding of the differences in the "fundamental natures" of women and men—as did this African-American appliance salesman in his thirties:

> . . . [although] with a man [when selling] you can be nice, you are nice, you are courteous, you are respectful, and you make some small talk.
>
> But with a woman it's: "How *can* I help you? Let me help! Let me assist you!" Satisfying her needs. It's subconscious—it's just automatic. There's no good and bad side to this treatment [of women]—it's just a good side.
>
> I don't think there's anything wrong with [treating women with "extra friendliness"], because women are different than men, period. I mean, a lot of people try and make out, "Hey—women and men should be treated equal"—well . . . women are soft, men aren't. Physically they're soft; they're pretty—you know. I never want to see any harm come to them. I mean, it's like: Women being in combat? Forget it. I can't imagine a woman being shot. A man being shot? No big deal. But a woman—she's soft, she's pretty, she shouldn't have harm come to her.

In addition, semipublic harassment clashes with the overriding definition of a sales establishment or classroom, and when the harasser is an authority figure like a professor or a server whose help the woman needs, the harassment can be momentous. A woman may feel less reason to be suspicious or fearful if there are others around and, in truth, if the man has seemed innocuous enough thus far. On the other hand, she may actively resent the man's efforts to interfere with the definition of the situation, especially if the situation is one in which she is trying to gain a living and especially if she is in one of those occupations, such as bartending or waitressing, where she regularly meets a high volume of troublesome remarks. She may, in addition, doubt the ultimate sympathy of the management of the shop or the school administration should she decide to complain about a customer or fellow student.

Interviews disclosed that the closer the context is to the anonymous street, the less likely women believed they would find a set of defenders. Harassment that occurs in public, particularly for women who face other situational disadvantage in public like disability or minority race, can have a significant, additive impact, just because of its frequency. While this impact may ultimately be an impact on self, there is also the more short-run, immediate set of experiences it can give rise to: in public places, women learn about and experience distinct vulnerabilities. Such experiences can be deep and lasting, involving others and stimulating fear. An otherwise competent, confident manager said: "After that day [when she was followed from store to store throughout a mall], I mostly don't go out alone much anymore. I take my husband or my baby or my mother-in-law." More than one woman, successful in a job, gave it up or changed careers because of customer harassment or harassment from men who could intrude into the context even though they were not customers.

Not surprisingly, routinely walking down the street on the way to a business or being in a place of business frequented by men made some women feel observed or scrutinized. One woman said: "Unconsciously, I know I case any place of business for men, and I feel different, worried or uneasy, if there are men there. I always feel they're looking at me, and I want to tell you, it's *not* a pleasant feeling." Some women could strategize by choosing semipublic places likely to have a comforting majority of women. Said one woman: "I like department stores. I like hair-style salons, dress shops, boutiques. You go from the street where the men stare to these places. You can just relax." However, this strategy is limiting—who wants to spend their public life in a hair salon?—and does not protect a woman from what she might encounter on the street. Again, some women had to strategize further with relation to race or health status, since those categories still afforded many troubles.

Sometimes public harassment by customers in the school and workplace diminished women's attachment to career and work outside the home. In this, it was indeed an effective social control to relegate women to the home. The ways in which men could publicly harass at a woman's workplace sent an uncomfortable message to many women: They felt that they were being "untraditional" in taking jobs or that men were sending them a clear message that they *should* feel that way. Women who had experienced the worst incidences of public harassment in the workplace—stalkings that resulted in threats or even rape, unwanted pursuit by a customer that ended in the customer's complaint to a boss, constant incidents of more minor harassments—sometimes came to feel that they did not, in fact, belong in the workplace at all. Some among these quit their jobs or changed the type of work they did. One such woman observed that her harassment by one man during the time she worked in a department store "proved men are right when they say women still belong at home, because I do, and now that's where I am. I should never have tried [to take a job outside the home]." Indeed, public harassment can have a notable effect on a family's finances—perhaps on a nation's as well.

Many women mentioned men who used knowledge of where they worked to practice public harassment. A former belly-dancer related this incident:

> While I was buying groceries two men approached me who obviously recognized me for my belly-dancing. They took the liberty to ask me where I lived, did I want some company, we could all have a great time together, etcetera. Obviously, I was uncomfortable, but I still tried to be polite and firmly told them, "No, thank you." From there I did my best to ignore them, finished my shopping, and left.
>
> It kind of scared me because these men knew where to find me: my work. Therefore, I didn't feel I could become too hateful with them. This situation left me with a very vulnerable feeling. Some men think nothing of treating women like a piece of meat and having no regard for her as a human. (Mohsenzadeh 1991)

The more open and vulnerable a woman's job left her, the more intrusive a man might become. Some occupations and some work situations left women open to men dedicated to instituting a sense of menace that lingered.

Incidents in semipublic places can also be surprising depending on the way in which they occur. Insofar as they are unpredictable and occur in many circumstances, they contribute to the offender's advantage and the target's disadvantage. For example, customers' harassment can be unexpected, as for this store clerk who was fondled and followed around the store by a customer:

> This particular incident happened on a weeknight, so hardly anyone was in the store. When it happened, my first reaction was surprise. I didn't see it coming. He put me in a very awkward position, which I was not at all prepared for. Nothing like this has ever happened to me. I felt really strange for the next few hours following the incident. Even though I'm old enough to know that I did nothing wrong, I still felt like I was somehow "bad." It's hard to explain that feeling, but it was almost like a guilty feeling, because I was worried that I had somehow invited him to touch me. I never wanted that, and I worried about it happening again. (Ferree 1991)

Women may experience fewer troubles in semipublic contexts, then— or they may effectively have commerce and job opportunities reduced. Another type of context exists partly to solve women's difficulties in both full-public and semipublic contexts. This context too both helps women avoid and cope with public harassment—and facilitates and fosters public harassment of its own.

THE PRIVATE IN PUBLIC: PUBLIC SHELLS AND INSULATION

In addition to public and semipublic contexts, there are some contexts in which public harassment occurs that fall into neither classification. These are "public shells," those barriers to public apprehension that make an individual a shielded private person who is seemingly only incidentally embraced by a public context. Often public shells are technological baffles to intrusion like the telephone or the car, or even the credit card and mail-order catalogue, which allow a woman to shop but obviate personal contact. In fact, many of the habits, conveniences, and institutions of modern life that provide shielding for some of a woman's public activity or enable her to secure other shielding also, paradoxically, allow greater access to her. Sometimes clothing forms a shell, as in Muslim dress that fully covers a woman, baring only the eyes.

These shields to accessibility must be considered a context of their own for exploitation by strangers, not precisely like any of the other contexts but allowing the same sort of incursions while ironically standing as protective measures. One of the most questionable blessings is the telephone, which allows women to summon help but also allows men, from aspiring lovers to tricksters to criminals, symbolic access to women's homes. Telephone access can engender the feeling that women may be being watched there and elsewhere, and prank or obscene calls whether at home or at work can widen the feeling of menace.

Another mixed technological blessing is the automobile. A woman's world could be limited to the home when driving was overwhelmingly a man's activity (Scharff 1991). Now that women frequently drive cars, they can travel in relative safety and with relative speed to a variety of public destinations, shielding themselves from many vicissitudes. However, as much as the car insulates women, it also provides circumstances that can pierce that protective shield: since men also drive cars, they can easily follow women who aim to speed away to safety. An African-American secretary in her twenties noted:

> A man came after me from the 7–11, shouting, asking me my name, and where did I live, and where did I work. Trying to get at me. I got into my car, thinking that'd do it. No way, because he just got into his car, and he came after me, and for a while I could hear him keep shouting things of this nature. ("Doe" 1992)

Many women reported men who had chased or followed them to their cars from work or on the street, or intrepid—and quite frightening—

men who had spotted them in cars and given chase, sometimes at high speeds and sometimes for miles. Women who worked in public venues often reported telephone harassment from men who might sometimes initially purport to be workmates, bosses, or customers, then proceed to harangue or insult a woman. Women sometimes feared that a caller was actually a boss or other superior, and sometimes they were eventually proven correct. Many women's homes were invaded by strangers making obscene phone calls.

THE CONTEXT OF RATIFIED TALK: THE EXAMPLE OF PUBLIC AID

There are few legitimate reasons for striking up talk with strangers. Among these are service encounters in shops and semipublic venues, brief greetings and comments on the weather or local conditions or other "undebatables," and, last, public aid encounters. I use the term "public aid" to describe helping behavior between strangers in public places (Gardner 1986). Public aid encounters can be used to examine and understand the tensions of gender relations between strangers. Although both sexes reported cases of cross-sex public aid that were unremarkable or remarkably generous, both sexes also reported dysphoric cross-sex cases where the other gender was implicated as appetent and exploitative (as many women said of men) or, weakly, asked more than their due (as some men said of women).

In public aid I include all situations in which one stranger is entitled to ask another for help in public places. Thus, "favors" such as door opening and closing (see Walum 1974), requests for or gifts of information like the time or directions, putative "loans" or effective "gifts" like a match or a tissue, the unrequested, sometimes extravagant help or unrequested gifts we give to those we believe are extraordinarily deserving, and help in the emergencies and civil disasters that make possible heroism and "Good Samaritanism" all fall under the heading of public aid.

Americans in general feel that any citizen has the right to ask for public aid and that every citizen is obligated to grant it, no matter the race, social class, or gender of those involved. Therefore, public aid is one of the backbones of the structure of public contact and mutual public support. If a citizen suspects that some groups will take advantage of public aid opportunities, then mutual public support and trust are undermined. Indeed, public aid is one of the features of an anonymous civil economy that signifies mutual trust among strangers, including strangers of diverse groups. We feel that we owe any citizen the courtesy of the favor of opening a door or picking up a dropped object for her or him; likewise, we owe any and every citizen the civility of providing information or the requested tissue, cigarette, small change, or pen.

Yet, petitioning for public aid can be a morally freighted event. The grantor is as inevitably in a morally superior position as is an impressive potlatch gift-giver. For the citizen in public, a gift is usually impossible to repay because public aid encounters occur between strangers who are unlikely to see each other again. The petitioner, just as clearly, is in the recipient's debt, even if what has been given is only of the magnitude of a pin, a pen, or a set of faulty directions.

Two versions exist of women's special situation regarding public aid: the ideal version and a version revealed by observations and interviews that suggests how women act and are treated. Nearly 75 percent of men whose interviews were used here (139 by count) felt that women were singled out for especially "good" treatment in public places; almost a quarter of these men (44) mentioned that extra measures of public aid, which they were required to give, comprised a portion of women's pedestaled status. Despite this ostensibly privileged status, women reported that actual treatment by men sometimes disappointed. Less than a tenth of the women who reported themselves disappointed, harassed, or discriminated against in public aid encounters said they expected a favored status vis-à-vis men; most expected the "common courtesy" they believed was due to all.

Women's Experiences of Public Aid

Cross-sex public aid produces a tension between a romantic agenda and an altruistic one. My observations and interviews showed that a woman's helpfulness or neediness was often taken by strange men as a signal of openness and desire to be engaged in further interaction or simply as an opportunity to insult a woman. Women informants for this study often reported that problematic gender relations in cross-sex encounters limited their willingness to get and to give public aid, sometimes making public aid encounters distasteful instead of the positive instances of reciprocity they might have been.

In consequence, women said, they sometimes found themselves cynical when judging public places or the men who, they perceived, regularly gave them trouble. Where women had once believed public places to be sites of interaction among friendly or at least innocuous strangers, after reflecting on "bad" public aid encounters women's attitudes toward public places—and the male citizens who also inhabited them—had changed for the worse.

Legitimate motives for asking and giving public aid are ideally only those of participating in reciprocal norms, that is, a sense of public responsibility toward one's fellow citizens. If one is a petitioner for aid, one should be willing to repay those same citizens (or the collectivity) by giving future public aid (Gardner 1986). Yet exploitation is as common as the woman who accepts an offered bus seat that she knows she does not need. Undermining acts are as common as the man who seeks any legitimate occasion for talk in public—like public aid encounters—to woo a woman or to secure her acquaintance, or blatantly to ask for her phone number or to make more intimate comments.

Thus, those who exploit norms of reciprocity do double damage: they undermine trust in and compliance with practices like public aid, and they also deny prospective participants the opportunity to recompense others in payment for past favors. One young female homemaker's story is revealing. When walking downtown, holding her sleeping baby, at a time of day when many men were on the streets, the diaper bag opened "and all the things fell out." Yet, she noted with growing desperation, "no man offered to help me, [none] even seemed to look at me, so I started to ask outright. The men refused. I was amazed. At last, a woman came by. She helped me, wouldn't you know." More than one woman mentioned that other women comprised a dependable class on whom they could rely; refusals from men deepened their cynicism.

Certain social categories are expected to exploit the possibilities of public aid. Women, on the basis of gender, reported that they both suspected themselves of overusing public aid from men and regretted their alleged overuse and that of their sisters; this excluded stereotyped "dropped-hanky" situations, which some women reported were in fact canny and productive practices. At the same time, women suspected men of routinely exploiting both petitioning and granting in cross-sex public aid encounters and, indeed, men were named, almost ten times as often as women, to be the authors of both deeds in observations as well as interviews. Sometimes I observed a man convincingly mimic a need for directions to a lone woman, then use the attention he wrested to insult or proposition her; women often reported such incidents.

"Dropping the Hanky":
 Women's Purposeful Exploitation of Public Aid

Both women and men were suspected of ulterior motives by the other sex. In fact, women have been counseled to exploit aid to secure the acquaintance of a man. The mythic case is of the woman who drops a handkerchief or package in order to snag a man to pick it up—a man whose acquaintance she uses the ratified talk to secure. Although men are suspected of exploiting aid to produce a nearness that will be either welcome or unwelcome to the woman, beliefs about women (at least noncriminal women) hold that they will overuse public aid—at worst an annoying situation for the man approached, certainly not a criminal or harassing one. If men exploiters are rude or inconsiderate at their worst, women exploiters seem, at worst, to seek romance when they believe it not to be their lot to make the first move.

Such advice ignores the problems that women have in public places and provides a counterpoint to crime-prevention advice that counsels women, in quite the opposite spirit, to beware of strangers asking public aid and to avoid the petitioner's role as well. Women trying to meet men are, on the contrary, told they may fake the need for information (see, e.g., Hanson 1982:60). A woman also can be advised to seek out a man unknowingly in need of aid himself, such as the stranger at the laundromat innocently loading his white underwear along with his red flannel pajamas; although such an encounter may take some amount of forthright bravery, such a man (who himself seems incompetent) will, in the end, believe she is charming, since "you've established yourself as a helpful, albeit offbeat, woman" (Hanson 1982:60).[5]

When women said that they had indeed initiated "dropped-hanky" encounters, they noted varying results and varying feelings about their experiences. A resourceful and confident Asian-American health-care worker in her mid-thirties, termed it "the best road to romance I've found." This woman reported she had "got three boyfriends when I dropped a large package that I had wrapped up some of my own medical books in—medical books are heavy—and got a nice man to help me each time." The aid led to dinner and then, according to plan, romance. (The downside was, for this woman, that her "incompetence" also played, she felt, into the "stereotype of the fragile Oriental woman"; thus her triumph was a trade-off.)

Some women saw simulating need for aid as allowable, in view of the onus on women who initiate courtship. My informant Susannah was an African-American homemaker who had met her husband Jeff five years before when she purposely dropped cranberries on him:

5. Such suggestions are not limited to women, nor are they limited to public aid encounters. One such advice book, directed to African-Americans, is Davis 1993: see chapter 5, "The Right Place."

I wouldn't tell everyone to try this, but it certainly worked for me. I was standing in line at Safeway just before Thanksgiving, and you know how long the lines are then. I saw a good-looking boy before me, so I dropped a bag of cranberries on his foot. I had my hands full. That boy was Jeff [her future husband].

Susannah defended this practice as a "woman's weapon," and she, along with about 1 in 7 of the women interviewed, specifically mentioned it as a useful, and used, strategy for meeting men strangers. But even women who said that such a tack had "worked" in meeting a man, or at least had provoked a conversation, sometimes remarked that they felt it was "humiliating" or "degrading to have to engage in charades." Although recommending the tactic, a woman who met a future boyfriend by requesting his help in starting the perfectly healthy engine of her car said, "I'd say, 'Go easy.'" She had felt "foolish, stupid, even though it worked, and I felt he was secretly laughing at me for being a fake. In fact, we had an argument about this when we were dating. I don't think a man would've worried about a similar 'fake' on his part." In fact, she was correct: Men informants considered simulating public aid where they had no true need to be instances of "pickups," attempts to transform an unacquainted to an acquainted status. Others felt that a woman who would try to initiate acquaintance with a strange man was morally loose.

About three-fourths of the women who said they had simulated the need for aid or the willingness to provide it said that a man had mocked them or embarrassed them by ignoring their overtures. They felt that if women were allowed to initiate contacts more freely with men they both were and were not acquainted with, they would not have to practice these misleading tactics.

Rights to Public Aid: A Male Perspective

Male informants sometimes spoke of the need to establish or judge a female stranger's "right" to receive help that men would have unthinkingly provided a man (as they occasionally admitted). Some evaluation undoubtedly goes on whenever a public aid encounter happens since any established state of talk can be precedent to robbery or another exploitative encounter; yet men, more than women, spoke of the necessity to judge the other gender for possible exploitation by those who did not—so men judged—really need help.

Some men also spoke of women's propensity to overuse men's alleged capacity to provide certain types of help. For example, many men spoke of women who used men's stereotypically greater knowledge about the mechanical mysteries of cars in order to have a passing man change the tire that a woman might well have changed herself.

Balancing requirements for politely granting extra measures of aid is as hard a task as securing those extra measures of aid. Somewhat less than a quarter of the men interviewed reported that they were baffled when women refused the more-than-ordinary aid that they sincerely believed any woman would need, recalling the old joke about the Boy Scout hurrying the unwilling old lady across the street. In this vein, a computer technician in his twenties related:

> Well, this happened last week. Well, I saw this older lady, I would say forty to sixty, coming out the grocery store, and she had a lot of bags and she was carrying a mop that I guess she had just bought.
>
> Well, my mother raised me to be polite to the ladies and to the old folks too, so I just walked up to her and I started to take the mop to help her along. And we had a wrestling match over that old mop—she just *didn't* want to let 'er go. She kept saying she could do it herself.
>
> I was just trying to help.

As problematic as the offer of unrequested aid can be, women also reported that they were equally troubled when they were refused sought aid.

Simultaneously with feeling obliged to provide a woman (or a person with a disability, or a child, or an elderly person) with a greater than normal amount of public aid, then, a man (or any evaluator) may feel the right to quiz explicitly these lower-status individuals to make sure that public aid is not being exploited—that the aid that will be provided is in fact immediately merited by the person who asks it.

Nearly all the men who pointedly mentioned that women overused public aid also offered anecdotes in which they explicitly queried or argued with a woman who said she needed or seemed to need aid. One young African-American food industry worker told a long tale in which he battled an elderly "but healthy" African-American woman off a bus seat he judged she did not truly need in "a battle of the butts." An Asian-American/white man meticulously questioned a white woman as to why she needed parking meter change, requested as a loan, and "why couldn't she plan ahead." He refused her the quarter, concluding, "She gave me no satisfactory answer." Rightly, some feel trust from public aid, while others feel judged.

There is always a *certification process* for any petitioner for aid, although customarily we hardly pause to consider if the person does in fact deserve a light, a tissue, or directions. Yet in cross-sex public aid encounters, gender relations rise to the fore. When a man felt a woman required more than customary amounts or types of aid, he reported that he scrutinized the woman, as in this instance of a young white college student in his twenties, who said he habitually scrutinized before certifying women petitioners for public aid (although not men):

> When a woman asks me to help her with something, I'll give her the once-over. If she's little or something, O.K. *But*—if she's hefty and middle-aged and looks like she lifts weights, then, no, she can do it herself. The same for getting up on a bus to give her a seat.

Men who evaluated a woman's merit often specified a set of characteristics for an undeserving woman that described her, and her appearance, as nontraditional and status deprived—in short, everything we do not expect a woman to be: middle-aged or old, ugly, or strong. Purportedly, to include such women among those eligible for aid would powerfully tax the time and strength of men strangers. A man whose words almost repeated the previous account said that apparently strong women could "handle it themselves. That's what I mean by evaluating rationally: if you didn't, you'd just be helping people all the time, never get anywhere." Yet I observed many occasions of men who gave public aid to other men—middle-aged and older men, men of indifferent appearance, and apparently strong men. The answer to this puzzle, of course, can be found in the basis of much of the etiquette and civility of public order, which is a heterosexually motivated romantic attraction that is awarded at a man's discretion. These tenets of the social order instruct that a man is not attracted to older or unattractive women, women who have not preserved the strength differential between the sexes, or women who can reliably be imagined to be the property of another man, as shown by the copresence of a child.

When aid was not given, men fell back on accounts that portrayed themselves as upholders of a new and egalitarian etiquette of public places. One man interviewed noted that "if a woman's arms aren't broken" there was no need to award public aid. Significantly, he also reported that a woman juggling a baby and a toddler had asked him for help in getting her coin purse out of her coat pocket in a movie line. He assessed her age—early twenties perhaps—then refused her, explaining that "men and women are equal now." Another man avowed that to give women aid was to "go against the equality of the sexes. This is the nineties, [and] I'm a progressive guy." *Soi-disant* liberalism was, then, no guarantor of public aid. Yet another man judged an "old woman who said she couldn't carry [her] bags . . . healthy as a horse, or so she looked to me"; he refused to give her aid.

When men refuse women of nontraditional appearance public aid, their refusal reinforces the value of traditional appearance, unattached youth, and fragility. Although a man might invoke "the equality of the sexes" to account for his refusals to provide public aid, these refusals also sometimes supported the very inequality his words condemned. In such cases, the causes named by men for their problems in social settings commonly contradicted the causes women named in similar incidents.

Significantly, women did *not* report that they withheld or believed they had the right to withhold aid from a man who might not need it. For their part, men only reported instances of women who had refused them public aid when the woman was not capable of supplying the aid, when it was clear that the woman was frightened by the strange man's approach *per se,* or when the man admitted that he had embroidered the conversation with other, sometimes smutty, talk.

Dilemmas result for well-meaning men as well. Such men sometimes took the trouble, for example, to attempt to demonstrate their innocence to strange women in need of public aid. Sometimes they themselves felt trapped by a dilemma concerning the strange women who distrusted them. In both reactions, the men wanted to help a woman in need, but recognized that they appeared dangerous to the woman. For the many cases in which a man does not intend to turn public aid into more than it must be, the man may righteously be offended if he is suspected. Women who hesitate, then, may receive reprimands that they are too suspicious or that it is unreasonable to suspect the man's intentions. In these cases, it will again be the woman's turn to apologize for her quite well-founded doubts—and books like this exist to enlighten well-meaning men.

In sum, then, a variety of costs and risks exist for both prospective petitioner and grantor in cases of public aid. These costs and risks vary according to whether direct or implied petitioning is involved. I also suggest that they exist in particular for members of situationally disadvantaged groups, some of whom are ideally provided with extra measures of public aid by custom and etiquette, as a person with a disability is felt to merit the proffered stranger's arm in descending a curb. Thus, women, as other "halo group" members, those who receive more aid than others, receive aid that they do not need and need aid that they are sometimes restricted from getting (Gardner 1986).

Although my interviews and observations showed that men made clear and common use of public aid encounters to foster acquaintance with strange women or to engage strange women in conversation meant to be shocking or lascivious, men—young men in particular—complained of strange women who they believed had attempted to secure their acquaintance through some variation of a classically alluring "dropped-hanky" gambit that might stimulate romantic notice. The crucial difference between men's and women's plaints was that men never expressed the fear that women did, nor did men accuse women of being more than harmless nuisances.

Public aid is unlike other types of ratified talk in public between strangers such as routine greetings and service encounters. In these situations information about the individual as a person can more easily be conveyed than in non-talk street assessments or in many semipublic situations, especially relatively rote and automatic service encounters. Moreover, acts of public aid assume high moral values of selfless helping, sharing, and sociability. If there is a context where gender should not intrude and gender exploitations should not occur, it is public aid. According to informants and my observations, however, this is not so. Public harassment is rife in public aid contexts. The undermining of public aid encounters is significant for gender relations and for the sociology of public places in general. Lapses in civility, of which lapses in gender relations during public aid are but one case, are an as-yet unacknowledged yet significant contribution to the incivility of public places in general.

Because women are subject to many forms of public harassment, of which lapses or refusals of public aid are only one variety, these lapses and refusals can have a cumulative effect, for they are added to any other abuses a woman receives. Too, since public aid offers the most promising situation for positive gains, it may be the one that is most recalled as harmful, disappointing, or simply exhausting. Both observations and interviews showed how unwanted public aid can be thrust on one and wanted public aid withheld, and these situations added to the burden of other public harassment. Despite the reports of women who said that they had exploited public aid encounters to spark romance or at least an acquaintance with a strange man, more common was the complaint that women who needed help from strange men did not receive it or received extraneous talk—perhaps insulting, perhaps evaluative about appearance, perhaps questioning the right to receive aid at all. With regard especially to urban civility, which is currently such a concern, women's experiences undoubtedly reveal a diminished potential for our routines and rituals of interaction between strangers to imbue public places with trust. Women's public harassment is thus neither new nor simple, and it can occur during one of the most potentially positive legitimate contexts in public places—that of public aid.

PUBLIC HARASSMENT: COMMON ABUSES

The presence of public harassment in these various contexts suggests not simply that frequent possibilities for harassment exist in the public realm but that each context and all contexts hold possibilities for a common set of abusive practices. (I will allude to these practices as I continue to write about participants and behavior; see, especially, chapters 3 and 4.) In general, common abuses in public places are of three types: (1) *exclusionary practices,* where a set of individuals is forbidden to or discouraged from entering into some or all public places; (2) *exploitative practices,* where small freedoms or outright intrusions are practiced on a set of individuals, effectively disallowing them the privacy others enjoy and subjecting them to, for instance, conversation, touching, close scrutiny, or being followed; and (3) *evaluative practices,* where one set of individuals receives the evaluative opinion of strangers in situations where such evaluation is normally not warranted. A specific abuse may fall into more than one category.

Exclusionary Practices

For most individuals who are not regular members of situationally disadvantaged groups, it makes only limited sense to speak of one's "rights" of access to or presence on city streets and in shops and restaurants. The members of a situationally disadvantaged group, however, may note that these taken-for-granted rights are still in the process of being morally earned. Popular opinion purports that if the members of a given situationally disadvantaged group are wise they will avoid certain areas, times of day, and cities where their kind is known to be badly treated. They may also be advised to moderate behavior that can reveal their category membership to strangers if it is not apparent. When members of situationally disadvantaged groups ignore this "good sense," they are said to be "flaunting" category membership or "asking for trouble."

Exclusion restricts access to public places so that category members are either not formally allowed presence in public in general, not allowed in certain areas, or are subject to features of public places that effectively prevent them from venturing into public. For the most part, I speak of exclusion as practices that are mandated by folkways. There is, arguably, another type, pertinent to some but not all situationally disadvantaged. This might be called physical exclusion, since it encompasses characteristics that define a region in physical terms— for instance, when a public place presents not only a morally but also a physically unpleasant, forbidding, or impossible environment for some people (e.g., those with impaired mobility or loss of vision). Thus, over and above whatever difficulties people with disabilities encounter in contacts with the nondisabled that limit the presence of people with disabilities, once having achieved presence, their comfort may be delimited.

Poorly designed or poorly modified environmental features are, of course, the material consequences of belief systems and behavioral patterns that hamper the full participation of situationally disadvantaged groups in public places. A moral climate is thereby created that can discourage presence in a region. This moral climate can be just as effective in winnowing situationally disadvantaged groups from public places as can restricted public transportation. Similar statements can be made about the furnishing of the environment to protect women in public.

Exclusion can be effected by relatively formal social control measures such as laws and rules of etiquette, by informal measures of social control like verbal and nonverbal behavior, and by the internalization of shame, fear, and guilt by the individual who is the target of exclusion. Examples are common: folk wisdom that counsels group members to avoid public places, as in the case of women and crime, and historical laws that restrict people with disabilities who "constitute a disgusting sight" from appearing in public (Compton 1989); laws that demand separate facilities for African-Americans or for women or disallow presence in certain areas of public places; the absence of physical features that provide for certain contingencies in public places, such as sheltered spaces, adequate lighting, or police call-boxes.

Exclusionary practices force a *reduced* presence that can appear to be the result of choice, as when women, gays, African-Americans, and people with disabilities say that they do not want to go to public places where they are not "welcome." Reduced presence can also be the result of what is clinically identified as agrophobia, which afflicts women, or *reasonable* fears for avoiding public places, which category members may describe as agoraphobia, as I have heard members of diverse situationally disadvantaged groups do. The presence in public places of more individuals with some type of disadvantage makes practical demands of both disadvantaged and advantaged in the achievement of acceptance, often on a many-times-daily basis.

Part of what a member of a situationally disadvantaged group can come to fear from exclusion is that, subtly or baldly, the individual will at some point be accused of not meriting presence in public places at all—something that can feel very like being told that she or he is not a citizen of the country after all. Thus, the situationally disadvantaged rightly come to fear the accusation that she or he should not be "out in public," that is, that she or he does not have the same rights in public places that others seem to have.

For women, exclusion has historically been enforced in a variety of ways: from etiquette, to a division of labor that prevents the woman from having the time to venture into public, to crime-preventive advice that instructs her it is dangerous to do so. Female informants occasionally reported that they were questioned about their right to be out at night or even early in the evening. Some women reported that they were asked what they were doing not only in a place that had an unsavory reputation but also in a "nice restaurant that served liquor." Six of the 293 women interviewed said they had been asked—in contexts ranging from buying gas, to "malling it," to distributing anti-abortion leaflets on a street corner—why they were not home with their children.

Ironically, exclusion is a paradoxical type of abuse with regard to public places since it effectively prevents the individual from receiving other types of public harassment. Thus, types of harassment are to some extent hierarchically arranged: Before the individual can even be considered a candidate for evaluative practices, she or he must be granted access to public places. Thus, to say that the individual's rights to presence are abridged, limited, or modified is also to say implicitly that she or he is shorn of the right to mere presence in public; rights to more-involving potential interactions in public places, such as public aid or romantic "pickups" that transform strangers into acquaintances, are truncated as well. How unwelcome any invasion is depends, of course, on the feelings of the invaded: A romantic pickup may be just what a woman has been hoping for as well as a mark of low regard or the reason for fear.

Exclusionary experiences, beliefs, practices, and laws suggest that it is too simple to say that interactions in public places are episodic or diffuse with regard to communication. If they are diffuse, it is ironically so, since diffuseness comes coupled with the capacity to make pointed messages of great symbolic force on the individual's life.

Exploitative Practices

A second general type of abuse is the exploitative practice, in which small freedoms or outright intrusions effectively disallow individuals the privacy that others enjoy. Behaviors that can be classified as exploitative include the intense inspection that can evaluate people with disabilities; touching, grabbing, pinching, and stroking; pointing and staring and taking photographs as if to verify that the appearance is real, as reported by some people with disabilities and by one red-haired, green-eyed African-American woman; valuative public shows in semipublic circumstances, such as historical slave market auctions for African-Americans and displays of people with disabilities at medieval fairs or more contemporary sideshows. Judging through the usual means of visual information, then, can widen the gulf between situationally disadvantaged and advantaged, turning the first into objects of interest and the latter into sometimes curious, sometimes brave onlookers.

In one exploitative practice, the member of a situationally disadvantaged group constitutes a point of interest, either curious, critical, or contemptuous, for others. If we need to depend on appearance to assess strangers in public, we make it more likely that we will scrutinize them and that they may be revealed as members of a situationally disadvantaged group. As a consequence of an out-of-place status in public places, members of some situationally disadvantaged categories are sometimes subject to the free gaze and minute inspection of others. Patterns of visual contact that are normative for public places, such as civil inattention and social recognition, can be abrogated. Scrutiny can be helped with artificial aids like cameras or binoculars.

We can experience strangers as veritable objects that draw our intense and riveted inspection—that is, we engage in a process that can be called "inspection draw" (Gardner 1992). One element of inspection draw can be thought of as forced witnessing, as happens in cases of sexual harassment.[6] The regular scrutiny that the situationally disadvantaged undergo when in public gives them, in fact, a kinship with apparently very different groups such as celebrities or the notorious. These latter groups may feel that, whatever else celebrity has brought them, fine examination of their every move is something for which they had not bargained; because of scrutiny in public places, celebrities may decide to make momentous decisions, such as donning disguises, concluding that they must end their shopping days forever, or even moving to secure what they regard as peace when in public places.[7] It is hardly a surprise when such-and-such a famous name has decided to relocate to the country to avoid public invasion; it is more of a surprise that women sometimes give public harassment as the reason for choosing jobs, pastimes and hobbies, shopping spots, places of worship, or even dwellings.

Inspection draw can be relative. For example, women sometimes say that, when they are in the company of other women either less or more attractive than they believe themselves to be, they note their own status flicker from visible to invisible. Not only can they receive varying "complimentary" street remarks on one outing, they may, depending upon the estimated attractiveness of other nearby women, gather interest from one stranger but be ignored by the next for an apparently more intriguing woman.

6. In a recent case, a woman cadet at a military school was chained to a toilet and was photographed there; elsewhere, a sports writer had prospective interviewees flash their genitals at her in a locker room. Tailhook disclosed that male naval personnel engaged in a highly ritualized kind of exhibitionism by doing the "elephant walk," a "manly" thing to do: they exposed their genitals to female recruits and other personnel.

7. Examples of the measures and reactions spoken of here are detailed in other chapters, especially chapters 2 and 3, "Contexts" and "Participants." My own work in progress makes it clear that people with disabilities, with members of

Thus, some members of situationally disadvantaged groups note that members of the public subject them to a sliding scale of interest. Knowing that inspection is forthcoming, those most likely to draw gaze will sometimes incorporate the inspection they are sure will follow as one of the marking rituals of presentation for their group, as, for instance, do cross-dressers (Fry 1974:162–163). Or they may evolve complex strategies for dealing with inspection, strategies in which companions may have to take part since they too will be examined and assessed. Inspection draw is often implicitly critical, yet it sometimes simply conveys that the individual can be examined closely and seemingly "verified."

Other means of harassment are unambiguously or more subtly appraising, but valuative nonetheless. Women, as well as members of other situationally disadvantaged groups, will find that public places manage to exploit every aspect of their existence. (Chapter 4 in particular, which deals with some aspects of behavior, demonstrates how many apparently armored aspects of the woman's presence can be exploited by the determined, or even casually interested, man.) Apparently functional conversation—such as that involved in service encounters or asking help of a stranger—can turn out to have lengthy adhesions, where the woman's sexuality or, simply, her personal life becomes the topic. There are exploitations of public presence whereby men exploit the situation of proximity to touch or grab or even hit the woman, to follow her, or to subject her (or parts of her body) to lengthy and insulting scrutiny. In all of these situations, a routine and unavoidable aspect of being in public is mined for the worst that the stranger can do. Nearly every public harassment has an exploitative aspect; many have an evaluative component as well.

---

other situationally disadvantaged categories, sometimes also take up the very same measures. In public places, then, we are all sometime-celebrities, and often unwilling ones at that.

Evaluative Practices

A third category of mistreatment is *evaluation,* by which I mean measures of public harassment that critically appraise, characterize, and rate the category member, as do street remarks for women in particular, and name-calling and exploitations of common verbal routines for all other categories. Stereotypy of the group is a necessary element of verbal and nonverbal evaluation, needed to catch attention and to wound—it must be relied upon because all more personal knowledge of the individual must be guessed at. (The crucial element of an evaluative practice is *not* that it is verbal, however. It is that the critical element predominates over that of mulcting a social routine, as in exploitative practices, or simply robbing one of the right to participate at all, as in exclusionary practices.) Evaluation may be either positive, in which case the authors will argue it to be complimentary, or negative—in which case the authors will argue it to be deserved and stimulated by the target. In the public world of stereotyped verbal evaluations, an educated young African-American man was transformed into the chattel of the white woman he accompanied. The woman noted that, as an interracial couple, they "mostly try to ignore rudeness. Every once in a while, though, you can't. The other day, a carfull of white teenagers went past us and they made comments about Bob being my 'slave.' One of them sang 'Way down south in the land of cotton—' and so on" (see also Gregory 1970:146).

Commonly, indirect evaluations occur that feature the imposition of a theatrical metaphor, in which the situationally disadvantaged individual is the avidly watched player on display and the advantaged person becomes the master of ceremonies, who is able to dictate the moment's entertainment. The advantaged person can choose to pretend that a passing woman is, for instance, a beauty pageant entrant that he can rate with a written number, as when a trio of young white men I observed "girl-watching" on the main library steps seemed to take studious notes on each passing woman, then trotted after each woman to inform her if she was a runner-up or a winner.

Finally, the evaluation may be a characterization that, ostensibly at least, seems complimentary; yet, it is no less an evaluation, a presumption made from the dominance and right to judge of the advantaged person. In this way, street remarks to women from men are overt compliments at times, but they are delivered in such a way and in such an atmosphere that the privilege of the commentator to judge and review (and to deliver a less pleasing verdict if he so chooses) is clear. One airline passenger who had to reveal himself to be Jewish to receive his kosher meal found himself also presumed to be honest and a teetotaler (Israel 1985:38–39). In this way, all evaluation in public places is closely related to the right of the situationally advantaged person to define both the situation and the other individual.

Members of situationally disadvantaged groups soon learn that almost any activity can be the opportunity for such gender-based harassment. A white teacher in her early twenties was in a public park where many people stroll, exercise, walk dogs, or just sit:

> I was waiting for my boyfriend on a park bench. While I was there, I was doing some mending. This middle-aged man came up to me. He looked perfectly respectable, and he was walking his dog. He sort of shook his head and said, "You're always knitting something, aren't you?" I said, "Pardon me?" I was surprised, because I didn't know him and the remark sounded personal and, anyway, I wasn't knitting [but sewing]. He then said, "My wife's always knitting something too—she's got nothing better to do, I guess." I sort of smiled, but I was disturbed. This was clearly an insult. But I didn't want to get involved with him, so I just said nothing. But then he said, "Well, see you later," as if I should be there tomorrow, handy for his comments. A little bit, I felt like a park bench myself.

Semipublic contexts can either facilitate or complicate reactions to evaluation, reactions that women label satisfactory. These contexts of disadvantage reinforce other circumstances of disadvantage such as the speed of an act or a getaway. Thus, a female student in a large high school was hit on the buttocks with a yearbook by a male student she did not know as he rocketed down the hall. As the force of the blow toppled her, she heard him yell that she had a "nice butt." Evaluations like these in semipublic contexts can leave women stymied. Although the student wanted to retaliate, she feared "I'd see him again. He might turn out to be my best friend's brother. Or"—the curse of the evaluative practice—"they might think I was a bitch, since it *was* a compliment. He said I had a 'nice butt,' after all." An intrusion can also come at the end of an otherwise nonevaluative conversation, as happened to a woman "in a bar one weekend when a guy struck up a conversation" with her. After a brief conversation, he rose to leave and pinched her buttocks while walking away. Her reaction was much like the young high school woman's: She was too mystified by the positive evaluation of a casual buttocks pinch and inhibited by the bar crowd to retaliate.

Contexts are sometimes a circumstance of disadvantage, calling to mind other disadvantages. Thus, a woman who might want to get out of a semipublic situation like a restaurant meal or a school game is restrained by the hope of securing food or the fear of embarrassment before peers. These realizations fortify disadvantages under which women operate as they extend vulnerability to another set of sites.

Often, however, interviewees reported that semipublic offenses convinced a woman that her only recourse was to leave the situation— the area, store, synagogue or church, even her job. To some women, then, exploitations were practical impediments to carrying out everyday, as well as work or school, activities. The nature of the impediment is a "category classification activity," namely, an act imposed by a man that exploits her presence and in so doing reminds her that a perpetual task for her is to achieve gender and that the worth of that achievement may be evaluated and commented on by men at any time. Such encounters caused one informant to leave a store without buying the furniture she needed when "the salesman was the friendly type." The salesman had taken every possible occasion to touch her shoulder or pat her arm or back; as she moved away, he moved closer, finally touching her hand—she then decided she "had had enough of that."

Occurrences of this sort can give a woman a sense of vulnerability and trepidation even about activities with those with whom she is slightly acquainted or with whom she has thus far felt she shared a situation or even a spiritual life. A young African-American college student reported such an experience:

> I got off the school bus by a student. As I was walking on the sidewalk, I noticed that my shoe had come untied. As I laid my books on the ground to tie my shoelaces, a student with whom I had rode the school bus ran over and smacked me on the bottom. . . . Another time, after church, when I was not looking this man whom I later found out was a deacon in the church kept rubbing his hand up and down my arm. ("Doe" 1991)

Of course, cases in semipublic places or between the semiacquainted could have other complications: A fight could break out in school, and the retaliating woman could find herself handled by official agents of social control like a security guard or principal; in places of business a woman could fear that her job was at stake if she was a harassed worker or that she would not receive services if she was the customer. Furthermore, in many semipublic cases where the participants are semiacquainted, a man would know where to find a woman, leading her to fear retaliation for her retaliation.

CONTEXT AND CONSEQUENCE

At stake in all instances of harassment are intrusions on the limited privacy any citizen expects to retain while in public, as well as threats to one's inability to maintain control and escape harm. Some abuses involve the production of physical pain (as chapter 4 in particular will show), and in many cases, public places become precincts defined by heightened vulnerability and fear of intimidation. Harassment in general provides lessons in the fragility of public places and, more generally, in the fragility of the social web. In public harassment, every aspect of the individual's simple presence in a public place can be intruded upon. This stands as a general reminder of the vulnerability of the individual's presence and privacy; more, it may stand to women as a reminder of their vulnerability not just in public places but in private and semipublic circumstances, too. When without significant penalty, public harassment abuse to women of whatever kind and in whatever context sends a symbolic message that men's rights and control are predominant and omnipresent and can be communicated even in an arena where all citizens—especially women—are most vulnerable.

These three types of public harassment and the many contexts of public harassment flesh out our general notion of what it means to be in public by showing the many defenses the individual must unconsciously mount and the many abuses that normal civility could protect her or him from. In the matter of abuses and in the salience of these reminders, situationally disadvantaged groups are made most aware; among these groups, women are consistently and unapologetically abused.

Furthermore, public harassment abuses are significant in terms of (1) their contribution to the situated self that women present in public; (2) their relationship to an informal social control in public places; and (3) their effect on the complementary situated self that men must demonstrate in public. The simple stereotypy of these abuses reinforces *Kaffeeklatsch* complaints of one sex about the other, enabling women to deprecate men who seem to want only one thing, and requiring men to seem to want it. In addition, public harassment abuses emphasize and reinforce other social problems, including: problems in public places, such as women's vulnerability to rape and assault; problems in private places, like wife-battery; societal problems that affect all women, like pornography; and other problems in contexts like the workplace and school such as sexual harassment and discrimination.

Insofar as public harassment echoes these other problems it makes women into a group expectant of social abuse and men into a group prepared to give it and practiced in its execution. This constant reinforcement of public harassment makes it more unlikely that women will be treated with civility in public places. Recently, women experiencing public harassment have begun to identify it clearly as a form of sexual harassment, as in the case of women students touched and hugged by men students who are strangers to them (I discuss this at length in chapter 5).

In addition to the dangers that women experience in public, women face a legal system that does not currently recognize these abuses as wrong and a prevalent architectural scheme that does not offer women special shelter or otherwise provide for their needs. Public harassment abuses are thus part of a discriminatory and endangering environment, and this adds to their force. To trace the path of these abuses is to begin to account for the ways in which a woman's sense of vulnerability is constructed, rationalized, experienced, and managed.

This chapter, then, has documented a set of potentially troublesome contexts and a typology of common abusive practices. It has also offered an explanation of the sense of vulnerability women can develop in public places and the ways in which their claims to civil treatment from others are in constant danger of repudiation and must be constantly defended. In sum, the occurrence of public harassment in so many contexts suggests that civility in public is not the given that it has been assumed to be by many analysts, or certainly that if one's presence in public signals a temporary ceasefire in the war of man against man, it does not seem to do so in the war between the sexes. Instead, even such common acts of civility as restraining from haranguing, scrutinizing, or touching another person are privileges that the individual earns partly by virtue of gender, and that must be bargained for and achieved, perhaps many times in the course of a single trip into public places. What a woman can hope to attain by presenting a seemly and attractive public appearance is simply to be left alone by those who will appreciate that she has bowed to the norms, as it were; what she can in fact attain is targetworthiness, since gender also makes her ripe for a variety of abuses. Many contexts support, even encourage public harassment of women, and on examination, women must admit that almost any man can, and typically does, commit public harassment.

The very structure of public places determines the type of communication that strangers can accomplish; in each context a woman will also find that gender can intrude. Women report that public harassment happens in public contexts such as the street, semipublic contexts such as stores and schools, and insulated settings such as in cars. Harassment can occur when women are shielded by other activities or other people, or during ratified talk in public places, as when one individual asks another for help. Examining the many contexts of cross-gender relations in public places is useful, since the women who were interviewed for this study said public harassment, despite its typical brevity, could have deep and lasting impact. Public place interaction is frequent, recurrent, and pervasive, and, as the next chapter reveals, can be practiced by any man with any woman as target.

CHAPTER THREE

Participants

THERE'S A STRANGER IN THE BAR, BUT HE'S ONLY
PACKING A PEN. BEEVILLE, Tex. Dec. 28 [1991]—The tall,
lanky Texan strode into the dance hall. He leaned up against the bar
and ordered a pitcher of beer. He surveyed the crowd with his sea-
blue eyes.

"You live around here?" he asked some of the young women
who stood nearly gaping at his posse of heavily armed men.

Spying a young woman in a down jacket and skin-tight jeans, he
put his arm around her and purred, "You and me, alone at last." . . .

George Bush, good ol' boy, is back in town.

December 1991 news release by Andrew Rosenthal,
special to The New York Times

All give, all get.
Woman informant, Indianapolis

One of the most pervasive myths about public harassment of women
by men is that it can satisfactorily be explained if the character, station,
or social class of the man offender—or the appearance of the female
target—is taken into account. Men's "low" class and women's "low"
appearance are thus used as moral judgments to rationalize an offense.
Certainly every one of the 293 women interviewed, regardless of class,
age, appearance, and occupation, had experienced public harassment,

and all but 9 classified it as troublesome; certainly every one of the 213 men interviewed, similarly without restriction to class, age, appearance, and occupation, said (eventually) that he himself had bestowed public harassment.

It is, in fact, indicative of how well known, expected, and universal public harassment is when it is highlighted in a movie such as *Thelma & Louise*—when a trucker leers, slurps, and gestures at two women riding in a car—or in a rap song, "U.N.I.T.Y.," by Queen Latifah. It is just as significant when the president plays at public harassment in the course of a sound-byte moment. Public harassment is not solely the practice of the lowly born or a crude working class, nor is it accomplished only for the purpose of racial vengeance, as many informants of both sexes and every race argued. A woman knows that, just as she is one of a constant and inexhaustible supply of targets for offending men, so too is the available supply of offending men a constant and inexhaustible one. For example, a woman who was pursued by a group of men through a mall, grabbed, and kissed later noted the event had increased her "general suspicion of males, and then also, it occurs to me sometimes that, even if I don't see this same man the next time I'm at Lafayette [Mall], any other man might do the same, or worse." Just as the last chapter showed that public harassment pervades all contexts, this chapter will show that all types of men can be harassers—and all women their targets.

For all participants, the experience and meaning of public harassment was modified by the set of what we, as a society, believe to be "legitimate" reasons for interaction in public places. Before I discuss what it means when an individual, female or male, is author or recipient of those breaches that make up public harassment, I will discuss the legitimate events that form the background against which breaches are experienced. Understanding that a legitimate contact is occurring can calm a woman, but she will also understand that a man can, when he chooses, transform any of these legitimate contacts into a distasteful, unwelcome, even ominous encounter. As we learned from the last chapter, all contexts thereby become suspect.

LEGITIMATE TALK, INTERACTION, AND CONTACT IN PUBLIC

Every citizen, of course, has the opportunity and the right to approach strangers, although some otherwise competent citizens, such as people with disabilities like stuttering or hearing loss, may be generally restricted from doing so or may meet frequent rejection when they do (see, for instance, Higgins 1980; Murray 1980).

Some contexts, constellations of participation, and, of course, appearances argue in themselves that individuals are involved in legitimate pursuits. Merely by being accompanied, for example, a citizen is less likely to be judged as inappropriate in public places: If two or more people are performing some inappropriate act it has the force of legitimate pursuit. Accompaniment also defuses urban paranoia toward the solitary, a paranoia that affects both sexes. Then again, having a companion furnishes an audience off which one can bounce remarks and gestures that show all citizens that one is aware of impropriety and would correct it if possible. I once observed a quartet of affluent young college-aged men, three African-Americans and one Asian-American—roommates, perhaps—laboriously carting home a 1960s Swedish-modern sofa that they had gathered from a pile of curbside refuse in downtown Indianapolis's Talbott Street district. As they walked, they took care to engage each passerby—indeed, even people across the street who were watching them with interest—through eye contact and some deprecating, explanatory comment. Such commentary is not just *not* public harassment: Made by others, it is a generous move that communicates to the other person that her or his delict has been recognized and explained away or forgiven. Made by guilty individuals, these comments show that commentators know how far their current behavior is from their usual activities and how little it represents what they truly are. Citizens do seem to react more charitably to inappropriate behavior by those in pairs or groups than they do to singles. Street remarks to the situationally disadvantaged, however, differ from explanatory glosses in that street remarks are illegitimate conversation. They are, in fact, commentary on women's behavior that is *treated as inappropriate*: A woman may not in fact be walking down the street toting a sofa, but she may as well be.

There are varied occasions for breaching "civil inattention," a term that sociologist Erving Goffman coined to refer to the ritual between strangers of eyes met, eyes dropped, then a studiously indifferent and nonthreatening middle-distance look (Goffman 1963). Goffman argued civil inattention to be the norm for much of social life between strangers in public places, and he argued also that it conferred the benefit of recognition while also conveying that the other was of no special threat. One occasion—typically a pleasant one—when this usual pattern of civil inattention is breached is when some obvious similarity exists between one passerby and another, which creates a temporary guild of like-minded individuals. This similarity makes a temporary fiction of the anonymity of public life and the uniqueness of any citizen, and verbal remarks and their nonverbal equivalents based upon these "kinship claims" may follow. Persons with dogs of the same breed, cars of the same make, children of the same age—are all licensed to give and receive comments when confronted by those who seem temporarily their kin. Other breaches of civil inattention are open to falsification and exploitation as, for example, the stereotyped case of the young woman who drops a handkerchief; similarity is especially open to misrepresentation.

Citizens anxious to meet other citizens of a desirable class, age, and/or gender may simulate an interest that another person of this class, age, and/or gender will be likely to possess. Currently, the popular literature for the unmarried advises women especially to attempt to forge some apparent or genuine similarity, then to use this similarity as the pretext to start conversation, much in the way that men traditionally transform themselves from unacquainted stranger to newly ratified admirer through the pickup or chat-up. A woman may, for example, be told to carry a camera in hopes of being noted by a shutterbug of the opposite sex (O'Connor and Silverman 1989; see also Gallatin 1987; Glanz and Phillips 1994; Sommerfield 1986). A person need only display the symbolic affinity: One may sport a camera in order to suggest familiarity with photography, entitling one to speak to other camera-wearers and possibly to receive comments from others without cameras but who have knowledge. This use of "badges," as such physical symbols may be called, announces some characteristic of the possessor that is usually unavailable to the public but that, once displayed, becomes a resource for focused interaction and conversation. In years past the bestseller ploy was the most often advised: One was told to carry a bestseller on the assumption that at least some of one's fellow citizens would have read it or heard of it and could be relied upon to announce the fact. Since the 1970s, the blooming of the message T-shirt and the ubiquity of well-appointed public joggers provide similar resources. Of course, other materials can be used to stifle attention and approach from others; predominant examples are portable "personal" radios, compact disk players, and boom boxes.

In claiming kinship, the citizen turns a situation of anonymous nonacquaintance into one of legitimate engagement, and it is the physical object concerned—the vehicle, the camera, the item of apparel—that allows this focus for talk and, perhaps, subsequent efflorescence of conversation. Rather than begrudging our materialistic society, then, we should, at least on this one small front, be grateful that it allows us so many avenues for demonstrating our more personal qualities and consolidating our social identities.

Finally, civil inattention can lapse when the citizen is accompanied by a member of a category that allows them to be approached at will with no pretense of stranger etiquette, as, for example, a child or a dog. Those who are physically "different" from the ideal—those judged ugly, the fat (Millman 1980:9–10, 79, 85, 184–185; Chernin 1981: 123–124), those with some disabilities—often constitute adult "open persons," to use Goffman's term for members of groups to whom so little respect is due that they may be approached at will (Goffman 1963). In the past and still today in some areas of the country, African-Americans and other racial minorities are sometimes spoken to as open persons by whites (McLaurin 1987:13–14, 91–93, 98–99), as well as suffering historically a wide and complex system of exclusion or separation in public places (Woodward 1955).

WOMEN ALONE

While completing the interviews for this book, I spoke with one woman who appeared to be the self-actualized model of the liberated professional women of the 1990s. A physician in her thirties, she was conventionally attractive, exquisitely dressed, counted herself a feminist, and was the competent and loving mother of two small children. Here, I thought as I interviewed, is a woman who will provide a politicized account of women's experience in public places—and so she did, save for her reminiscences of her early days as a medical student living alone in Indianapolis. There were, she said, "lots of nights I just wanted to get away from the cutting and cadavers, from the gomers [hapless patients about to die] and blood, and take myself out for a terrific dinner, maybe Chinese or Mexican, my two favorites." However, as much as she wanted to go, she found she could not:

> I just couldn't bring myself to eat alone in a restaurant. It was the 1980s, but whenever I sat down alone, I thought I could feel people looking at me, asking, "Why's she alone? Why can't she get a date?" And restaurant people treat you differently—the old myth about women alone tipping less. I gave up. I got frozen Mexican meals and I just stayed home.

This intelligent, feminist professional woman was afraid to venture out to a restaurant by herself on an occasion when she badly needed a meal out to restore her well-being. Instead, she says she contented herself with staying at home and eating frozen food. Explaining such a mundane irony was, in fact, one reason I began the research for this book: I had heard similar stories so many times that I wanted to discover, if I could, how such a situation could continue to exist.

This informant was no different from many to whom I spoke: Even today, women believe that part of what is communicated when they appear in public alone is that they are not sufficiently attractive or accomplished enough *as women* to secure a male companion. For many women, being out in public alone was like starring in a theater role but having no lines; that is to say, as women alone in public, they came to see themselves paradoxically as both central and nugatory to the public order, and both within a brief span of time. A woman who is at one moment the cynosure as she enters a restaurant may subsequently find herself unable to catch the waiter's eye to pay the check.

WOMEN ACCOMPANIED: ESCORTED, BEFRIENDED, WITH CHILD

Another context in which women may appear in public without fear of harassment is when they are accompanied. Informants said that, depending on by whom they were accompanied, there were varying advantages for the respect with which anonymous others, men especially, treated them. A woman alone might be ignored at counters and her place usurped in queues; she might be subject to vulgar street remarks from strange men. Such experiences can lead women to believe—as some Indianapolis women said—that their incomplete status, once remedied, would evaporate. In fact, this was often the case with regard to how a woman was treated by strangers. Sometimes, however, I observed that the way in which a woman was treated by her companion constituted a burden of its own.

Accompanied But Unprotected

Even when accompanied, a woman's momentary separation from escort or friends marks her as a suitable target for men's public harassment. Women reported exploitative and evaluative abuses when, for example, a woman went to get a soda in a movie theater, left an escort in a restaurant or bar to go to the restroom, or shopped in a different area of a store than her companion. The haste with which these women suffered abuse highlights how fragile a woman's presence in public is and how much this presence requires bolstering. For example, at the exact moment she turned to leave her husband's side in search of a cinema snack counter, a woman in her forties felt the arm of a strange man snuggle around her waist. Another study described a woman with some friends at a movie. They "went ahead and got their seats. I wanted some popcorn, so I stood in line and waited. Someone behind me pinched me. I was really upset, because this was the second time something like this happened" ("Doe" 1991).

When a woman momentarily alone is offended, it changes the nature of the disadvantage: It is no longer a brief intrusion that she can disattend or ignore. On the contrary, the woman's purposeful ignoring will possibly be picked up by the other(s) in her party; even if it is not, she may be uncomfortably reminded that more is happening to her than to her escort or friends. Further, she cannot ready herself for abuse, for not only are these intrusions ones she cannot *seem* to anticipate, no really suitable set of countermeasures exist for her protection (a suit of armor being likely only to bring out men with can openers). This makes these situations radically different from those, for example, in which crime is a factor—there are many measures women are advised to take to avoid crimes in public places (see chapter 1). And, since appearing in public places with another is often prescribed as a remedy for the troubles that women experience there, offenses that happen when a woman is with a companion show how ineffective accompaniment is for a woman:

> My most recent experience I had was on 16th Street the night before the [Indy 500] race. I was walking with a group of ten people, about half guys, half girls. I just suddenly felt someone grabbing my rear end and, when I turned around to really blast this guy, no one

was looking at me to prove he did it. So I didn't ever figure out who it was. What really kind of shocked me about it was that I was with my cousin and her husband and their friends, and even though my cousin made sure there was always a guy next to me because of how wild things get down there, some guy felt the need to touch me even though I was with so many people, with guys walking right next to me. I couldn't believe that someone would have the nerve to do that. ("Doe" 1991)

Some women who have a husband or a boyfriend have a strong sense that their "taken" status should be noted or known, although in truth there are only a few, sometimes subtle, ways in which that might be accomplished: a wedding ring, the copresence of children, managing to introduce into the conversation a prior claimant for her romantic attentions even when he is absent. In the case of an absent prior claimant, a woman can feel she has the right to remain unmolested not because of her own rights as an individual, but because she has a husband or boyfriend. Some women said that being accompanied was little better than being alone, and sometimes worse, for it gave women a spurious sense of protection that could all too soon dissolve.

One woman, a white lesbian educator in her fifties, resented the "obligation to go outside with somebody along with me. It's like you had to go to the lavatory in pairs when we were in grade school." As much as she resented this obligation, she often found herself, she said, pairing up with a woman friend or a gay male friend "simply because it makes life easier." Accompanied by a man, she felt "normal":

This is what I'm supposed to be. If I'm with a woman, we're "two girls out on the town." If I'm with a man, I'm dating or with my husband. You can see it in people's eyes. You can see them smile at you—they've placed you now, and they know how to react to you. Otherwise there's always this suspicion: Why is she out alone? Is she a dyke? Is she too psychotic to even have a friend? Public places are for straights, and straight couples at that. If that's not what you are, you have to prove yourself.

As she dissembled, of course, she too publicly supported these romantically paired heterosexual norms.

Of the nearly 300 women interviewed, all but about 20 mentioned that accompaniment was an advantage. Only about 2 percent believed that to be alone was to somehow be free, and each of these had a feminist orientation that was translated in public as the ability and determination to enjoy the anonymity of public places. Of these women, 4 were African-American and 4 were self-identified as lesbians or bisexuals. (In the face of the threat posed to all women participants from all men participants, it is intriguing that any number of women—even only 2 percent—can find public places liberating.) Most women said they followed traditional etiquette for public places, whether they felt it sincerely represented the balance of power within their relationship or their true feelings about the gender relations symbolized; many women said it was simply "easier" this way, "less of a hassle" or "production," for example, to persuade an escort to relinquish a bill than to convince a waiter to present a bill to a woman. Yet the picture that traditional etiquette paints of the escorted woman is one that emphasizes all the elements of symbolic incompetence (discussed in chapter 1), so ease is achieved at some cost.

My observations and interviews documented the following examples. In a restaurant, a woman can still be conceived of as someone who is incompetent to choose a wine herself, choose and order a meal, convey special wishes to a waiter, pay for her meal (not to say her escort's), push in her own chair or pull it out. On the sidewalk, a man escort is thought to buffer a woman from the dangers of the street; the traditional man takes the elbow of the woman engaged in taxing enterprises like crossing the street and sometimes helps strange women with packages, or opens doors or pushes elevator buttons for them. A woman in public is competent to walk, to sit, to eat, and to speak to her male escort, but little else is specified by traditional etiquette.

A woman can find, therefore, that she has traded a publicly evident incomplete status for one that is less obvious. Sometimes she will rejoice at the work that she feels this saves her: "I don't want to bother reading the whole menu anyway," sniffed a young white homemaker. "I can just drift through a date in a dream—I don't have to think about a thing but enjoying myself," rhapsodized a middle-aged African-American nurse.

If a woman is a student of power relations, she might note that there are two situations that leave her more advantaged with regard to the private world of the couple, and sometimes with regard to the public world too: to appear in public with a same-sex friend and, even more beneficial, to appear in public with a child.

A female friend shares her status with regard to etiquette and, thus, is no rival in terms, for example, of selecting wine or seeming competent enough to cross a street unaided. In fact, some 25 women (of the 293 interviewed) volunteered that they were comfortable in public when with their female friends. For one woman, the problem of how to choose a "safe" seat in a movie theater "just never comes up" when she is with a female companion. More important for Indianapolis women, informants noted that a female companion in general, and a group of several female friends especially, had enabled a woman to have some of the few playful, daring times that she had experienced in public. Invariably, when a woman said that she too had practiced gender-based public harassment on men, it was when she was with several other women (and typically when they were all young, often between thirteen and sixteen).

Even fewer problems of symbolic power arise when a woman appears in public with a child (generally, with regard to the advantages accrued, the smaller the better). Typically, any child with whom a woman appears is assumed to be her own, which speaks to the strength of the family as a template and also, to use Harvey Sacks's term, a "membership categorization device" for understanding others (Sacks 1972). Family values, then, are forged and forced in public, too.

Because children are open persons in public, the woman with a child will find that she is open to comment on the child, on the presumed similarity between her own appearance and the child's, on the lauded development of the child (or ruefully noted lack of developmental milestones met), and on a small set of other reasonably safe open topics. A woman learns acceptable answers, misleading even if palliative. She will also become aware that, although copresence with a man offers symbolic protection and relief from some duties and copresence with a young child means that those duties once more become one's own, nevertheless public proof of motherhood (and hence, by the way, presumed heterosexuality) has distinct rewards. There are the rapt, approving smiles and somewhat glassy, hypnotized stares from many strange women and even girls and the sudden warmth, charm, and volubility from some strange men—sometimes the very men who have, moments before, publicly harassed a woman when the woman's child was not in evidence. In sum, when discerning women compared male escorts, the company of female friends, and accompaniment by a child, these women sometimes concluded that accompaniment by a child was the best bet. Eleven women said they had purposely "borrowed" the children of others as "safe-conduct passes" in public places to ensure that they would be more likely to escape harassment by strange men. Often, too, accompaniment by a child neutralized what could otherwise be racial harassment, providing prospective harassers a benign topic—the wonder of children—to obviate their possible attention to race. Both white women and women of color mentioned that they felt accompaniment by a child could have this effect, which was not necessarily guaranteed by the presence of an adult of either sex.

If accompaniment modifies women's behavior in public, it also affects men's. Public harassment by men when in teams or groups outdid that of women in terms of complexity, daring, and frequency.

DRAMATIC SOLOS AND ENSEMBLE PERFORMANCES: MEN ALONE, MEN IN GROUPS

There is more than one type of public harassment that takes place between women and men, judging from whether one man, a pair, or a group is involved. In the representation of group public harassment, as in many other areas, fiction often provides a more vivid portrait than does social science and can emphasize the recreative or sportive elements of group public harassment. Fiction sometimes shows public harassment like insults or "girl-watching" as recreative. Examples can be found in books from James T. Farrell's *Studs Lonigan* (1965:122–123), to Thomas Pynchon's *V.* (1973:32–34), to Alan Sillitoe's *The Loneliness of the Long-Distance Runner* (1960:148–149). Academics have also shown public harassment like insults, "girl-watching" and "cruising," and related activities in a similar light (see Feigelbaum 1974; Cherry 1974; and Riemer 1979). Gerald D. Suttles's classic *The Social Order of the Slum* (1968) skillfully places girl-watching in an ethnic context. A young African-American/Native American salesman informant said of his own behavior and the behavior of other men in groups that the group dynamic stimulated participants to prove masculinity, since when "you're with your guy friends, you get all cocky. You got the balls. You can do anything when you got the balls, especially if you've been drinking an' having a good time."

In terms of the rationale that men (and many women) offer for public harassment, pair or team harassment is most often written off by traditional gender-role advocates as recreative or sportive, using terms like "just play," "little boys' games," and "just boys having fun." Some also argue that team harassment is heightened flattery—after all, this harassment represents more than one man's opinion, doesn't it? Like solo harassment, team harassment can also feature apologies or mitigations (as can solo harassment, of course). Team street remarks offer natural opportunities for one man to offer the remark and another to be team apologist and critic, so that the first man is not put in the position of retracting his own action—a division of labor that allows a woman to feel offense at a wrongdoer and simultaneously mollified by an apologist. (Sometimes these are done by the same member who originates the harassment.) Insofar as men routinize these performances, they can perpetrate harassment with the least amount of planning and with the smoothest quality of performance.

Group harassment is the primary constellation in which public harassment can become melodramatic. Themes of group harassment can be divided according to the ways in which they reflect men's demonstration of (1) the right to evaluate and the right to advise or comment and thus define the situation, behavior, or individual, and (2) the right to proclaim a formal or informal theatrical metaphor in which public places are used as regions where women are players and men are audiences, or vice versa. All of these combine to suggest men's mastery of public territory in terms of their right to assess, comment, and evaluate.

It must be noted that the stage metaphor has a distinctive application. When men practice stagelike public harassment, becoming creative, Klieg-lit players, they practice an interesting inversion. They perform, but it is not to be judged by the audience of women targets but rather to institute claims of attention or to discomfit women. These men do not have stage fright—it is their audience that does.

Finally, urban planners, designers, and architects often contribute— at least theoretically—to the assumption that public stages of the type required by those who offer street remarks are beneficial to the sociability of the city landscape (the works of William Whyte are an example). In brief, these planners view public streets as "participatory landscapes"; successful public spaces, in this view, introduce and accentuate the "dramatic" aspects of private life, presuming that one's private life and public relationships contain aspects worth dramatizing.[1]

---

1. See, for example, Francis (1989:148), and Whyte (1980). That is not to say that architects, urban planners, and sociologists have completely ignored the marked and disadvantaged place of the woman among strangers. See, for instance, historical overviews like Stansell (1986) and Stimpson et al. (1981); treatments of women's patterns of travel like Pickup (1984) or patterns of car use like Scharff (1991). Authors are sometimes specifically concerned with women's shopping behavior or their participation in the workplace. Though there are some general works, such as Franck (1985), Hartmann (1981), and Lofland (1973), few have a feminist agenda. Among those that do are Fox (1985) and Lofland (1984).

As far as women's interpretations of what motivated men in group situations, many women believed that, for a man, being with other men led to the obligation to "prove his masculinity," and that such proof could easily be given by offending a woman. When men were in groups, many women thought, they were likely to "need" to prove their worth or to seem self-confident to others in the group; women were put at risk as a consequence of this need.

Often, a team—of men, at any rate—uses an explicit sports metaphor. In the stage of the streets, sports imagery furnishes an evocative, explicit set of metaphors. Men rate women as judges rate athletes, perhaps verbally or with written cards that are held up; men sit as spectators in sports arenas, crying out their opinions of women's appearance with team-supportive fervor or visiting-team contempt; some men may root for one passing woman, while others of their friends root for another. In short, in many overt ways men can model public harassment on the activities on a sports field, and can use this to support a rationale that what women call harassment is in fact just a "game" or done in the spirit of good clean fun.

The choice of the playing field in practicing public harassment is itself stereotypically masculine. It becomes intriguing when women who mount reversals or turnabouts of public harassment against men strangers choose sports metaphors themselves—for instance, writing or yelling scores in evaluation of passing men. When women informants did this, they reported using a language with which they themselves often felt more discomfort than their targets. For more effective turnabouts, then, women no doubt need different and more imaginative strategies.

There are more covert ways in which public harassment, especially when done by men in teams, recalls sports. Street remarks—those verbal evaluations I will deal with at length in the next chapter—are canonical sports metaphors. Less so are exploitations of presence like unwanted touch and following. Unlike verbal evaluations by teams, exploitations of presence done in teams do not typically have one man who baldly evaluates a woman and others who play her defender; this audience contains only critics. For example, one man usually delivers the touch, while the rest of the team takes up his line, laughing with him, ignoring the incident, appreciatively congratulating him, or mimicking his look of innocence so that the woman who seeks out the offender is confounded. In the case of following, women reported teams of men who acted in relays, one pseudo-surreptitiously replacing another at the end of each man's tour of duty, and teams of men who tracked women in a pack, a particularly terrifying practice even when the men laughed, joked, or protested innocent and admiring intentions.

Rather than a division of labor in which participants demonstrate a seemingly different alignment to the unfolding action, the balance of the team in public harassment is the interpretive backup of a Greek chorus, underlining men's right to proprietorship in public places. A team performance also aids each individual perpetrator in depoliticizing his offense: that is, he can more easily argue that larger social issues are not at stake and that his offense is not consistent with any other set of abuses to which we have become sensitized, like rape, sex discrimination, or sexual harassment in the workplace. Any definition of the situation by multiple performers with one woman as the target will offer the force of numbers in support of the team's "majority" interpretation. Simultaneously, as other members of the team offer concrete corroboration of the offenders as harassers, many harassers also make it more difficult for the woman to tell herself that something unimportant or easily forgettable has happened.

Informants said that men in teams and solo performers as well often structured public harassment so that women's words and actions were taken as fodder for smiles, grins, ridicule, mocking, laughter, and pointing; women's proper behavior was treated as if it was risibly wrong; and women were caused to feel they had committed some act, like tripping or presenting a touchable breast or ugly appearance, that humiliated them—a humiliation that men then used as cause for laughing at women. In short, men engaged in "foolmaking" (discussed in the next chapter), with strange women as their unwary targets. For groups of men, smiling, grinning, or even laughing was a relatively low level of ridicule. Women said groups of men sometimes staged far more elaborate jokes or jests. Men made fools of women when they purposely caused them to commit some public infraction or misstep, then used the infraction as grounds for criticizing them. In exploitations of presence, for example, women reported that they were tripped, deliberately bumped, or rammed and that the perpetrators seemed mightily to enjoy the women's discomfort.

Men working as groups or teams brought to bear a force of numbers that supported the definition of joke or play. Much public harassment was enacted by men in teams vis-à-vis one woman, greatly weighting the force against the woman and making the offender harder to identify when the act was not witnessed. Often one of a group of men enacted the harassment for an audience of others, and the division of labor was sometimes invisible to the woman. Indeed, the joke succeeds all the better when the woman cannot fathom who is the author of the offense. If a woman appears mystified as to the precise culprit, accurate retaliation is stifled and she may publicly display her frustration. Both these occurrences can be fodder for enjoyment: A white woman in her twenties was standing in line at a fast-food restaurant when "somebody grabbed my ass, very painfully. I still don't know who, since when I turned around there was three white guys standing, smiling, in line behind me. They laughed at my angry look, because I couldn't tell who to get mad at, I think."

Women related that teams could function protectively for harassers. In cases of team offenses where one man was the perpetrator and the others were the audience, the audience sometimes assumed a protective wall, refusing to identify the perpetrator. Some women, however, devised a solution to this determined anonymity. Thus, after a "hard rear grab," a teenaged white college student confronted three men, who refused to tell her which had done it; she therefore symbolically "slapped the one in the middle [so as not to] let them think they could get away with something like that." Team performances also have a presentational advantage—the men supply a ready-made audience as well as pointing out performances, ensuring that some who see the performance can be counted on to have the same attitude and to provide the desired response.

Teams can help men depoliticize their offense. In this way, a sexually loaded remark by one man can be reinterpreted as harmless or well taken by a second participant, as in the following case. A white woman in her forties walking in downtown Indianapolis noted a pair of African-American men closely observing her. One looked her over, grinned, and said, stretching out the first word, "Bi-i-i-g tits." She did not respond, and his companion said to the first commentator loudly, "Must be she already married, otherwise she be nice"; then both chortled. It was not, then, that the first speaker had insulted the woman; the woman had offended him by not responding to his overtures and had to be reprimanded by the second speaker.

Thus, a problematic characteristic of public harassment for women is the split of functions sometimes evinced by the men who commit it. This takes place in both single and group harassment and it echoes the ambiguity apparent in many aspects of public harassment. Often when there are two or more men as speakers, a division of labor is presented for the female target—one man gives a respectful greeting, the other an evaluation vitiating the degree to which the woman can tell herself she has received politeness and no more. Thus, two African-American men spoke to an African-American/Asian woman in her twenties, the first exclaiming, "How're you this fine day?" and the second chiming in venomously under his breath, "Slut." Sometimes one man will encompass both functions himself; he utters a greeting remark and follows it with an evaluative one.

There is sometimes a good guy–bad guy split when two men are involved. Typically the good guy speaks first, but not always; when this is so, women's hopes for civility are raised by men's kindness, only to be dashed by men's cruelty, a pattern found elsewhere in the public order in cross-sex relations. Such a split of functions often happens in men's rating games. Whether men rate women from 1 to 10 or use some more esoteric metaphor of the moment, commonly one member of the pair or team will belie the game's assessing nature by greeting a woman respectfully, which insures that the woman will remain unsuspecting and good natured long enough for the rating to be made.

In general, divisions of team labor are also complex, should a woman wish to react or retaliate. Since typically at least one team member acts the part of sincere admirer, leaving his partner or partners to represent male salacity, the woman who is the team's target is left further stymied as to how to retaliate. Because one member at least is overtly respectful and appreciative, even apologetic, at least during the first part of the encounter, she may hesitate to criticize the team's less desirable member or members. The split of functions between offensive and apologetic in general leaves some women feeling confused, even taken advantage of. The second comment shows up the first as a sham, even if a woman attempts to consolidate the first definition by replying to it as what it pretends to be. Knowledge that a public harassment abuse may turn out to be ambiguous in this way reduces a woman's opportunities for swift response, since it is a situation that demands she rapidly choose the sense in which she is to take the remark, the greeting, or the evaluation. If she chooses the greeting, and if it has an abusive sequel, she has chosen to make the best of the man's rudeness; this may happen not once, but ten times in a single day. Therefore the woman who tries to put the best face on any team public harassment may come to feel her good humor to be badly overworked.

The Eloquence of Solos: Star Performances

If team performance features men as a well-coordinated, humorous, often aggressive troupe, men alone sometimes cast themselves and the women they harass as notable performers. Women differed in opinion as to which participants, lone or team, were more feared and more threatening—it depended on contextual factors. One player classifies and defines a situation—as happens in all evaluative practices—and men alone did this, as did the woman. At times, a woman's skillful management of such a situation began to seem mannered patter itself—a routine by the man seems to have evoked a routine from the woman. For example, a single white Midwestern nurse in her thirties said that the occasional gas station attendant would tell her that "you're the prettiest girl that's come in all day," to which she would modestly reply, "I must be the first girl to come in here."

Both team and solo performances can be vivid. Having talked to hundreds of women, it would still be hard for me to say which is the more memorable, hurtful, or dangerous in women's opinions generally. That seemed to depend on the precise incident, the woman's mood, and a variety of other factors including her habitual strategizing with regard to public harassment. Sometimes one florid act by a lone man at an impressionable time left a lasting impression on a young girl. For example, the emblematic gestures of public harassment could indicate spectacular approval, as when a young Indianapolis homemaker noted "my first pat on the derriere is the first and best thing that happened to me in public," or lascivious intent: "Walking down the street when I was eleven," said a typist in her forties, "I saw a middle-aged man dressed in a suit, and the man made obscene movements with his mouth. I'll never forget it." In this way, these momentary occurrences could have a half-life far beyond what might be expected, remaining with a woman for years.

In short, women become aware, although they do not always express it, that any man or group of men can publicly harass them—no matter how young or old a woman is, no matter whether she is pregnant, with a child, or escorted or befriended—and, further, that any public harassment can have a relatively devastating effect on a woman. Women can learn something more. They can learn what an African-American/white homemaker in her fifties learned:

> While walking down the street on my way to pick up my grandbaby, I noticed this real good-looking woman. She was black—well, she was more yellow, like me, maybe that's why I homed in

on her. She was dressed very well, too. As she was proceeding ahead of me, I noticed this man come out of a building. He looked familiar, so I kept watching as I kept walking. Sure enough, if he didn't sidle up to her and say things in her ear—I could see, anybody could, she didn't like it none—and then I saw him take a great big old handful of [her] butt.

Just at that time I realized how I knew that man: He was my minister, who'd just been preaching last week how the Women's Lib was leading the men astray.

Women can learn what a white homemaker in her sixties learned when she spotted her husband "cackling" and insulting "a peroxide blonde" when she chanced to board the same bus as her spouse: All men, not just rednecks or crackers or men of one race or class or educational attainment, commit public harassment. Moreover, any woman, no matter her looks, age, or temperament, can be a target. One practical application is this: If all men are culpable, it behooves us to take broader and more severe measures in countering public harassment and, if all women are targets, it behooves us to do more as a society to protect women.

MEN'S RESPONSES

Men repeated many of women's most racist and classist analyses of public harassment. Like women, for example, most men felt that only uneducated men harass, or men of a race different than that of the speaker. Like women, men said the likeliest sites for women to be harassed were crowded or, alternatively, dangerously empty streets; buses and other forms of public transportation; queues and lines; places where the individual was part of an audience, either in a stadium or theater or gathered informally on the street; and semipublic places like bars, dances, large parties where one did not know many people, fairs, and celebrations with a "carnival spirit" like the Indianapolis 500 or a fair such as Black Expo. This list is of course a fairly comprehensive specification of public places, and thus, it emphasizes that all public places are arenas of opportunity for male dominance rights.

Most interesting, however, is that more than 90 percent of the men interviewed for this book began by denying that they committed public harassment, even when quite innocuous examples were discussed and even when a man was the interviewer. However, by the end of the interview, each of those men had given a "justified" (or unjustified) example that identified him as the author of public harassment.

"ALL WOMEN GET IT": THE DEMOCRACY OF WOMEN TARGETS

To argue that it is only lovely or young women who receive public harassment is to explain it away. When women and men suggested this, what they usually meant was that young women received ostensible "compliments." What they did not mention was that the ostensible compliments often become outright insult and contempt. Through interviews and observations I learned that women of all ages, appearances, races and ethnicities, and sexual preferences can receive gender-based public harassment. The tone of the harassment varies—not the recipient. It may be my ninety-one-year-old mother, or yours. Currently, neither is likely to be secure about her reaction.

"ALL MEN DO IT": THE DEMOCRACY OF MEN HARASSERS

In the same way, many women and men informants argued that public harassment was the province of only some men, at some times, and in some sites. If accepted, these arguments would delimit harassment by author or context. In fact, they are mistaken characterizations, and more than once the person who put forth this popular wisdom gave— only seconds later—an incident from her or his own experience that showed that the constituency of harassers was a broader one than she or he seemed to realize. The gap between beliefs and experience was striking when a man claimed to be of a race or social class that did not harass, then promptly admitted doing so.

In fact, public harassment is a feature of a heterosexually romanticized public order, recapitulating traditional presumptions about gender relations. As such, it is practiced by men of all types, races, and classes. If a traditional woman wants to argue—as she will need to—that the power differential she sees in public harassment is due to something besides the dominance of men, she will have problems completing her argument: Every man is a potential harasser as far as public places go, and every woman knows it—or at least the information unwittingly given in the interviews suggested that the woman could realize it from her own experience. Although most women said initially that only a certain type of man publicly harassed, every woman who limited offenders by class later either modified her statement or gave examples of men who did not fit within the class she delineated.

Traditional women commonly come to have a practical knowledge of public places that differs from the rhetoric of romantic attraction they espouse. Through experience, they come to understand that although they may stereotype and identify classes of male offenders by occupation, race, class, age, and/or appearance, a male member of *any* social category can commit public harassment. An other-race construction worker might say nothing or merely nod and greet a passing woman—as I have observed for cross-sex pairs involving any two races; a same-race businessman in suit and tie, redolent of fine aftershave and toting a burnished briefcase, might invite a woman to grasp his head with her legs and press her crotch against his mouth—as I observed such a man do to a woman who blushed bright pink and hurried on.

Often women saw some categories of men as in themselves too innocuous to pose a serious threat, such as the aged, children, and those classed as mentally retarded. One woman in 15 said this, then promptly gave an example of an elderly man, a young boy, or a mentally retarded man who had in fact harassed them. If such a man did abuse a woman, he was an exception, they suggested. They placed the memorable offender in an exceptional or residual category, such as that of insanity or mental retardation. Such categories are populated by those who prove that public harassment can indeed be committed by all men.

This was the case for a white middle manager in her thirties to whom I spoke. She had been raped (by a white stranger, as it happened); however, she expressed little resentment about men who habitually practice public harassment like following women for blocks (as the rapist had done to her), verbally humiliating women (again, as the rapist had done), or spending long hours simply watching women where they work (she had worked in one of the center booths of a mall, and the rapist spent some weeks acquainting himself with her routine and staring fixedly at her before stalking her). She said, "My guy? He was just a weirdo. Insane. No sane man would do that"—although nothing else she said bore out the suggestion that her attacker was mentally ill. It was, however, her opinion that most problems in public places came from African-American men, although she could recall no instance where such a man had troubled her. (In such cases, I suspected that accusations of "trouble on the streets" were merely a convenient overflow for racism.)

Yet another woman explained that she had been slapped in the face by a man she herself had slapped (much more mildly) for grabbing her buttocks with both hands and squeezing painfully. Her harasser, however, was "just a bad apple—there are some in every barrel." My own observations, as well as women's inconsistent interviews, indicated that harassers were of varying colors, classes, sexual orientations, and ages, that is, many apples from many barrels.

Women formed classes of men they considered likely offenders. I will use the case of Rita, an African-American nurse of about thirty-five, to illustrate how women weight these categories. As a nurse working on the night shift at a large Indianapolis hospital, Rita said she had little choice about clothing that would enhance her appearance, so she took care to look her best when off duty. That appearance is already quite a pleasant and impressive one: Rita is tall, 5′7″ or so, strongly built, and articulate and amusing, and she projects a confidence and competence I felt were genuine. I was not surprised to learn from a friend who had worked with her that Rita's coworkers tended to shift responsibility onto Rita's shoulders, and that nurses, physicians, and patients bent Rita's ear with their personal problems. Her long hair is braided into cornrows painstakingly beaded every few inches. Her hairstyle alone, she said, made her the target of approaches from strangers, often hostile ones from white adults, usually admiring ones from other African-Americans and from white children.

Rita related many incidents of public harassment. She also firmly stated that in most instances she could handle what had happened to her. A man's foremost job, Rita said, was to respect women—women strangers as well as "his women," such as his mother, girlfriend, and daughters. She said that there were three categories of men whose "attentions" she did not mind—old men or retarded men and handsome, successful men. Of exploitations of presence like touching, grabbing, following, and scrutinizing in particular, she noted that they "really irritate me, especially on the street from someone I don't know." But Rita's reaction depended "on who this man is or seems to be to me." She could not see herself "racking up an old man, just for some harmless butt-grab"; she could not see herself "racking up the kind of [younger] man I'm trying so hard to get to notice me." Of course, since Rita exempts "old men," she eliminates them as romantic candidates, as she elevates "young" harassers.

She also added that a man she categorized as mentally retarded would escape her wrath, yet she admitted that she had experienced harassment from even those categories of men she tended to excuse. She reported that she had been harassed by two men, one of whom hit her buttocks and both of whom laughed at her afterward. When she confronted the offender, the man accompanying him explained that the offender was his retarded brother. But, Rita said sharply, the retarded man was apparently not so retarded that he did not know the difference between a woman's buttocks and a man's.

Rita also said that harassment occurring at some sites or in some contexts would be less likely than others to irritate or annoy her. She felt she could better assess whether a man was "decent" or "of better quality" at work, for example. Once she had made this evaluation, she knew what to expect of him.

In sum, having erected a typology of offenders, many women, like Rita, tried to pare their catalog of inoffensive offenders to just a few. They also pointed out that they sometimes suspected even the old or the retarded—that is, the "legitimate offenders"—of having "evil motives," as one woman said. The construction of such hierarchies may mitigate the conclusion that "all men are guilty until proven innocent" and depoliticize harassment by looking to race or class—but it leaves the woman with a sense that she can deal with offenders since they are limited to a few unpopular groups.

A Hierarchy of Dangerous Men: Race

Of the categories most important in identifying offensive men, white Indianapolis women mentioned race most frequently. A white homemaker in her forties described herself and the public places she had observed:

> I'm originally from Alabama and a real old-fashioned Southern lady. No true gentleman insults a lady where I come from, and I've noticed the same here. Low-class men do things, I've got to say [that] Negro men do things. Gentlemen, by which I mean white gentlemen with the proper upbringing, don't. You just don't see it, do you?

In fact, not only had I seen "gentlemen" harassing women, but I concluded that she had too: All her stories of harassment involved white middle-class offenders. (Interestingly, she magnanimously included "Hebrew gentlemen" among nonoffenders.)

For women of color and racially mixed women, race was often a lesser concern in gender-based harassment, or one that came into play with what they perceived as racially charged, not sexually charged, public harassment.

Occasionally a perspicacious white woman would suggest that African-American men sometimes tried to compensate for the fear Whites knew they inspired. A white woman of sixty noted: "Black men often seem to have an air of caution. . . . Black men have crossed to the opposite side of street, almost as if they shouldn't walk toward me. As if they shouldn't come near me." Men's sensitivity must be considered along with their harassment, then.

As I have said, in forming categories of men likely to offend, 9 out of 10 Indianapolis white women most often called on race and class at some point in their interviews to delineate membership categories of possible offenders. Asian-American women and African-American women were more likely to speak of a man's race alone as a predictor of public harassment. Thus this strategy delimited the threat to be identified, reducing the population of possible offenders from all men strangers that a woman encountered and that therefore must be feared or shunned to those of a race and class different from her own. In forming these accounts, white women especially were very likely to espouse a racist and classist criterion to make public harassment comprehensible (although not necessarily less frightening unless the man was of the woman's own race or ethnicity). In fact, when a woman concluded her account of the basic harmlessness of public harassment, she often finished by separating the act from the offender, as did a white self-described "farmer's daughter" in her twenties who was knocked off her bicycle on a busy street in downtown Indianapolis when hit on the buttocks by a group of teenaged African-American boys. Her account acquired a racially significant loading:

> You have to realize that most men are pretty "pro-women." After all, that's who they're going to marry. And so most of this stuff that happens to me doesn't really mean anything.

What disgusted me this time is, these were Black boys. That's what makes it different and scares me bad. My dad even wants me to buy a gun if I'm going to live in the city. We're going to Don's Guns [a large chain of Indianapolis gun and ammunition sellers] next weekend to do it.

When I asked her if she thought she would carry this gun everyday on the street she replied, "Oh, most definitely. My dad says, 'It doesn't do you any good at home in a drawer in the bedside table!' But don't worry: I got a permit." And she had—she showed it to me. The resulting picture is one of an unself-consciously racist woman, one who might charitably forgive men of her own race if they knocked her off her bicycle in busy traffic, but one who contemplated purchasing a gun when other-race strangers did so. This picture bluntly circumscribes stranger trust and fear and shows them as belonging to race and ethnicity more than sex.

A more pointedly charitable, although undeniably condescending, version of the same type of racist analysis was offered by white women who saw African-American men as ineluctably drawn to white women; such men sought the only contact they could have through public harassment. "Well, of course it's Black men who do it, because they've got it tough, and how else could they meet a white woman?" said a middle-aged white nurse who also felt that the many incidents of same-race public harassment she recounted "didn't really hurt anyone."

White female informants suggested a somewhat liberalized version of this charitable condescension, saying that African-American men, fearing to challenge white men directly, seek understandably to humiliate white women, who are convenient targets unlikely to strike back. This analysis emphasizes the innocuousness of public harassment by exculpating African-American offenders because they have suffered badly at the hands of whites. Both versions are very much like the analysis of public harassment as due to men's nature: If men are beasts, then white women often cast men of color as true brutes.

"LEGITIMATE" AND "ILLEGITIMATE" OFFENDERS: LOOKS AND CLASS EVALUATIONS

Looks and class were also criteria for judging the severity of harassment. Young working-class and middle-class women of all races had a tendency, more than did upper-class women, to be mollified on the basis of a harassing man's appearance and adjudged class. It did not matter if a woman was single or married for this to be a factor. Some women therefore said they preferred a handsome harasser to a plain, unkempt, or ugly one, and a wealthy-looking harasser to a poorly dressed or shabby one. Thus, when "a hippie-type Harley-Davidson type, fat, with long hair, does something, it makes me want to puke, and not because I'm scared of him, either," said a young white file clerk; faced with "the *Playboy* type, I don't mind almost anything. I appreciate and even enjoy it." In part, rating harassers by looks and class allows women to romanticize the encounter and persuade themselves that public harassment is indeed tribute to their qualities from worthy would-be Lotharios. Certainly age plays a related role.

Often concerns of class appeared in the guise of excusing comments from men who were spoken of as good-looking, businessmen, "clean," or simply "high-class." A woman might say that a harasser had looked like a man with whom she would want to be seen in public, escorted on a date. This tentative romantic evocation of courtship was then used to embroider a romanticized account.

Like his "nature," a man's class might be the reason a woman would forgive him. Although offensive, he was often not culpably so: Such men "knew no better," as more than one woman said, because they were "uneducated" or "unrefined." "They haven't been exposed to the societal graces the way we have," asserted a young white college student; "they're factory workers and such. And old guys forget."

Finally, women were less inclined to be tolerant of boys who harassed—boys of seven or eight were commonly reported as public harassers. These women found them "disgusting" yet ultimately harmless—disgusting because they were starting so young, but no threat in a physical confrontation. One exception involved race: A middle-aged physically fit white woman reported that she feared a "Black boy of seven or so" and especially African-American boys in groups. More feared than the young boy was the teenaged boy, especially when with a group of friends: A white woman of forty was at a drugstore counter with her husband, "when a kid, couldn't have been twelve, leaned over on the stool next to me and ran his hand up my stocking and smiled at me, like I should enjoy it. You don't much worry, because what's he going to do to you, at that age? But you worry about what he's going to do to you in ten years." Thus, among other things, public harassment by youths or boys communicated a dangerous precedent.

COMPLEX CONSIDERATIONS: THE EFFECT OF WOMEN'S JUDGMENTS

Taken together, as women often chose to do, a complex context could relieve harassers of their responsibilities or their guilt. Women named hierarchies of race, looks, and class, and complexities of context and mood, too. Women especially noted a hierarchy of events in public harassment, and men often agreed. Reactions to public harassment also depended to some degree on the general type, and other circumstances, of harassment. It was, for example, easier for women to explain away, even romanticize the act of ogling as complimentary than it was to derive a compliment from a man who had licked them or who had followed them, wordless, for blocks and blocks. It would be likelier for a woman to accept an intrusion as complimentary if it did not involve direct physical contact; yet intrusions that implied future physical incursion or assault, like persistent following, could seem especially sinister and lead women to believe that a man was planning rape or other violence.

Even women willing to classify some actions as complimentary customarily drew the line someplace. Others, most often women of color, reported a well-worked-out algorithm. A single Asian-American college student of twenty-one said that she, for example, felt "really good when guys compliment me," but that other aspects of street remarks neutralized or negated the innocuous tinge, including whether the man was Asian-American, her own mood and feeling about herself, her feeling of safety. "To tell the truth," she said, "there are a lot of things to think about a lot of times, because this happens to me all the time, everytime I go out." Thus, women typologized likely offenders, along with sites and events, as innocuous or harmful.

Cumulatively, the effect of these weighings and judgments, hierarchies and typologies, was to let many harassers off the hook: A woman might judge a handsome or well-dressed man who followed from stop to stop on her bus route as "an admirer, though I was a little afraid at first," as a young white hotel maid said. But the same woman railed against the "trashy boys" who followed her around a mall. And members of all races often argued that offenders were likely to be of a class, race, or ethnicity other than the target herself; a woman sometimes said that same-race men functioned as her welcome protectors if the minority was thought to be small enough of stature, as for some specific Asian-American and racially mixed women. The same careful attention to the nature of offender, site, and event, however, contrasted strongly with my observations of and informants' words about behavior, which was indubitably malicious, lewd, and humiliating more often than not, as the next chapter demonstrates. What women's sometimes masochistically forgiving explanations were reminiscent of were the vernacular *apologia* we have all heard for man-to-woman offenses, from the alleged accusations of a Supreme Court workplace harasser to a sports hero alleged to be a wife batterer. The complement, typically unstated, is that the woman excusing the public harasser also accuses herself.

CHAPTER FOUR

Behavior

If a man is gracious and courteous to strangers, it shows he is a
citizen of the world.

> *Francis Bacon, "Goodness, and
> Goodness of Nature" (1625)*

You say something to a girl on the street, today it's harassment.
She'll take you to court. It's getting hard to be a nice guy anymore.

> *Andrew "Dice" Clay (1994)*

Of the many ways that public harassment affects women, this chapter
concentrates on four. In addition to examining these four characteristics of harassment, I will explore the ways in which harassment typically works at an advantage for the harasser but places the harassed at
a disadvantage. Not every incident of harassment involves every characteristic. Cumulatively, women's knowledge and experience of these
characteristics helps to explain why even apparently manageable incidents become hurdles and why women feel an overall heightened vulnerability in public places.

A SAMPLER OF PUBLIC HARASSMENT:
ACCESS INFORMATION INTRUSIONS, STREET
REMARKS, AND EXPLOITATIONS OF PRESENCE

Public harassment includes scrutiny, exhibitionism, enmeshing service
encounters, public aid exchanges, or greetings with innuendo and ro-

mantic overtones, and determined following. Here I discuss three types of harassing conduct by men to women, each of which places a different aspect of the self at stake.

Each of these three kinds of public harassment demonstrates a different aspect of the public harassment women receive and suggests some consequences for the "situated self"—the portion of the self that is characterized and tailored for public places. The first section, on "access information," discusses concerns for women in public places that sometimes follow a woman into the private sphere as well; an example would be what might happen when a man discovers where a woman works or obtains her phone number. The second section explores "exploitations of presence," the same set of communicated messages and conundrums relayed on nonverbal channels that exploit an individual's presence in a public place. The third section on "street remarks"—those comments and evaluations that women, and others, receive from strangers—describes talk from the members of advantaged groups that attempts to open up conversations with members of situationally disadvantaged groups.

ACCESS INFORMATION INTRUSIONS: "GETTING TO" WOMEN IN PUBLIC PLACES

The first type of public harassment is a man's attempt to gain access information about a woman, that is, information about her future whereabouts. At stake is a woman's fear of what may happen to her in the future and the wish to keep customarily private identifying information (name, address, phone number, place of work) private.

Access, in Goffman's sense of openness to and availability for interaction, is an especially salient concept for gender relations in public places. A desire for access, or at least the ostensible desire for access, is the source of many street remarks and exploitations of presence; foiling access is at the bottom of much crime-prevention information directed toward women. "Access information" is a related concept, and can be defined as "the information given that would lead to discovery of an individual's immediate or ultimate destination or a place where the individual can later reliably be found." In this sense, access information is a present contact that focuses on future contacts, as access trades on a present that seeks a future. Thus, men's attempts to assess access information often require a verbal exchange, or state of talk. That citizens will enter a verbal exchange is given; the situations surrounding access information show the problems that women have in states of talk in public places that men do not.

Women must guard against stranger contacts in the public domain, instituting a suspicion that can carry over to other areas of their lives. The women and men interviewed agreed that rules and practices for disclosing access information are not gender neutral among strangers. About a tenth of women informants explicitly reported that they had conflicting pressures on them: they desired to remain accessible to others in the limited ways possible to them in public places, they sometimes wanted to spark acquaintance with men, and, of course, they always wanted to remain crime-conscious and not divulge a name or address to a potential criminal. Women also reported that these pressures gave rise to the development of strategies to deal with strange men (I discuss the contingencies and success of these strategies in chapter 6).

The object of acquiring access information is to gain access to the person at some future time, or merely to suggest that such future access is possible. Thus, knowing a woman's home address, her place of work, or her name or telephone number functions as access information, as may knowledge of what her house looks like or knowledge of the general area in which she lives or of her habitual hangouts. The more determined the person in search of access information and the more inaccessible his target, the more slender the knowledge he will build upon—as happens with female or male skiptracers, dedicated fans, or *paparazzi* (none of whom necessarily has women targets, of course).

Technological devices like telephones enable seekers to secure access information, and technological baffles either foil the accumulation of access information or defuse their suspected threat (see Lapin 1983). Of these baffles, the telephone answering machine is sometimes touted as the means to discourage annoyance callers who presumably enjoy threatening access as a thrill or as pure power. Again, access information can differ for tracker and tracked, depending on the degree to which each feels activities must be masked. Thus, a young woman giving a false name or telephone number at a bar can choose to present the information she gives as correct, or she can choose to communicate her prudence by suggesting she has an unlikely or funny name:

> How much I trust a man depends on my intuition about him. If I feel comfortable, I may tell him the truth about everything, even my real name and my home address. But if I feel uncomfortable, I'll try to close the encounter as soon as I can, or else I'll adopt a joking, slightly flighty manner. This joking then allows me to present him with some phony name, and if he catches on that it's phony, it doesn't really matter, because I've already set out that I'm just kidding, and I can always fall back on that. I'm in charge in these situations.

In the same way, the man who trails a strange woman on a city street in order to get a rise or reaction from her sometimes fails to mask his stalking as he might; some men stalkers say specifically that they enjoy the woman's reactions. On the other hand, the aspiring burglar seeking to discover where a wealthy mark lives will make her or his actions discrete, down to the measure of dressing in the same style as prospective victims in order to arouse their suspicions less (Barnes 1971:27).

The results of gaining access information vary from simple, although sometimes threatening, trailings, as is commonly the case for women in public places, to stalkings that are meant to preface crime, to intent to do mayhem, as is the case for criminals with ulterior motives. Access and openness rightly concern all women who spend any time at all in public places, as most must. Women, especially young women, find many reasons to class public places as sites of sexual harassment in everyday life (Stanley and Wise 1987). Women also feel substantial fear of public places as possible sites of crime, especially rape, and have good reason to do so (Bart and O'Brien 1984, 1985). Yet, along with this trepidation, young heterosexual women also feel particular pressure to form acquaintances among members of the opposite sex, a pressure and a fear that have also been noted in other populations such as, for example, gay men (Starr and Carns 1972; Taub 1982).

Women who identified themselves as lesbian or bisexual sometimes argued in interviews that the lesbian and gay bar and restaurant culture removes this burden of finding strangers who may become lovers, since they are guaranteed a population of potential mates or simply of people with whom a brief flirtation may be enjoyed. Although lesbian bars and restaurants certainly have their dangers from the hostile heterosexual population, in this way they present a distinct advantage. One related disadvantage, said a white lesbian professional in her twenties who reported she had only sporadic interest in the dating scene, was for the lesbian who entered such a bar or restaurant only to have a drink or a meal. This woman was annoyed to find that many others were there for express purposes of romantic or at least temporary sexual affiliation and that they made "having a meal out the same sort of hassle I imagine it can be for a straight woman alone."

Some popular advice articles and books counsel young women in the big city to sham the need for information like the time or directions or help in a physical task in order to achieve the goal of meeting men (see, for example, Hanson 1982). To women, then, public places can appear to be places for the exercise of men's power and privilege and, at the same time, places where they believe they must stimulate acquaintance with men.

Access information between the fully acquainted is normally not a problem, as acquaintanceship presumes willingness to present oneself as accessible in at least some way. There are also rules and customs of polite behavior that prevent exploitation of access information, exemplified in the nineteenth century by an intricate introduction and calling-card etiquette (Young 1882:31–41, 52–53). In our own time, the individual realizes that she or he is expected to phone before visiting a friend and that, furthermore, she or he must phone only at certain hours; the individual may also realize that, having learned the schedule or plans of a fresh acquaintance, the individual is not expected to volunteer that she or he has just decided to participate in the same event. Likewise, in rural settings, the locations for all individuals in a given town may be well known to the whole town for least part of the day, although one is often expected to act as if this were not so. Here again, consensual rules for handling access information issues are worked out by custom and etiquette. Knowledge of whereabouts (and other access information) can be linked with the suspicion that the knower may be up to no good. With access information, more than any other area of public harassment, women seem suspected of the most extreme kind of access, that of prostitutes, about whom access is unrationed and purchasable and access information is free to all.

Streetwalking and Walking Streets: Prostitution and Availability

In Western cultures as well as in some Eastern cultures, presentation in public places has been historically linked with prostitution. To be sure, "streetwalker" still means a woman who, by making herself available for paid sex in public places, denotes an accessibility that is strongly sanctioned—in other words, a sex worker. Thus, presence in public places for women is associated with moral laxity. Indeed, the concept of the house as a woman's protective domain has a long tradition; in early advice books for women it was often argued that women should make their homes symbolic cities, since actual cities were not their proper domain, or make their homes symbolic fortresses, since these homes and their associated values were fragile (Pizan 1983[1405]: 8–11).

At certain times and in certain cultures, to be present in public places was to proclaim oneself as a prostitute, a woman who had no right to limit her sexual availability (Cohen 1980:20–21). So that respectable women might go out and not be mistaken for prostitutes, some cultures have designated special badges or costumes for prostitutes (Otis 1985:80) or restricted them to segregated areas in shops or theaters (Goldman 1981:142–143).

Even ordinary women's fashions can connote availability to women themselves. Some women interviewed felt that fashions available to them proclaimed a general accessibility, even a moral looseness, that was difficult to manage publicly. Three women said that they covered jewelry with their first name on it; otherwise, one said, it made her feel as if she was wearing "a sign that said, 'Take me, I'm yours.'" Other women said that, when skirts "were down" or long, they were more comfortable when in public. Revealing fashions, such as the short-shorts and hot-pants of the seventies, made more than one older woman recall their feelings of vulnerability: "I felt I was naked on a billboard," said one with distaste. In the same way, Muslim women who reside in the West often say that they retain native clothing in public places to reduce visual access to their bodies (Stanley and Wise 1987:172).

For women in public places, availability is canonically actual, promised, or threatened availability to their bodies and specifically to sexual parts of their bodies. That these bodies are also available for property or other crimes is a lesser consideration. In many Middle Eastern societies, restraint of women's public accessibility is especially important, since it is a clear signal of sexual availability. In Islamic countries institutionalized clothing like the veil are means of signifying women's inaccessibility even when they do venture into public (Abu Saud 1984: 37–61). This belief has led to virtual appropriation of the public sphere by men and the private sphere by women (see Abu Saud 1984:25–26;

Dorsky 1986:53–73; Mernissi 1987:137–147; and Minai 1981:20–67).
Some have argued that this split is not necessarily inimical to Muslim
women's self-development, although this certainly depends in part on
what the opportunities for men in the public sphere are and are believed to be within a given society (L. Abu-Lughod 1979:637–657). In
peasant societies in general, the separation of the daily rounds of
women and men establishes and constantly reinforces gender as a central variable and force in a society (Harding 1975). Public and private
territories have been identified with men and women, respectively, in
studies of community, where areas that are public spaces have been traditionally analyzed as male preserves (Lofland 1984; Reiter 1975; Wylie
1975). And in feminist utopian or reform movements, a radical redefinition of women's "domestic space" has historically been a notable feature (Hayden 1981:135ff.).

The Search for Access Information

Clearly there is a potential tendency for every public circumstance in
which the woman finds herself to be fragmented by men's intrusion.
Often, as with many street remarks, men can be shown in retrospect
as apparently not needing or wanting to continue an encounter beyond
the harassment of the moment—not, in fact, to have access information or the feared ultimate goals of access information in mind. Other
street remarks are disturbingly different because they are inquiries
for items of access information, as when a young African-American/
white secretary told of the time a middle-aged African-American man
at a lunch counter importuned her for her name, phone number, and
place of work until she finally "left in fear," abandoning her lunch.
Such inquiries or efforts at inquiries can leave women distraught.

Once a woman allows a man to gain a wedge of opening recognition, the exchange can disintegrate into a roundelay of persistent attempts to gain further, then further access. Questioned about directions on the street, one middle-aged white woman was then asked for

her name and number by a "perfectly respectable businessman," also white and middle-aged. While eating her lunch on a park bench, a middle-aged Asian-American woman suffered a young white man who squeezed in next to her; he muttered about selfish people who occupied up too much space, then took out a piece of paper and pencil to record the phone number he confidently asked of her. A white homemaker in her thirties was in the process of changing her baby's diaper as inconspicuously as possible at the back of a nearly empty movie theater when one of the moviegoers, a young African-American man, graciously asked her if she needed help, then if she would give him her phone number; "I think maybe he did it because I have a mixed-race baby," she said.

At any point in a woman's public passage, then, she can meet a man interested in delving into personal information that she is neither prudently expected to display nor disclose except in narrow circumstances. One young African-American saleswoman expressed every woman's nightmare of vulnerability:

> I quit working altogether, and it was because of the actions of a strange man toward me.
>
> Before 1990, I used to work at a sales cart in the middle of a mall. No sooner did I start to work there, than I noticed the same man—white, middle-aged, well-to-do—hanging around. At first he bought small items, gifts like, from the cart, and we would exchange a few words, like you do with any customer. Just trying to be pleasant, you know. Later on, he'd stop by but not buy nothing, and he would make comments about my appearance: I had beautiful hands, a lovely mouth. Still I thought nothing of it—but it began to make me uncomfortable.
>
> Then I began seeing him everyday, standing away from the cart but watching me or sitting on a bench watching me. Now I really began to get worried. And then he followed me out to my car, and then he followed me home twice. His comments now were really vulgar, and he tried to grab on to me. I called the police, but they never could catch him because at that time he started coming around

irregularly. It was impossible to predict when he'd come. I quit my job.

Now I'm terrified. Since I quit my job at the mall, we live O.K., but we could sure use the extra money. I don't work at all now and haven't since it happened. Whatever kind of job I can get, it won't have to do with meeting the public. Also, it's changed my attitude toward men: I'm scared now for myself, and I'm scared for other women too. I don't understand how someone could hurt people like this.

Another woman told a similar story, this one of a man who took considerable pains to learn her office and home schedules; when he finally confronted her, after months of determined stalking, he screamed "that I was a whore, I was easy, I was loose, looking for it. But I say, if I was so available, you'd think he could've found me in less time." This harasser accused her of sluttish availability, his very pains declaring that her unavailability would have been taken as inauthentic and disdainful rejection.

Another 37 of the 293 women interviewed offered that they knew of men who had, they were sure, taken pains to learn their schedules and thus often "just happened" to show up at a certain place at a certain time. It might be a workplace, but it might be a public place bordering as closely as possible on the woman's own home, as when women noted men who consistently took the same apartment elevator as they did, jogged or ran at precisely the same hour each day, emptied the trash at the same intervals, or washed their cars in adjoining backyards at the same point in the week.

Women also described men who consistently turned up at the market, dry cleaner's, or newsstand at the same time of day or week; these places were farther from the woman's home and the occurrences revealed a great perseverance in learning a woman's schedule that discomfitted the women more than did incidents nearer home. In this category was the man who seemed to have taken the trouble to learn the "complete schedule" of a graduate student in her thirties:

"Suddenly I saw him at the Safeway where I shop, the newsstand, the same path I take when I go for my walks." Women often said that regardless of the subsequent interaction they were disconcerted by the evident industry men showed in learning about them, and they had become suspicious of the use to which this information about their work or private lives might be put.

Disclosing access information is said to invite crime and victimization for women. Women reported that they believe that strangers, men strangers especially, were more likely to use access information to bother women by harassing them on the phone, trailing them to their places of work or to their homes, or plotting some crime against them. Advice books for women on crime prevention profess to help women by recommending behavior that will not "invite" crime. A wise woman will be acquainted with the dangers of divulging access information:

> Never give intimate details about yourself to strangers, women or men, with whom you strike up a casual acquaintance. It's one thing to be friendly and cordial, but indiscriminately mentioning your address or phone number, or describing your home may be dangerous. (Hair and Baker 1970:165)

Popular belief and popular literature also note that rapists have often seen or watched their victims before, even if they are not acquainted with them, and that persons who make obscene phone calls and Peeping Toms are also likely to have met their targets. This arguably makes them—like the faithful, avid, and obsessive fans of celebrities—quasi-acquaintances of the women they watch from afar.

Yet women who try to "prevent crime"—that is, who try to avoid being selected as victims—are cautioned never to appear so suspect of crime that they damage their appearance as open and feminine persons. Further, women often interpret as "merely" fashionable clothing styles that are sexually alluring to men. This disparity between interpretations of chic and of sex is heightened to the degree that we continue to expect women, more than men, to be concerned with and be expert in appearance and fashion.

Items of Access Information

Of the individual items that make up access information, women can establish a hierarchy according to which items are the least potentially dangerous to reveal. For example, upon reflection, a woman may decide that accurately revealing her first name alone is a safe procedure—it supplies the implied warmth of first-name acquaintance with the assurance that there would be many Jennifers, Julies, or Sarahs to sift through to find her again. Both first and last names, correctly divulged, however, may enable a strange man to gain knowledge of her address and phone number through the simple expedient of the phone or city directories, assuming she has a listed number. Similarly, simply revealing a phone number suggests a woman is not so much in peril as she is if she reveals her address: the phone is less invasive in that calls may be answered or not and, even if answered, abruptly disconnected if the caller is undesirable.

One item, however, may be manipulated by the woman to her advantage, and that is knowledge of marital or boyfriend status. If a woman wishes no further contact or wishes to limit an encounter to the current conversation, she manages to inform a male stranger that she is married or has a boyfriend. A mention of a boyfriend or husband is a polite turndown often used at bars or elsewhere, either when a woman is waiting to meet someone more to her liking or when she is simply not interested in anyone's company. A dozen or so women reported that they took care to thank prospective interlocutors in streets, shops, restaurants, and bars by saying, "No thanks, I'm waiting for my husband." As far as this necessary insincerity makes women feel like deceivers, and as far as it undermines the ease they feel in public and the trust they feel in strangers and in men generally, it is regrettable.

Access information intrusions are a type of public harassment that sometimes turns out to be trivial, sometimes momentous. In three of the more extreme cases reported, women experienced situations where men plainly, but seemingly humorously, stole a credit card to get a name, stole a carbon to get a phone number, or playfully rifled a woman's purse to determine if her true name matched the one she had given him. The credit card and carbon were returned and the purse was handed back respectfully, but the women concerned were shaken rather than reassured that these strangers were playful admirers.

EXPLOITATIONS OF PRESENCE: SCRUTINY, FOLLOWING, TOUCH

In addition to the public harassment of access information exploitation, women also receive a type of public harassment that can be described as an exploitation of public presence. Such harassment involves an abuse of the routine situations in which a person is near or comes into the ken of a stranger when in public. Although dominated by a few types of intrusion, exploitations of presence include diverse types of behavior. These tend to be stereotyped in kind, but they are unpredictable in actual time or situation of occurrence, and in what "class" or "type" of man the offender may turn out to be as well, which is of importance to women in assigning a cause for public harassment. Exploitations of presence can consist of words and of behaviors that we customarily classify as "nonverbal," such as touching and scrutiny. At stake in the set of harassments I call exploitations of presence are the physical harm or body violation that can come from unwelcome touch or caresses, or the intimations of physical intrusion that come from protracted scrutiny or trailing.

Some types of exploited presence, however, are not accurately described simply by reference to either verbal or nonverbal behavior. These involve acts, like following, that can seem menacing even if they have no ill outcome or do not involve much in the way of close contact. Other types involve acts that result in some amount of interpersonal violence, although it may be limited—at the low end of the spectrum of violence. Such acts are, for example, being hit with a magazine, jabbed with a ballpoint pen, or poked or prodded with a stick. Equally, exploitations of presence can have more violent potential: A woman can be hit hard, so hard she trips or falls or is tossed from her bike or motorcycle. Exploitations of presence can include what I will discuss shortly as "street remarks," verbal evaluation from strangers.

Hitting, grabbing, pinching, and prodding are one frequently reported type of exploitation of presence, a physical one. But this direct and physical intrusion is not the only type of exploitation of presence. The three main types of exploited presence are touching, following, and scrutinizing that involves both extended eye appraisal and the gestural communication that goes with it; but there are other varieties of exploited presence as well including exhibitionism and nonverbal assessments like lip-smacking and wolf-whistles. Moreover, the various types of exploitation can occur simultaneously, and words are sometimes a part of the exploitation.

As with many troubles that occur in public places, popular advice and lore call attention to only the most minor exploitations of presence, devalue the sense of vulnerability they promote (which, I would argue, is essential to their success as performances), and isolate them from other troubles in public places. This advice also separates female victims from persons in other social categories who experience these troubles. Women often politicize exploitations of presence, considering them marks of men's domination or sexual harassment in public context; yet, inconsistently, a woman's interpretation sometimes romanticizes the events or at least her own alleged responsibility for stimulating them. Exploitations of presence clearly demonstrate the tension between romanticized and politicized interpretations of public harassment (discussed in chapter 5), and analysis needs to demonstrate when women call on either a romantic interpretation or a political one, and show to what ends both interpretations can be employed.

Women reported that other ways to exploit presence were to impede or mark a woman's path, to throw an object at her, or to cause her some small surprise injury with a sharp object. Like scrutiny, following, and touching, these offenses are not only used against women but against members of other situationally disadvantaged groups, too. Informants were hit or poked with a fist, a stick, a ruler, a crutch, a cane, or a rolled-up magazine, and had received these blows in the crotch, on the buttocks, or on the shoulder. One woman had watched a carnival worker poke passing women in the rear with the cane used in a ring-toss game whenever he saw a woman whose appearance he "seemed to enjoy."

Using pointed objects to cause minor injuries (and to produce a startle reaction) is a genre in its own right, especially in large cities, where it may amount to a fad. Periodically, such a specialist gains momentary journalistic renown, as did the Pin Wielder and the Dart Man (*The New York Times,* 1991:A-16). Here, especially, the element of surprise—sudden pain ruffling what is seen as a woman's calm or dignified exterior of composure—is apparently part of the thrill for offenders. The women I interviewed had been stabbed with pencils and pens and with what they believed were sticks and pins. Part of the message communicated in such instances is the attacker's apparent indifference as to whether these acts might cause serious injury: One woman was hit "a quarter-inch from my eye with a pointed stick by one of a crowd of men—I never figured out which one." In these instances, women are stymied from identifying the man not just because their vision is practically impaired, but because they sometimes are frightened of the man's retaliation.

Women are thus seen as persons who have no right to present a calm, unruffled demeanor in public places; if women seem to be dignified, there are a range of publicly harassing practices to disrupt their exterior calm, and many exploitations of presence are among these.

Scrutiny

Not every exploitation of presence uses following or touch. Some breach the customary pattern of gaze, which, for civil inattention, is making eye contact briefly from a distance of eight or ten feet, averting the eyes once contact is made, then raising them once more with a middle-distance focus to rest on a point slightly to the side of the passerby (Goffman 1963). Breaches of the gaze pattern can happen when eye contact is not promptly broken or when gaze lingers too long upon some part of the passerby. And a special vulnerability of women is their rear view—etiquette volumes remind men to precede women strangers and acquaintances off public transportation and up and down stairs (Corinth and Sargent 1970:65; Post 1969:93). Men are even to minimize touching that is functional when helping a strange woman debouch from a bus or mount a curb (Vanderbilt 1972:246).

Scrutiny is a regular practice for many citizens when they are in the presence of someone considered a celebrity or person of renown. Americans are aggressive in their habits of watching, for example, celebrity strangers, a pattern said to be absent among the population of Great Britain, which is more respectful of all individuals' privacy when in public. For Americans, not to crane one's neck, gawk, or peer at a celebrity can mean giving up an infrequent and irresistible opportunity. Thus, although for the most part scrutiny is practiced by men alone or in pairs or groups vis-à-vis lone women, it can also be practiced in quite organized and evaluative fashion by either gender when the targets are held to be of general interest, as with athletes, artists, celebrities, or the notorious.

Some 65 of the 213 men interviewed—among them were men otherwise quite sensitive to how women experienced public places—noted they considered women a potentially pleasing feature of the landscape, and sometimes they used very nearly these exact words. Other men spoke of the joys of "girl-watching" and "cruising," of women "so pretty they should pay them to decorate the street," of other women who "should keep home—they're like urban pollution and blight," and of a man's "right to sit back and just enjoy the show [women] put on, the same as if I was at a museum." As Hummon (1985) points out, these evaluative judgments pepper our urban ideology.

Some women, especially younger, white women who identified themselves as heterosexual, also said they increased efforts at maintaining an appearance that they thought would be pleasing to men in hopes of gaining men's attention. (Some women, both heterosexual and lesbian, said they did the same for purposes of passing through public places unharassed: In this case, they used a pleasing appearance that was, as one middle-aged lesbian professional said, "apparently heterosexual," as a guarantee of safety.) Even a woman's symbolic presence can provide opportunities for watching and gesturing appreciatively, as I observed when I saw a cheerful young African-American man walk past a department store window whose female dummies were in the process of being dressed—he waggled his eyebrows and wolf-whistled at them.

Following

Following a woman—an action for which there are few innocent glosses—can inhibit her feeling of freedom or alter her enjoyment of activities. Following a strange woman can be practiced by acquaintances as well as strangers, as when disgruntled boyfriends and husbands stalk a woman with a view toward anything from menace to murder.

Following occurs in public places of all types, from football stadiums, public parks, and hiking trails, to semipublic arenas like places of business. An often-reported locale for following is a darkened cinema, in which a man follows a woman from seat to seat. A white secretary in her forties was enjoying a movie when "suddenly a man sat down next to me and put his hand in my lap. I of course moved, and he moved too, and he followed me around four more seats in the theater." Following is an exploitation of public presence that often effectively traps or confines a woman—or occurs in a niche where she is already "trapped," as when one young college student was followed into the women's room.

Men sometimes used following punitively, women reported. For instance, following was used against women who would not acquiesce to other intrusions or would not cooperate in attempts at pickups. Even a car was not always an effective shell:

> This happened last week when I was driving downtown with my best friend. A car pulls up next to us, and it's full of guys, and they start whooping and hollering really obscenely. I was very offended, and I was careful to give them no attention at all, but they kept following us from place to place where we went. We were scared to get out but at the same time, we had errands to do. Finally they quit, but by that time we'd missed a class—we were scared to go to school because we were sure they'd get out and would follow us further.

Exploitations of presence like this can often be conflated with a general sense of intrusion—being unable to trust that another individual will quit an encounter on schedule or when one expects, leaving a woman feeling mired in the interaction.

Attempting immediate access through following stands as one method of denoting desire for contact. In some sense, public harassment by stalking in this way constitutes a kind of bastard introduction or at least attempt at the same: Following seems to express a desire to interact with an individual, even though face-to-face interaction may never be achieved. Celebrities also provide an example here, for they sometimes find that fans trail them along the streets with very little idea, apparently, about what to do when they actually catch up with the objects of their pursuit (see Hill and Weingrad 1987:311–312 for a vivid example).

Following may be done with no word exchanged, or it may be accomplished as part of a street remark or greeting, conversation in a shop, or an exchange of what began as pleasantries at a bus stop. In part, the practice of following women for long distances while they are on their errands or on their way to their destination is an attempt to determine where the woman lives or works and is often felt as such, for nearly half the women informants mentioned that one of their fears was that a man who followed them would learn where to find them later.

Touch

Certain reactions to the presence of others in public places are considered normal, nonthreatening, even canny or circumspect. For example, initially evaluating a stranger's appearance visually to ensure that the person is no threat and that she or he is not in one's direct pathway is a legitimate, even necessary part of presence in public places, but this functional gaze has strict limits on the area of the other's body it covers and on its length if it is to be judged civil. Following and touch are also allowable but circumscribed among strangers. They are legitimate only in quite narrow and delimited cases, such as pursuing an individual to return something she or he has dropped, the functional touch that is a part of emergency aid to strangers, or the touch incidental to crowding or to service transactions while, for example, returning a customer's change. (And typically even these instances are sometimes verbally explained or excused.) Last, there are cases of exploitive touch by malefactors intent on deeds other than public harassment; here harassment is a byproduct or a shield for a worse deed such as shoplifting or pickpocketing. For example, pickpockets engineer proximity to nudge or bump victims, who resent the intrusion but seldom suspect that it masks theft. Criminal uses of touch only mime exploitive touch, indicating that on the continuum of wrongdoing there is a worse-yet class.

Women sometimes said a single incident of touch was the reason for changing their feelings toward men, public places, or both. A white woman in her twenties told of the time, some years past, when she worked at a large department store, and an African-American man persisted in patting her buttocks:

Briefly, I kind of felt like I was attractive. I wonder if I'm prejudiced because he was black—still, it wasn't right. I asked him to
leave me alone. He ignored my plea and grabbed me, right there in
the shoe department. . . . I still wonder how and why it happened.
It's changed me: I'm not as friendly or personable with people. I'd
say I'm like a turtle not going anywhere, because I spend all my
time in my shell. (Ferree 1991)

As I can suggest for public harassment in general, one hazard for a
romanticized interpretation of touch is that it can give way, on reflection, to a puzzled cynicism or simply a fear that makes a woman leery
of all public contacts.

When words accompany touch, the man typically takes the line
that the woman appears desirable and that her attractions have stimulated his touch, either in appreciation or for verification, to make sure
that what the eye notes is real. This verificatory component leaves open
the possibility that a man's original judgment of attractiveness can
change to its opposite; it also allows a man to then display the possible
emotional reactions to a well- or an ill-favored woman, such as surprise, delight, and approval if she is found well-favored or disappoint-
ment, scolding, and disapproval if she is not. In any case, the line
taken is that it is a woman's appearance that has actuated a man's intrusion, as when a man squeezed one woman's breasts, then suggested
to her that he had to do so to make sure they were real. An African-
American woman said a white man had pinched her buttocks, then
told her he needed to make sure they were as firm as they looked.
Other women, who had direct contact with the public as cashiers, for
example, had men who had touched an arm, face, or hand, then told
them how soft their skin was.

Of course, a man sometimes suggested he was disappointed with
what his investigative touch told him, and some men made it clear they
touched and verified in horror, not admiration. Thus, some women
noted they were probed, handled, fingered, or otherwise sampled, then
confronted with a man disappointed over unfulfilled expectations.

Revoking judgment was offensive in another way: Not only was a woman first deemed "worthy" of offensive touch, but she was then deemed not worthy of the offense, much as if she had been a beauty contestant who did not manage to make finalist. A Latina cook was headed into work when a man hit her buttocks; she protested she would "'break your fingers.' So the old man replied to me, 'Your ass is not all that great for you to want to cut off somebody's fingers.'" Not only did this man offend her, he doubly offended her: she was not worth the offense in the first place.

Sometimes such retorts were mixed with critical or offensive racial or ethnic messages, and women—if prone to be offended at all—sometimes felt in cross-race offenses that they were victims of racism as much or more than sexism. Some believed they were particular magnets for a man of another racial or ethnic group, as was one woman who said, "I'm blond, he was black. That's why it happened," or another who said, "He was after my ass because I'm an Oriental boy toy, or so he thought. I've had this happen before. White boys think that's all I'm good for." Having literally and palpably taken the measure of an other-race woman he has touched, a man might suggest he had sound data on which to base further racist appraisal. A white man rolled an Asian-American woman's breast between fingers and thumb, then laughed, "Don't get mad, honey, you haven't got enough to be excited about. Most white women have a lot more." Thus, words sometimes accompanied touching. Typically, the verbal component established or reinforced the line that a woman's looks ineluctably led a man to touch, pet, grab, kick, or hit her. Site or situation could further reinforce the line: A woman pumping iron at a health club had a man walk over to her, plump a quadriceps, and simper, "You've been working on your thighs, I see." Adding words that interpret a man's actions as actuated by appearance provides a later point by which to legitimate his actions if need be. And, by adding verbal evaluation that justifies the touch, the man at once sexualizes and depoliticizes an offense, implying that he could not keep from, for example, patting such shining hair or brushing his lips against luminous shoulders. The remarks are seeming legitimations of contact—the man would not have caressed unattractive hair or hand. Adding remarks thus suggests that a man's offense is less serious and more comprehensible than it might otherwise seem.

In sum, exploitive touch suggests that civility in public is not the given that it has been presented as by many analysts and that women's privacy must be accomplished silently as well as by words. Instead, even such common civility as refraining from touching another person is a privilege that the individual earns partly by virtue of gender, and that must be bargained for and achieved, perhaps many times in the course of a single trip into public places.

In exploitive touch, the woman's body is literally the object of play (or prey), and this is bolstered by a ludic reading given to the encounter, which may feature foolmaking. Humor is communicated in different ways. Women said that often men's demeanor and facial expressions reinforced the notion that the woman was the butt of some obscure joke, the point of which probably was that she would have no effective and entirely satisfactory recourse. If the streets are, for purposes of cross-gender interactions, a theater, then it is Artaud's Theater of Cruelty—an improvisational romp where the customarily uninvolved audience can be rapidly transformed to participants, then dupes, and finally victims. Street remarks illustrate the sequence.

STREET REMARKS

There may presently be fewer pleasant ulterior motives for making the best of street remarks. One popular article on crime prevention for women, for example, holds that women should not show fear during the street incidents since rapists often test their victims in this way (see Dobell 1977). With this reasoning, women's groups may feel that street remarks constitute a handy theater in which to practice assertive behavior (see Porath 1982).

Street remarks are evaluative, advisory, or other types of expressive comments delivered by one stranger to another in public places. Thus I include as street remarks labels given ostensibly as flattery, clearly critical commentary, and name calling, insults, contempt, and other verbal and paralinguistic abuse. I exclude explanatory and apologetic glosses intended to excuse the individual's behavior to others, and I also exclude stereotyped greetings or exchanges—what I refer to as "undebatables" or secured topics. The remarks are unobjectionable because they are innocuous, focusing on overwhelmingly common subjects. At stake in the street remarks men deliver is the woman's estimate of her own appearance and conduct—an estimate that, street remarks will suggest, can be optimistic or pessimistic.

Secured topics are among our culture's legitimate or easily rationalized talk in public. One may request what I have called public aid (see chapter 2), that is, information or services—a match, the time, directions—requested of a stranger. For any area and time, there may in addition be a set of secured topics—a locally legitimate set of subjects for conversation that often carries with it a heavily patterned or rote turntaking, from whose snugness little deviation is tolerated. Examples are the local sports team, the weather and other relevant natural occurrences, or an item of news so well known that anyone can be imagined to know it. Sometimes undebatables pop up suddenly to embrace more than the usual number of potential commentators, as in the case of a political coup, an assassination, the death of a famous person, or devastation to a local hero or national champion.

The citizen also has the right to catch other citizens in behavior situationally inappropriate for public places: Looks may be pointedly given, conversations started, comments thrown. In these conversations, street remarks are involved, although they are somewhat marginal ones: As much as one citizen feels a right to comment on liminally inappropriate behavior, the citizen demonstrating the inappropriate behavior will feel a right to go about her or his business undisturbed. The man or woman who walks down the street in wedding gear, hopping on one foot, or carrying a spray of balloons will be obliged to take almost any intrusive look or comment in good spirits; she or he, by appearing as a less than properly comported citizen, is thus an open person *pro tem.* Citizens caught in inappropriate pursuits are also required, and are often anxious, to provide explanations or respond to the looks and comments of passersby, thereby demonstrating that there is some reasonable gloss for what appears to be a situationally inappropriate pursuit or that there is an extenuating circumstance.

Evaluative street remarks, however, differ from these more mundane citizen-to-citizen remarks. At one extreme of innocuousness, street remarks can seem expressions of admiration or pleasure, as when a passing woman tells another that she likes her coat. However, these more pleasant, unambiguous remarks are likely to be between equals; when such a remark occurs between a situationally disadvantaged person and a situationally advantaged person, the former may retrospectively be thankful that nothing frightening occurred.

Thus, remarks are especially potent when coming from a member of a situationally advantaged group and delivered to one not so advantaged. Using mostly visual clues to the target's group membership, the offender criticizes, comments, or labels, leaving the target with a philosophical set of management strategies or simply the fervent hope that she or he will be left alone and that others will mind their business. Often, then, street remarks are occasions for verbal abuse and name calling from, for example, apparent heterosexual to apparent homosexual, from a member of one race to a member of another, from nondisabled to disabled. Occasionally, too, street remarks are facilitated by other structural possibilities for interaction between strangers in public places, for example, by the "passer's privilege" that exists in many communities or neighborhoods. This is a norm that may or may not be fulfilled: The individual has a right to choose to orient toward or not orient toward, to greet or not greet another stranger when coming near or passing another; when not greeting another, it is understood the individual will affect not to see or focus upon the other or will divert her or his attention to some alternate target. Passer's privilege is regularly abrogated when women are routinely expected to greet strange men. Passer's privilege leaves a slot, a felt lacuna, so that the individual may ready her- or himself for the possibility of both being greeted and being ignored, taking care to invest little energy and direction toward either possibility lest the other occur. In these slots, women often find that a street remark occurs instead.

Sometimes a woman engages in some action associated traditionally with the achievement of male gender, receiving spirited commentary from men. This is presently the case for joggers in some areas, where women in particular are subject to commentary and conversation and, more particularly, women who overtake men and are thereby seen as besting men publicly at their own game. Linda, an African-American woman of thirty, enjoys "dressing up" when she goes into public places and says she has little problem accepting men's evaluations, even the vulgar ones, in all but the following situation:

> When I run, it's different. I am also an excellent runner, and I can pass by most of the male joggers I see, leave them huffing and puffing. Every time I do this, and I do mean *every*time, the man I leave eating my dust does one of two things. Either he tries valiantly to pass me in turn (and usually he can't) or he starts harassing me: Who do I think *I* am? Am I some kind of stuck-up showoff?
>
> No, Mister, I'm just like you, I'm trying to get a little exercise, a little relaxation. In the way that I do it, I just happen to be better than you. That's no reason to be ashamed, since you probably be better than me in some other area. But that's just the way it is, so accept it gracefully.

Eloquent Innuendos

Double entendre and innuendo, both characteristic of street remarks, can also be seen as a man's right to alter meaning—to play with words for an audience, either the woman, or his friends if he is in a team. Often, especially when a team of men is involved, double entendre takes the form of one man speaking not directly to the passing woman but in a manner that clearly indicates she is the subject of the talk and the intended overhearer. Men emphasize the double entendre with eye contact inappropriate to a conversation solely among team members: A man's talk is often ostensibly to his fellows, but his gaze is focused on the woman who is his actual target. An Indianapolis woman spoke of walking in public past a group of keenly observing men:

> The way men talk can get very involved, very elaborate. Like this one time I went by these three old guys sitting on lawn chairs in a tough, working-class neighborhood. I guess I am big-bosomed [she is not, particularly]. One says, scraping me with his eyes, something about planting melons in the garden, and the other two go on about how their melon crops're coming along nicely. . . . Well, they got what they wanted, because I could feel myself blush beet-red, red as a fire engine. . . . I didn't feel scared but shamed, and at the same time not sure enough of what they meant to get mad at them.

The employment of double entendre can make props of actual or elaborated characteristics of a woman, so that a woman with a cat T-shirt whose legend told others that she loved her Persian heard a man loudly say to his friends that he, too, liked pussy. Almost anything can provide ammunition—if ammunition is needed—when men choose to indulge in heavy-handed imagery of a patently vulgar sort.

The right to redefine a situation, as innuendo does, speaks of power and domination; in private, presumably redefinition must be helped along by willing subordinates, but in the vacuum of the public realm the redefiner is often the most recent speaker. In public a man can choose his role—as either vibrant actor or judgmental audience. Included in this right to redefine is the right of inquiry, although the question a man has in mind may seem minor, nugatory, or embarrassing to the person to whom it is addressed. In by no means all cases do potentially embarrassing questions seem to result in embarrassment, however: for example, not every potential instance of redefinition involves verbal innuendo. When a man or a team of men rate a woman with scorecards, soberly and silently (as happened at the PanAmerican Games, which took place in Indianapolis), they communicate an elaborate metaphor without heavy verbal hints—they establish a double meaning all the same.

Another characteristic of street remarks is that they are often evaluative and, ostensibly at least, evaluative in a positive way. Thus, men's, and sometimes women's, folk interpretations hold that these remarks are compliments. A proper compliment, however, is not given in public to the unacquainted, especially the unacquainted of the opposite sex, as is the practice of men who offer street remarks. When a woman responds with "thank you," as is natural among acquaintances, a man sometimes escalates the exchange into outright suggestiveness or abuse. In these cases of compliments that turn out not to be compliments, men use a flattering remark or look as a stimulus to lure the woman into ratification of a mutual state of talk; the ratification then is used as a springboard to reveal the man's real feelings, trading on the attention gained by the initial compliment. Or a man may speak of parts of her body that are normally not to be evaluated in public—as when a man informs a passing woman that she has "good tits" or "bad tits," depending on what his expert judgment has led him to decide. So evaluations are not invariably positive, leading women who suspect that they are about to receive a street remark to fear it will be an insulting one.

It is the right of every citizen, woman or man, to remark in public upon the inappropriate behavior of persons not known to him or her personally. In men's street remarks to women, however, men treat women engaged in a perfectly satisfactory achievement of gender as if their performance was in some way flawed; that many women react to this with anxiety or confusion is understandable. Men who treat women as if they were acting inappropriately thereby create a partial justification for their own behavior, for they are certainly allowed to breach the rules for civil inattention when they note a citizen behaving inappropriately. Men's street remarks take on the task of publicly available criticism that was, early in the history of the republic, the function of devices such as bilboes, ducking stools, pillories, branks, gags, and scarlet letters—all eloquent symbols. These punishments were not, of course, restricted only to women, although classes of women considered deviant, such as scolds, were certainly singled out to receive them (Earle 1969).

Women may think that men find feeble pretexts for approaching them, as when a New York African-American woman, who classed herself as overweight, wore a fake-fur leopard coat and was informed by a strange man that she looked just like Jackie Kennedy, who was featured in that day's paper in a real leopard coat (Verta Mae 1972:14). Typically, however, there is no trace of the compliment in the accusation and often nothing that can remotely be found offensive. Not all slips said to be showing actually are.

When a man comments on any aspect of a woman's presentation, even seizing on understandable or admirable aspects and transforming it into an offense or delict, he thereby reinforces the right of all men to be rightful proprietors and legitimate commentators in public. A young woman carrying a single, thin paperback book walked past a quartet of men seated on the bench of a mall; "Gotta do that schoolwork, huh?" bellowed one, and another said, "Hey—what're you doing, writing a term paper or something?" As a middle-aged woman carrying a small briefcase waited for a bus, a passing middle-aged man called to her, "You oughta take the train when you got that much luggage, Sis!" Such magnification resembles improvised riffs more than logical connections or likely guesses. Comments that make any trait the woman displays an aspect of a secret sin or foolish impropriety can make even sincere compliments into cruel mockery, exposing what a woman may feel is her corrupt inner self.

Still another characteristic of the man-to-woman street remark is that it tests the woman's self-control. Men's street remarks provide constant tests, trials, and sentences difficult to commute, as when a young woman walked past a young man who cleared his throat slightly, then a bit more audibly, then a bit more audibly still, and, when she still did not respond, yelled in her wake, "Yeah! I'm talking to *you*, stupid! Listen up!"

Part of the ambiguity that results comes from the conventional requirements for civil inattention; that is, individuals are not supposed to be attentive to strange individuals beyond certain limits. Too, traditionally prescribed women's behavior forbids women to speak to "strange men." Yet the overt form of a summons or call for attention makes a claim on women, though it is a claim by an unacquainted person.

Not every characteristic of access information intrusions, exploitations of presence, or street remarks is present in every occurrence, but these features are common enough to hold as a basis for public harassment—and perhaps other harassment as well, since they represent, at bottom, canny, unscrupulous advantage by one person when another is disadvantaged or unsuspecting.

DISADVANTAGE AND THE DEFINITION OF PUBLIC PLACES

The embracing characteristic of public harassment is that the man risks little, while successful exploitation costs the woman much.[1] The man's offense is often stealthy, quick, silent, and unseen; the woman's victimization is often visible, marked by strong emotion, and visually, even theatrically compelling. Advantage-taking in gender-based public harassment reinforces men's proprietorship of public places and their imposition of a metaphorical stage in public—in fact, it supports men's general right to define and redefine incidents of public harassment.

Taking advantage is also an abrogation of civility. Taking advantage helps to ensure the production values of the play—that is, the

---

1. Of course, this is the embracing characteristic for all public harassers and all victims, not just gender-based harassment.

surprise and suspense for the woman and for the perpetrator and his team when the woman actually receives the act of harassment. Individual characteristics of public harassment—diverted attention, ambiguity, unpredictability, and surprise—guarantee that harassing incidents can be practiced (and suspected) anywhere and everywhere in public.

Diverted Attention

A woman's diverted attention is often a transition to a surprise encounter. This changes the definition of the situation and, necessarily, the woman's involvement. One prerequisite is that a woman's attention must be elsewhere. Often public harassment is attempted when circumstances put the woman at a disadvantage in terms of being on her guard. She may have her attention occupied for the moment or be involved in a situation that commands some attention and an interactional agenda, as when the physical requirements of a task demand full attention. Women reported exploitations of presence when skating, bicycling, changing a tire, or parceling out greasy French fries to children—all circumstances in which men chose to hit or punch preoccupied women. A woman may be physically unable to move, either because of crowded circumstances or because she will consequently have to relinquish her place, as in a queue. Thus, women reported being touched in packed stadiums, in theaters, and on crowded public conveyances. A woman's presence may be exploited when she is physically occupied, as when her arms are full with books or a child, when she is handing out pamphlets or collecting for charity, or eating an ice cream or rifling through her purse. Sometimes offenders pick the brief moment in an otherwise innocuous situation when a woman is suddenly and momentarily vulnerable, as when she bends over to pick something up or has her back to others in a crowd or on a bus.

If a woman's attention is diverted or occupied, she will be less likely to retaliate and may have a satisfyingly (from the man's point of view) startled reaction. In other cases, exploitations are so subtle that the acts themselves are ambiguous. In these cases, women may be more upset.

Ambiguous Acts

The incursions themselves are sometimes subtle and ambiguous, both in the character of the act and in the definition of the situation. For instance, a man can construct a verbal chain of progressively less plausible and more offensive comments or questions, relying on the woman's politeness to the first, then on her involvement in the interaction to glue her to more and more innuendo, finally ending in touch. An encounter that initially seems to be friendly—a bus-stop greeting, a request for help, or casual questions about an item of clothing a stranger might want to purchase for his wife—can be revealed as something quite different. A woman in her twenties had such an experience at a grocery store:

> A male friend and I was standing looking at some food on a shelf. All of a sudden, a strange man who was standing beside us was looking down at my feet. I had cropped pants on, knee high, and flats with no socks. This man bent down, touched my shoe, and asked, "Are those real leather?" I said yes. Then he wanted to know where I got them. I told him I did not remember. About that time he put his hands around my ankle and lifted my foot off the floor while rubbing his other free hand over my ankle and bare foot. He then proceeded to try and take my shoe off. I yanked my foot back and said, "No, I don't think so." It did not happen this slowly, of course, but more quicker.

An African-American librarian in her forties said that during a notable encounter, "we started talking about the weather, then umbrellas and galoshes, and somehow it ended up he was touching and feeling all over my raincoat." As a result, "I don't start talking about anything so much with a strange man now."

The act itself may be delivered in such a subtle manner that a woman may be left uncertain whether she has been offended. Sometimes, for example, touch is administered so lightly, almost tenderly, that women reported themselves uncertain of whether they had been fondled. It is always possible to argue to oneself that a man has not been following one, that his presence is coincidental. For one informant, a married white woman in her thirties visiting London for the first time some years ago, subtle touch and following were combined by a straight-faced man in the following way: She felt a persistent feathery touch while riding in a subway car, and she managed to persuade herself it was her imagination. She then was followed off the car by the offender, who proceeded to lightly stroke her on the long way up the escalators. Ogling is sometimes done openly enough, but when the woman attempts to meet the man's eyes he shifts or shields them or pretends great interest in something else, thus mitigating or qualifying scrutiny. The effect of both types of troubles is increased when the unpredictability of these offenses is taken into account.

Range of Offenses and Unpredictability

Incidents of public harassment cover a wide range in every category in which they occur. Any single incident will be unpredictable: A woman may sense or suspect that public harassment is coming from a given strange man, but she will never know precisely what it is that is coming. That is, a street remark can be a stereotyped comment, label, or slur, one that the woman has heard many times before, but it can also be an unlikely, even bizarre comment, and the woman could find it all the more difficult to mount a response. In these latter cases, the harasser might also be treated to a startled or shocked reaction from the woman. Similarly, if a woman prepares herself to be on the lookout for exploitive touch, she must prepare herself to prevent not only the stranger who pinches her breast or buttocks but the stranger who grabs her hand and strokes it, licks her cheek, nibbles her ear, or tweaks her nose; these were all occurrences that women reported.

Likewise, there are many ways to attempt to secure access information from a woman. Even normally predictable and routinized legitimate talk between strangers, such as service encounters at stores, greetings, and public aid transactions, can be mined for an opportunity for the suddenly inserted phrase or other intrusion.

Some street remarks are unique, which may seem to personalize the comment, thus arguing to the woman that it must be something equally unusual about her appearance or conduct that has actuated it. One woman heard a man say, "If you were my sister, I'd have incest with you!" A young white Midwestern college student noted her "all-time favorite comment" was given by a man who called to her, "You know what? That sweater you got on is my favorite color of fly fishing lure!" Another effect of a bizarre or unlikely comment is to throw the woman off her stride, making retaliation difficult; yet another effect is that an unlikely remark is almost impossible to anticipate, so that the woman who seeks a set of strategies or retaliatory remarks will be hard pressed.

Touching in particular provides a man with infinite opportunities. He will have an almost inexhaustible set of possible acts to contemplate performing, along with an almost inexhaustible set of targets available to him. Yet he may have to exercise considerable exertion in reaching any single target, perhaps leading to his literal downfall, as in the case of a college student in his twenties who related that, while standing on the rim of a campus fountain and "whooping" at passing women, he lost his balance and fell in. Understandably, these downfalls can be keenly appreciated by the woman target, as an African-American/white construction apprentice related:

> When we were in high school, a bunch of boys we didn't know went by us in a car. This was on a back road, and they was going slow. The reason was, one of them was leaning out of the car window and trying to smack us on the rear. He reached too far and fell out, and, at the same time, the car racked up—not bad, but it racked up. We almost died laughing.

Thus, the sheer inventiveness and unlikely character of certain intrusions can puzzle the woman, who can have prepared no practiced, not to say slick, response for a man who, for example, hugs her while she is on a skating rink or falls down in mock-tribute and grabs her legs as she walks through a restaurant.

Surprise

A publicly harassing incident can come as a surprise because of the character of the act, which might be performed quickly or when the offender manages to appear quickly and on the run. Such acts were especially effective in discomfiting women, since they blocked retaliation: "I didn't want to ignore it. I wanted to hit him for what he did. I had really no chance, it happened so fast," said an older health professional. If an offense unfolds rapidly enough, it can escape detection by others who might possibly come to a woman's aid, and speed can reinforce the woman's illusion that she "imagined it." Finally, a speedy act helps produce a startled response in women, and therefore also produces a lush display for the man or men to enjoy.

Methods for ensuring speed were varied. Informants related that men sometimes engaged in activities that promised speedy passage past offenders or targeted women passing speedily when the men were stationary. Some men publicly harassed while skateboarding, riding in cars or on motorcycles, ice skating, or bicycling; some men practiced public harassment on women who were skating, bicycling, jogging, or on scooters. Speed also lessens the chance of correctly identifying the offender, who can escape quickly. Public harassers may intend only to swiftly deliver routine pats or pinches but may deliver worse, as was perhaps the case for the woman on a bike who had her buttocks slapped by a man on a motorcycle—she was knocked over in the process.

Barriers to sight can offer a functional equivalent to speed: one man darted out from behind a bush to press himself against a woman; another lounged in a doorway, with only his arm venturing out to pinch the woman's buttocks. Some incidents of public harassment, like any attention to a woman's buttocks or acts of following, are characteristically—although not invariably—delivered behind a woman's back. Some offenses occur because a woman's back is turned and she cannot perceive the approach, as when she is in line for the movies or when she is followed down the central walk of a mall. And distance is the functional equivalent of speed for street remarks, the more so when one party is moving rapidly away—as when a street remark is shouted from a speeding car.

Limited Recourse

If a woman believes she has no, or ineffective, recourse, she may be forced to choose between continuing her participation in her current activity and enduring the continued propinquity of the man (and thus the chance that her presence will be exploited again). Thus, caught in a checkout line with a man who rubbed her breast, this woman hesitated:

> Should I say something to this guy? Or should I just leave the store? If I leave, what happens to the milk and eggs? Do I ditch them on the way out? Do I give the guy an angry look and plunk the milk and eggs down next to him? (And is it the store guy's job to return them then, or is it mine?) Either way I lose: If I say something to him, he might get mad at me, or he might make fun of me. If I dump the milk and eggs and go, I look stupid to everybody but him—*and* I don't get my breakfast, which is what I came out for. And the final and best question: Why is it women have to think about all this shit? I'll bet you the guy who felt me up isn't giving it a second thought.

Caught between a number of possible lines of action, a woman can be frozen into inaction, as in the case of one woman in a packed movie theater: "I was forced to sit by a young man who was out with his younger brother. During a romantic scene, he reached over and rubbed

my leg. He then got up and left. I waited a few minutes before insisting that my date and I leave also, because I did not want to risk a confrontation with this guy." But even women disposed to protest or take
action found male offenders guarded by many aspects of the situation:
"You turn around, and you can't decipher which guy did it. So you
end up taking out your anger on the wrong people. It really aggra-
vates me," a young African-American secretary said.

Through searches for access information, through exploitations of
presence, and by uttering street remarks, men claim proprietorship of
public places vis-à-vis women; among these proprietary rights are
symbolic possessorship of public places. Following, for example, suggests a comfort with and an ownership of public paths and environs.
Touching and gaze demonstrate one of the privileges that accompanies judgment rights, the right to evaluate women, as do street remarks that rate and appraise a woman's appearance. Touching and
gaze are evaluative because they are often explicitly rationalized as a
man drawn by alluring appearance to follow, ogle, or touch a strange
woman. And touching specifically centers attention on a single body
part, thus reinforcing—as street remarks often do—a tendency to treat
women's bodies synecdochally. More than enabling male proprietorship, however, exploitations of presence hold women up to ridicule.

Exploited presence thus also stems from the player's rights to determine and transform the definition of the situation from serious or
neutral to playful. In street remarks, part of a man's action may be to
play with words before his friends, twisting meanings and supplying
innuendo to sexualize and evaluate a woman's presence in public. To
play with words for an audience of friends when in a team recalls
playing with a woman physically.

One young woman at a high school basketball game was grabbed
by a young man sitting with his men friends:

[I] enjoyed being in crowds, so I was prepared to like this game.
But this boy was seated behind me, along with three, four of his

friends. I didn't know any of them. I got up to cheer when our team made a basket, and that's when it happened. When I started to sit down, I felt somebody take a big chunk out of my ass. I wanted to turn around but I couldn't—I heard him and his friends start laughing. One of the friends gave him a high-five and said, "*Good* one, Charles!" I could feel myself turn red and tears came to my eyes.

I told myself I'd ignore it, but everytime I thought of it I started crying again, I couldn't help it. I don't remember the rest of the game. Don't remember who won.

I have discussed three kinds of the many kinds of public harassment that affect women. From this discussion, I have abstracted characteristics that facilitate harassment for men and impede retaliation from women. It would be a complex task to relate these characteristics in any simple way to workplace and school harassment, private harassment, and harassment in quasi-acquaintanceship. Workplace and school harassment (as between professor and student or employer and employee) and harassment between the quasi-acquainted (such as celebrity and fan) often begin as ambiguous acts, to be sure: The victim will be unable to tell at first whether the professor's polite expression of interest or the fan's glowing letter of appreciation will lead to nothing more, or to sexual blackmail in the first case and celebrity stalking in the second.

Other types of harassment may, or may not, be characterized by the same sort of range and unpredictability that public harassment embraces. Certainly workplace and school harassment often have bizarre or elaborate expressions: The lessons of Tailhook have demonstrated that (Office of the Inspector General 1993), as has the well-known and widely discussed testimony of Anita Hill. For incidents of wife battery or even celebrity harassment, however, individual acts of harassment can devolve into a boring predictability: the beatings that always happen on a certain day, at a certain time, and follow a virtual script; the hundredth or thousandth fan who clutches and busses a celebrity. Even here there are differences, however. Once the professor sexually blackmails the student and once the fan moves into the celebrity's home, there are official and institutionalized measures to follow, nowadays often mitigated by a lawyer or member of the EEOC. And for the celebrity there are those who make their careers by shielding celebrities from exactly this kind of harassment.

While public harassment often depends on diverted attention because of the nature of communication in public places, the employer can depend on the woman's riveted attention for the efficacy of his sexual harassment. For some private woes, like battery, and for some quasi-acquaintanceship harassment, like unceasing and threatening fan letters or telephone calls, it hardly makes sense to speak of attention at all, since these ills reach into the home or other private spaces where one's guard is down—they take advantage of havens, not frontiers.

Nor does it make sense to speak of workplace and school harassment and private harassment as "surprises," at least in remotely the same way in which public harassment is startling and surprising. Instead, the victim might have had a series of clearcut "warnings," as for the husband who has told his wife for years to toe the line or he will beat her—and then does. Or a given profession, such as acting, might have routinized expectations of harassment by fans (the grateful and enthused, as well as the obsessed) as obstacles that come with the territory. Because public harassment remains an unadmitted and ergo underground problem, we do not yet have the routines to handle it, and we have been taught to ignore the repeated threats.

Thus, the different types of harassment—public, private, quasi-acquaintanceship—in truth share no invariable characteristics. Women in search of ways to deal with harassment apart from public harassment will find that the skills they use to cope with and manage harassment in one context will not necessarily guarantee them success in another. Even the ability to manage diverse types of public harassment and an appreciation of their common characteristics, then, can be useless to women in other contexts.

CHAPTER FIVE

Interpretations

The feeling I get when I'm touched by a strange man, and I can't quite tell if anything's happening or not, and I'm scared to do anything or even say anything—did you see on the TV? The best I can tell is, it's like I'm Anita Hill and he's Clarence Thomas.

Married white accountant in her thirties

Imagine yourself walking down the street. Someone passes from the opposite direction, and as they pass, they hurl at you the most vile epithet for your group that you can think of. Now imagine that you are African-American, and the other person is white. Imagine you use a wheelchair, but the other person does not, or imagine that you stutter, a usually silent stigma in public that is revealed when you must ask the other person for directions. Imagine you are Asian-American, and the other person is African-American.

Imagine you are a woman, and the other person is a man.

How does your interpretation of what happened change, if it does, depending on your group membership? Most people match their interpretation of what happened to the group membership of the people involved. If you are like many people, you will be unhappy, disturbed, or outraged at every case but the last. In the last case alone, the presumption of romance intrudes to cloud what has happened—as it intrudes on all gender-based public harassment.

This chapter will examine the two major rhetorics, the romanticized and the politicized, by which women now interpret and account for public harassment. For men, one of these, the romanticized, predominates.

Many of our expectations for the performance of etiquette imply a heterosexual romanticization, even eroticization, of public order. Many assume, for instance, that a man's evaluative comments on a strange woman's appearance have something to do with his estimate of her as a potential romantic or sexual partner. More accurately, he uses his evaluation of her as potential partner not only to express an opinion but to express his right to express an opinion. This romanticization and eroticization are upheld by the delicts of public harassment, as well as by the dictates of etiquette. In fact, what the individual must support is the demonstration of the public norms of identifiably heterosexual society; what one does in other spheres, in private places, or in bed can then comfortably be peripheral to the case. Thus, it is not really one's romance-worthiness that is at issue: it is the approved standard that one must be willing to support, sustain, and represent by modeling it in public.

An individual harasser therefore used public harassment abuses to explain what he objects to as well as what he approves of. Public harassment therefore can be an emblem of the harasser's ratification and support of the existing hierarchy of heterosexual preference and the existing romantic basis for attraction, centered on appearance-based evaluation. In public places it is not so much that "love at first sight" rules the day, as that "a reliable estimate of gender and sexual preference" does—and ought to—rule the public realm. Thus, in sustaining public order, the individual is habitually called on to sustain values that she or he does not actually support elsewhere, and the individual sometimes agrees to do so. As individuals appear to support behavior and countenance norms they do not in fact practice, they subtly undermine their own activities and perhaps their identity. In this way, one gay man I spoke to said he had often felt pressured to comment on passing women strangers or at least to scrutinize them, as he saw other (presumably heterosexual) men about him doing. For him, what resulted was a gulf between private and public selves that he was called upon to adopt, first as a gay man, second as "a red-blooded American male." Insofar as the individual attempts insincerely to pass as a member of a category he is not, he ratifies and legitimates the *status quo* of conventional life in general. In the process, he may also knowingly be false to a more deeply cherished private self. A final irony, of course, is that his cohort of "red-blooded" public harassers may be as insincere as he is, either because they too are homosexual or because they are heterosexual practitioners who feel it is necessary to comment, touch, and stare but in fact have little interest in the women they abuse. The goal, to fit in by being apparently appetent romantic heterosexuals, can be accomplished through public harassment.

In earlier chapters I referred to the romanticization and the politicization of the public order. Some women (sometimes many women) try to explain what is happening in public harassment by using the template of a heterosexual romantic or erotic attraction: that is, they use a romanticized interpretation. Some women explain public harassment by using the template of a feminist politicization: that is, they refer to harassment that occurs in public places as being on a continuum with sexual harassment in school and workplace and violence in the home and street. Most women interviewed, including those who identified themselves as feminists, ended by using a mixed romanticized and politicized rhetoric. No matter how outspoken a woman was of public harassment, she often fell back on criticizing her own appearance or behavior as culpable—tacit admission that romantic attraction was at the root of public harassment by men. A parallel in race-based public harassment would be the African-American informant who suggested that, had she not had such dark skin or such nappy hair, the white men who screamed "Nigger!" at her from a truck would not have done so.

This chapter will suggest as well the principal ways in which men account for and interpret public harassment. Men also used (although rarely) a politicized rhetoric for dealing with public harassment, but it was often the verso to politicized rhetoric: Men who interpreted public harassment as politicized sometimes did so by envisioning it as a reaction to the women's movement, seeing it not as proof that they themselves were abusers in the street as well as the workplace, then, but as proof that, given women's current strident political stance, public harassment was punishment well deserved and appropriately meted out. That it might not go to those who had "earned" it escaped the attention of virtually all men politicizers. Although women and men typically placed public harassment within either the romanticized framework or the politicized framework, they sometimes employed both—uncomfortably, for some women especially.

Women and men were likely to interpret incidents of public harassment differently: Even when women and men used the dominant and widely disseminated romanticized rhetoric, they—quite reasonably—did so, if nothing else, from their own points of view and with what was at stake for their own sex foremost. What this chapter reveals above all is an estrangement between women and men in their views of one another and in their goals for their own sex. As both genders explain and account for public harassment, they also unwittingly reveal their assumptions about the opposite sex. These revelations suggest we have far to travel merely to understand the diversity of the opposite sex, much less to make peace and live with respect.

ROMANTICIZED AND POLITICIZED INTERPRETATIONS

These two interpretations of public harassment, the politicized feminist and the romanticized traditionalist, involve rhetoric. I define rhetoric, for the purposes of analyzing interaction, as a theme or stance noted consistently throughout a spate of interaction or with regard to a topic or subject. By the very language and through the morphology

of tales of troubles or tales of triumph, politicized or traditional accounts embody certain social histories and scenarios. They also imply
certain assumptions about women, men, and the relation between
them, as well as their potential to change their behavior.

Both romanticized and politicized accounts can be categorized according to the alleged causes for the harassment. In making this typology, I have tried to concentrate on women's estimates of offenders' intentions, issues that women saw beneath the offense that gave it more
significance, and general philosophies of the sexes.

Women can find interactions in public places not merely significant
in terms of how they are generally perceived in the society, but significant of the general governmental and legal situation their group finds
itself in. A young student said:

> What happens to women in public places shouldn't happen to a dog.
> We can be yelled at, pinched, patted, and it goes all the way to rape
> and violence. It's just a symbol of how the society sees us: We're
> worth nothing. Places that men feel comfortable aren't for us. No
> one has to respect us, and there you see it, everyday on the street.

A middle-aged secretary offered the same politicized interpretation:

> They say you're pretty, but that's just an excuse to harass you. I can
> see a man saying to Geraldine Ferraro she's pretty while he pinches
> her, and she has to take it, just the same as I would. "Pretty" is sup-
> posed to cloud your mind to getting felt up by some strange man. It
> shows you the power that men have over women, even today.

Another example of feminist politicization would be the comment
of the white homemaker in her thirties who said of being pinched or
spoken to by a strange man, "It's no different from your boss or your
professor saying something vulgar or something they shouldn't." But,
of course, public harassment *is* different, and that is partly what makes
it difficult to manage and to erase. What I have defined as public harassment is not always illegal, or its illegalities, where they exist, are
not widely enforced; cross-sex public harassment, when recognized,

will no doubt open the door for enforcement of public harassment by women where racial insult and gay-baiting by women, to name two related types of events, occur.

In politicized feminist accounts in general, the central problem of public harassment was seen as a result of undeserved and longstanding inequalities between the sexes. These feminists believe that discrimination and harassment are reflected throughout women's lives, and that without remedy, women will continue to be disadvantaged. The model politicized woman is one who takes a no-nonsense stance against discrimination and harassment whenever they occur, even among strangers. The particulars in the accounts of these women often varied according to a woman's race: Some African- and Asian-American women and lesbian women of all races said that their experiences with more extreme public harassment had race or sexual preference at its root and reported that this had prepared them for what one young African-American lesbian termed "being harassed 'just' as a woman." One young woman saw "being Black and being a dyke as a training ground for being a woman. I'm glad—I wouldn't know how to handle a lot of things otherwise." Membership in other situationally disadvantaged groups, then, might provide welcome, if regrettable, practice for handling public harassment.

In the traditional romanticized account of public harassment, the claim may be made that public harassment does not exist or that what sounds like harassment ("Whoa! Slut! Whore! Gimme some! I *like* it!" yelled by a man at a passing woman who has not made eye contact with him) is actually nothing worthy of note. Or it can be claimed that such speech actually flatters a woman or is uncontrollably actuated by her choice of dress or her physical appearance. Or the claim can be that such an incident is a response to a man's deeply held obligations to tease, to play, or to demonstrate devoted, even lavish heterosexual preference. In return for accepting these male "obligations," a woman can rely on other obligations she knows to be his, insisting that he has breached etiquette. As she herself acts as a "lady," he too is to act as a "gentleman."

Romantic values, of course, can be recognized and cited by lesbians and by gay men. One gay health professional was walking home from a concert on "a perfect evening," when he

> saw the perfect woman, also coming out of the concert. She had Marlene Dietrich legs. Legs that wouldn't quit. Legs that I'd die for, by the way. I whistled my appreciation and she gave me a glamorous smile. She was wearing full makeup, beautiful lipstick.
>
> A perfect moment, as I say—except that whistle was all I had in mind, and I think she might've been disappointed when I kept on walking.
>
> But I might have imagined that.

The romance of public places is heterosexual because it is presumed that something significant *could* eventuate between opposite-sex strangers. When a woman does take pleasure in being admired, typically she does not imagine that her man admirer is measuring her legs against his own, for example, or that his interest is purely clinical and limited since seeing her legs is all he would ever want from any encounter with her.

Many women, especially those who took care to identify themselves as feminists, made a point to say how offensive men's public harassment was. It constitutes a social problem that as yet has no widely known name (as some regretted) although it is on a continuum with school and workplace harassment. An interesting finding, however, was that identification as a politicized feminist or as a more traditional woman did not affect the level of emotion with which a woman reacted at the time of the harassment itself.

For many informants who explicitly identified themselves as feminists, their own knowledge or interpretation of feminism seemed to have dutifully raised their consciousness, but it had not yet provided them with solutions or suitable strategies to deal with public harassment.

Sadly, identifying themselves as feminists often seemed to leave women *more* frightened, and with less idea of what to do about it, than their outspokenly traditionalist sisters. In part, this is undoubtedly due to those feminist women who have increased their knowledge of the world of men's violence toward women, and that knowledge has left them reasonably shocked and frightened. I suspect that this is also because feminism can open women's eyes to abuses by men but can rob them of the capacity to employ "traditionalist" measures for coping with sexism. Tradition might include reference to etiquette norms, but it also harkens back to a woman's understanding of biblical or koranic dictates that kept the sexes on an uneven keel. A white middle-aged working-class clerk, who strongly professed an identity as a traditionalist and explicitly rejected feminism and "women's lib," said of low-level public harassment incidents in general that an offending man "was not being respectful of me as Adam was of Eve, and that's why things of that nature are morally wrong"; a young African-American college student said much the same, referring to the Koran. Neither had any compunction about speaking frankly to and taking confident active measures against male strangers who had spoken or acted rudely toward them in public. This suggests, then, that women's practical understanding of feminism, at least in this one Midwestern city, has failed to provide women with practical measures for combatting public harassment. Unfortunately, however, whites and African-Americans were consistent in expecting traditionally polite behavior only of men of their own race, thereby revealing something about how little each race feels it can expect from the other and demonstrating that the traditional relationship between the sexes goes only so far in supplying confidence and spurring action.

Of the traditionalist women who reported taking active measures, Asian- and African-American women were prominent among them (in fact, roughly 50 percent in a sample that did not include an equal number of women of color); young, white, heterosexual women were worst represented here. Of the women who said they used measures more likely to have a lasting effect, such as contacting an offender's boss or phoning or writing to the company for which harassers worked, virtually all were women who identified themselves as feminists, lesbian and bisexual women, and (again) Asian- and African-American women were prominent among these.

Thus, women who had a strong regard for the traditional sex roles that included a "privileged" etiquette for women, one that featured men as available to cosset or protect women or be their deserving betters, sometimes did take relatively "active" measures; that is, these women did not invariably numb themselves or studiously ignore what was meant to provoke. Examining all women's accounts of public harassment, then, will say something of the power of both the politicized feminist interpretation of public harassment and the romanticized traditional vision of the sexes to express women's dissatisfaction with public harassment and enable limited retaliation.

A FINE ROMANCE: WOMEN'S ROMANTICIZED INTERPRETATIONS FOR PUBLIC HARASSMENT

Most women arrive eventually at strategies for accounting for public harassment. Broadly, this accounting may be divided into four types of claimsmaking activities by a romanticized vocabulary of events. First, there are those that claim that public harassment is essentially innocuous, and buttress their claims by mentioning that women as well as men are among the offenders, that offenders can be reliably specified by categories of class, race, appearance (often a cover for concerns of class and race), and sexual orientation (often under the guise of reference to a man's "masculinity," lack of same, or the use of a specific homophobic slur). Second, there are accounts that argue that men's nature is to blame and present as proof men's ineluctable sexuality or their adoption of allegedly boyish traits such as showing off or teasing; the simplest version of this explanation held that "men just can't help it." Third is the claim that men in fact flatter women—that men only *seem* to be insulting, hitting, groping, trailing, ogling, or engaging in

unwanted conversation. Fourth, women who use romanticized rhetoric often claim that the acts are basically breaches of etiquette; what
happens is undeserved criticism by unappreciative observers. Unfortunately, this claimsmaking style opens the gate for critical espousers to
note that women too breach traditional etiquette when they dress inappropriately, act loosely available, or in other ways denigrate the portrait of the traditional woman who keeps comfortably to her home
and ventures out only when need be—and then with proper respect
for the situation at large.

Public Harassment as Flattery

Assuming that romanticized etiquette operates in the same way in
public places that it does in less public gatherings, many nonfeminist
women, and many men as well, argued that public harassment was in
fact "complimentary." This account is, when examined, a particularly
difficult one to sustain. There are probably few compliments between
close friends that feature obscene slurs, threats, and slaps, yet it is an
explanation that is customary for public harassment.

Current etiquette books and advice articles often support this rationale: They counsel women to interpret street remarks in particular in
the most flattering light possible by saying, for example, that a street
remark "goes a long way toward filling your need for spontaneous,
frank praise" and, furthermore, that it is "merely (and this is the best
'merely' I know of) a tribute freely offered and meant to be just as
freely accepted. . . . Unphony, no strings—simply one person vocalizing
pleasure at seeing beauty in another" (Geng 1979:76). These works of
etiquette rely on interpreting public harassment as positive, helpful,
and salutary simply because it is anonymous.

Traditional folk interpretations counsel women that much public
harassment is innocuously intended and flattering; it is the reward due
to the woman who correctly projects beauty, femininity, and attention
to appearance. Such an interpretation suggests not only that it can

help the woman feel better about herself in the immediate situation but that "when a street compliment has made you feel beautiful, you can project that aura to the men who are really in your life and just passing by" (Geng 1979:75). Thus, it can be an anonymous practice or socialization session for the woman on how she can expect to be evaluated in private circumstances. In fact, flattering incidents of public harassment could, some women claimed, actually help a woman. Incidents like these could at times make them "feel better about themselves," feel like "real women," boost self-confidence, and socialize women in the skills of pleasing men.

The exact way in which public harassment made women feel better about themselves was, of course, gender related and, within this, related to presumed heterosexual interest and judgment of appearance. Scrutiny could, said some women, make one feel appreciated "as women," "as an attractive woman," or "like a good-looking girl." Wisely, no informant was waiting for a strange man to inquire as to how she fared with regard to inner and spiritual beauty, or pinch her, then ask how her portfolio was doing. Thus, these tributes, when they were considered such, were also taken as responding to the ability of the woman to properly convey her gender and appear heterosexually attractive and interesting, but to nothing else about the individual. Even when women welcomed them, these events reinforced traditional gender divisions, powers, and rights—in particular, men's tendency and right to judge women based on appearance and to convey those opinions.

Of course, a famous harasser could make an incident all the more memorable. Harassment from a celebrity? It *must* be a compliment— or so some women reported thinking at first. At a government function, a Midwestern worker felt a hearty pinch. As she turned around to confront the pincher, she saw a smiling man who confidently informed her, "Well, now you can say you have been pinched by the governor. Today is your lucky day!" Another woman had scrupulously saved to get a front-row ticket for a play featuring her favorite actor. Excited by the evening, she decided to walk home, then gradually became aware that a man was following her, muttering obscenities to her. It was her idol, whose photograph she promptly tore up once she was home safely.

Gallantry as Proof of Flattery

In making the argument that public harassment is truly flattery, women often mentioned that men bestowed public harassment on those not truly compliment-worthy. This observation was used to bolster claims of men's charity, even chivalry, in harassing women. Indeed, public harassment argued to be "gallantry" is the public equivalent of such private occurrences held up for praise as the man who marries the unattractive woman or the man who nobly goes through with the charity of the "pity-fuck." In every one of these incidences, the man gains not only a sense of power from the harassment or the advantages of marriage or bed but also the image of a desirable and moral nature, while that of the woman involved is correspondingly diminished.

Some women noted that men sometimes committed public harassment in such a way that the act neutralized or at least minimized the offense, thus making it as likely as it could be that a woman might feel commended. Women might count this as another proof that public harassment was charity or flattery rather than hostility. For instance, an African-American law student was walking by "a bunch of white boys going the same way when one bowed as I went by and said very seriously, 'Very beautiful.'" She continued, "This elaborate and formal ritual" was proof of their sincere efforts to compliment her; moreover, "they spared me my race. It could've been nasty, if they'd said 'Nigger bitch!' for example." A white homemaker noted that she knew that the middle-aged white man who pinched her painfully as she waited in line at a public utility office was in fact trying to "pay me a compliment," because "he patted my butt afterwards, then he carefully smoothed out the fabric on my skirt. I felt it was respectful of me."

A man can attempt to classify himself as an admirer of the woman, not a competitor of a presumed spouse, and thus as an even more stalwart upholder of the heterosexually romanticized public order as a champion of married life: I watched one woman listen to a man yell, "Hey! Hey! Look at me! I know—I can *see* you're married [she wore a ring and carried a baby], but you're beautiful all the same!" She smiled—as did several of the ten or fifteen people observing the incident.

The men in these examples may have defused offense partly for their own protection, which sets these situations apart from skillful street remarks or modified exploitations of presence. These men cast themselves as neither disrespectful lechers nor serious suitors, thereby bypassing the possibility that they could be seriously refused and implicitly substantiating the romantic ideal. Such ambiguous tangles of implication and definition make it all the more difficult for women to act when they resent public harassment: When women try to react assertively in circumstances where marriage or romantic companionship is invoked, they seem to criticize not just harassers but values of marriage and family as well. Of course, regardless of how they are mitigated, these occurrences of harassment nevertheless reinforce traditional gender relations, substantiating that it is a man's prerogative to evaluate women. Mitigation here implies the author's right (even duty) to calibrate the impact of an action rather than the recipient's right to avoid it.

Different is a man's apology for the act (unless that apology itself is offensive, which compounds the public harassment). As women noted, men sometimes demonstrated that they meant no harm or regretted the harm that was intended when confronted by women who were hurt by public harassment.

Certainly an apology is more pleasant than not attempting to retract or neutralize damage; yet men who did apologize made the attempt when they noted the woman's reaction to public harassment—they did not apologize for assuming the right to commit public harassment in the first place. The woman who countered a crude comment, ogling, or a lascivious gesture or pinch with a pained look sometimes received an apologetic assertion that the harasser was only kidding. In essaying a pained look, the woman drew in part on the man's obligation to act the gentleman, not the brute. There is, indeed, an apparent gallantry to these retreats, but it must be noted once again that the person who makes this attempt at repair is much the same as the motorist who rushes to secure an ambulance for the broken body she or he has just run over. Compare this with a case involving race: Imagine, for example, if the Asian-American woman who had a gang of whites and African-Americans following her and yelling "Slant!" and "Yellow bitch!" had received the explanation that they were "only kidding."

Middle-aged and older women, especially white middle-class women, specifically pointed out that they believed that the rate at which they received public harassment had diminished. (My own observations suggest that, while extravagant "compliments" diminish, contempt increases.) Because middle-aged and older women said they considered at least more minor acts of public harassment complimentary, they now found themselves pleased at intrusions that would have left them indignant when younger. They applied, they realized, a sliding scale of offense: One white middle-aged office worker now counted "pinches, and pokes, and grabs" as compliments, whereas when younger she would have "decked the man who dared to look at me too long." Such women were all the more likely to support harassing men as generous gallants who chivalrously offered the women what they now thought to be rare praise. In terms of the woman's everlasting obligation to achieve gender, middle-aged and older women discover that they are faced with a task that they cannot accomplish when in public places.

Traditional women said that one situation offered men an arena for gallantry, even undiluted heroism: when men gave a street remark or "appreciative" pinch or look to a woman from behind—only to discover when they drew level with her that she was either not so attractive from in front or not so young as they had thought (and hence in either case someone who had no right to be the possessor of an attractive posterior). A man confronted with this new and sudden knowledge commonly said he felt himself duped, and commonly showed it. One middle-aged man said, of a middle-aged woman he mumbled praise at from behind, that when he came face to face with her he thought that "what she did was like passing bad checks—she had nothing in the bank to cover it." If this is the gallantry and heroism to be found in public harassment, then these encounters reveal gallantry and heroism themselves as flawed bases for interaction.

The women involved in such encounters can feel themselves unworthy tricksters. A woman in her fifties who had purchased, then finally abandoned, a short skirt that regularly landed her comments and scrutiny said of such an incident that she then felt she "had no right to wear the skirt in the first place." Indeed, popular advice and lore expressly warn middle-aged and elderly women against adopting potentially deceiving items of apparel—clothing, makeup styles, or footwear, for instance, that is "too young" for them. This advice comes from a book for aging women:

> Boots have now come into fashion view: choose them with care. In black or brown, they are warm and practical. Hip-length, in shiny leather, in white or crazy colors, laced through brass hooks, they promise a youthful appearance to the young man following you on the street, a disappointment when he catches up with you. (Russ 1972:83–84)

Thus, part of the reason for aging women to mute their attractiveness and avoid inappropriately "youthful" dress is to avoid generating awkward situations. Of course, all apologies and all skillful mitigations are a response to the immediate character of the harassment offered, not to the power structure that has allowed the man to commit harassment in the first place. Therefore, even repair work must be analyzed as an unsatisfactory depoliticization of offense.

There are, however, many ways in which public harassment does not seem to be easily classifiable as flattery, and even women who traditionally romanticize harassment are occasionally troubled by these situations. Part of what may catch their attention is the speed with which an apparently complimentary street remark or other harassment can rapidly become a vulgar invitation or assessment, or even the speed with which it can be rescinded should the man decide the woman is no longer deserving. When a white woman heard an African-American man yell that she looked fine and that he would like to carry her books, she was inclined to smile, but when she thanked him but told him no, he yelled, "Shit, baby, you ain't all *that*. I was just trying to be nice anyway" (Ferree 1991). In such cases, a man makes a remark, receives a rebuff or lack of response from the woman, then takes her lack of response as the rationale for withdrawing his original estimate—which then does not seem a sincere compliment after all.

When a woman goes to what she feels is considerable trouble to maintain, alter, or modify her appearance in order to secure men's attention, she might be all the more likely to feel that a wide range of public harassment was evidence that her efforts had not been made in vain and thus all the less likely to question the character of the attention. (She might also carefully distinguish between public and private spheres and public and private attentions.) Thus, a woman who had had breast reduction surgery to "escape public notice" said that when a group of men surrounded her in the downtown business district and yelled "Show us your tits!" they lauded the appearance that she had achieved at the cost of much pain and much money.

In fact, twenty-three women informants revealed that they had had cosmetic surgery to alter the way they were treated in public (I did not routinely ask this question). Eleven of these women reported that they had had cosmetic surgery to make themselves more attractive to men and suggested that attention in public places was an expected part of that. Eleven, on the other hand, told me that they undertook cosmetic surgery at least in part to escape that same attention. If nothing else, public harassment would seem to be a great support of plastic surgery as a medical specialty. Thus, one young African-American file clerk told me that she had had her breasts enlarged to ensure that men on the street would look at her with what she felt was admiration: "It cost me two months' salary to get these breast implants," she said, "and you best believe that I did it so guys would look at me. I don't care if they feel me up, or what they do. That's what I paid all that money for." These are quite serious modifications—face or breast surgery, liposuction, and leg recontouring are the most common surgical measures—to endure for the sake of peace in public places. If women go to such lengths to pass down a street undisturbed, why cannot men be expected to marshal willpower enough to change their behavior?

Public Harassment as Courtship

Women who supported the romanticized interpretation of public order sometimes argued that what seemed public harassment was in fact a legitimate effort to meet a woman whom one would date, perhaps marry. For many women informants (and for me), this was a troublesome interpretation to support, since women are traditionally counseled to withhold availability to strangers and since some occurrences of public harassment—a pinch that later produces a bruise, a playful push that sends the woman sprawling on the sidewalk, or, in one case, in the gutter of a busy downtown street, for instance—carried little promise for any subsequent courtship. Then too, customary public interaction, at least on streets and other transitways, is typically too brief to support anything but what would have to be classified as an arranged marriage—one in which the bride had little say.

When accounting for public harassment as courtship, women occasionally expressly commiserated with their public harassers. These men, women might say, were burdened by the many difficulties of making friends in the city or perhaps had been rejected by a girlfriend or spouse and were casting for a replacement. Some of these women used public harassment that had occurred when they were with an escort to buttress the argument that a man had courtship on his mind rather than that women were of such little worth that they might be harassed even when ostensibly protected. In these situations the escort presumably often sympathized with the harasser rather than the woman, as some women reported. Other women suggested that a defending escort's actions used public harassment as the occasion for solidifying a courtship already in progress—rather a romantic incident all the same, since their escort's protective involvement could be taken as proof of romantic love. These women saw themselves as comfortably sought after by a faithful defender (the escort) and a pawky rival (the harasser). Instead of thinking that they had suffered public humiliation, some women—typically young middle- or working-class white women—concluded that they suffered an embarrassment of riches, a tactic that saved face for the woman and implicitly excused her harasser by placing him in a legitimate, romantic pursuit:

> At a Mellencamp concert, I was in one of the first rows with Gabriel, my boyfriend. Gabe and I were having a great time, dancing around, when suddenly I felt someone pet me on one breast and then someone else petted me on the other. I couldn't believe it. I turned around, and I saw a bunch of guys, and one on either side of me, and I started to tell them they were creeps—but then Gabe did it for me. He really raked them over the coals.
>
> I felt pretty great. Those guys were pretty cute—maybe I'll go back there and I'll see one again and he'll ask me out. And [Gabriel] let me know how much he cared and that he wouldn't let anybody else make a move on me. And I'm very happy with how to handle the problem. I let my boyfriend handle the problem—that's the best [way]—and I didn't have to do a thing, and I learned how much he loved me besides.

When escorted, such a woman might portray the offender as a plausible rival. Although the offender had no real right to touch her, speak to her, or commit other public harassment, he was not criticized for trying. This was at once a romanticized, depoliticized interpretation that assumed the encounter was in fact a genuine, albeit illicit, court-ship approach.

Other women who were more likely to be older and higher on the socioeconomic scale and less likely to be white and heterosexual still used the romanticized interpretation to evaluate what were seen as courtship approaches, but these women tended to feel that, although they understood public harassment as a romanticized approach, it was inappropriate and it disrespected the prior claims that a partner had on them: Harassment could, in fact, be taken as an insult to the entire family system.

As I said above, some of the reported harassment by men blurred an abuse by mitigating it with an appeal to a strange woman's husband or boyfriend, thus the harasser aligned himself with mainstream social values of family and heterosexual romance. When a man patted the buttocks of one African-American teacher while she was walking down the street carrying her month-old daughter, she concluded: "He was good-looking, but—where did he think I got [my daughter]? That's disrespect to me, but also to my husband and to the whole institution of marriage." Her statement implied that to acknowledge correctly legal offspring should stimulate respect for all members of the institution—herself included. Another woman spoke of disrespect to the small children with her, rather than to herself, since her three- and four-year-old children might have "absorbed a contempt for family values" when her harassers all but pitched her onto the sidewalk as they yelled, hooted, and hit her breasts as she tried to cross the street with the children. Still another woman spoke of being goosed at a mall as wrong "because only my husband has the right to do that." In contrast to upholding a woman's own dignity, interpretations like these upheld the dignity of others and the ownership of women by husband and children, even children of very young ages.

If politicized accounts suggested that public harassment was weighted with significance far beyond the immediate situation, so too did romanticized accounts. Whether women cast public harassment incidents as opportunities for crucial proof of affection from boyfriends or as slights to social institutions such as marriage, the family, and womanhood, they elevated these typically brief, everyday encounters between strangers to incidents of larger romantic and familial concern.

Interestingly, a woman's husband or boyfriend did not actually need to be with her for her to resent what she identified as an attempt of a rival. This testifies to how incomplete these women felt when alone in public and to the tendrils of power and influence that the men in their lives had. They felt that wearing a wedding ring, being engaged on a family task (such as conspicuously purchasing fishing tackle for a man that they specified to the clerk as a spouse), or being accompanied by a child were signs that their presence should be regarded as protected. In such cases women noted that their sense that they should be flattered warred with their sense that the offender had failed to regard a husband's prior claims.

Public Harassment as the Result of Men's Natures: Men as Rampant Beasts

Women who romanticized public harassment were likely to support the idea that acts of public harassment stemmed from the allegedly unalterable character of the strange man who was offender, thus in fact accepting the intransigence of men as a social category. To these women, men are equipped with a certain nature comprising character, constitution, genes, brain, and hormones, and really have no choice but to be constantly sexually appetent; women, then, are left with no recourse but to endure or to strategize in minor ways when public harassment occurs. One woman who identified herself as "firmly traditional" said that changing men's behavior toward women in public was as likely as "changing a leopard's spots, and a lot more dangerous." African-American women were especially likely to allude to some vaguely biologically based rationale for men's public harassment of women: in fact, nearly 75 percent of the African-American women interviewed did so. (In contrast, white women of the middle and working classes were especially likely to espouse and elaborate on women's responsibility to categorize correctly the membership of potential offenders.) One African-American law student said, succinctly, after "a brother had hit my butt and insulted me," "They've got dicks. That's what they think with. They got no choice. I got no choice either. That's why I forget about it. Else I stay home." Such a statement, especially from a "promising Black professional," as she identified herself, speaks of an alienation between African-American women and African-American men.

Other women were more inclined to use quasi-sociological analyses of men's public harassment, suggesting that public harassment was comparable to pulling on a girl's pigtails or dipping them in the inkwell, male-initiation rites of primitive cultures, or simply demonstrating "machismo," a term women used to cover a great variety of acts that could be thought of as rude but might be judged to be battery or sexual battery should our lawmakers choose to consider them. When women cited machismo as a spur for public harassment, they often sympathized with the harasser, implying that it was, on the whole, too bad that men were bound to constantly strive, approach, and be sadly disappointed. A twenty-year-old white receptionist noted:

> All men are insecure with their masculinity. This is our culture that does this to them. If they were headhunters, there'd be no problem. But now it's very hard to be a man. You have to keep it up, keep proving it. They *have* to tease women constantly, touch them, try to talk to them, do anything they can. Otherwise, they'd be wimps. You've got to feel sorry for them when you think about it, don't you?

This woman had been hooted at by construction workers on her way to work for weeks, so that she eventually took to creeping around the back of the building to take a service elevator.

Many women perceived the inherent heterosexualist romanticism of public places. Did a man yell, catcall, grab, pinch, follow, or leer at a strange woman? If so, these women felt the act demonstrated that he was an appropriately virile heterosexual (and she, by turn, was a fit object for the attentions of a virile heterosexual). A youthful white secretary visiting Indianapolis from Chicago was walking through the aspiringly trendy shops of the Broad Ripple area alone one afternoon when she felt a hand creep up her shorts from behind and quickly squash one of her buttocks with a vicelike grip. She noted that the offender "must have wanted to avoid seeming like a fag, because Broad Ripple's full of fairies." Interestingly, this makes homosexuality a final cause of public harassment of women by men: It is in order *not* to seem gay that straight men allegedly sometimes harass. The woman who believes this is in some measure homophobic or at the least heterosexist. Her tolerance of her presumably heterosexual harasser reinforces her feeling that notable differences exist between heterosexual and homosexual men.

Women who said that heterosexuality was "proven" by public harassment were touchingly naive, of course: They took at face value the male heterosexual entitlement of public harassment. I spoke to gay and bisexual men who had harassed women (although there were few). I spoke to some heterosexual women who had been harassed by men they took to be proving their masculinity, as indeed they may have been—but, since I knew the men in question, I knew the masculinity to be homosexual. I also spoke to one heterosexual man who told me confidently he had harassed a woman he called "a hot number"—a woman I privately knew to be lesbian.

Women who were inclined to theorize more about society said that "men's nature" leads to a truly awe-inspiring sex drive, which made them look at every woman, even strangers in public, as potential sex partners. However, many women who mentioned men's "strong sex drive" also noted the characteristics that accompanied it, such as "a sense of superiority," "dominance," and "bossing women around." To suggest, sometimes pityingly as these women did, that men who publicly harass women do so out of insubstantial masculinity or attempted bravery is, in some measure, to justify their offenses. It also presents public incursions as marks of men's failure when they are, quite clearly, marks of men's domination and effective power over women—an effective power that can depend on women's acquiescence, even though it can be a prudent acquiescence.

Yet, for the most part, women perpetrated views of men as biological, social, and genetic lost causes, as doomed to misbehavior and crime by nagging penises and male hormones, just as many men believe women are doomed by their reproductive organs and female hormones. Men, it seemed, not only were rampant beasts when in public places, they were unregenerate and untrainable ones to boot. Men constituted an inevitable threat because of their "natures," however a woman specified nature (genes, socialization, brain, hormones, or penis). Ultimately, biologically based explanations in particular were more depressing and pessimistic than they first seemed. They enabled and sustained a view of men as recalcitrant, obnoxious, and biologically determined creatures at the mercy of society and body—slavering offenders at worst, cutups and cards or fearful Mamma's boys at best. Moreover, to take such a view of men's natures made it difficult for women to claim to strategize successfully or, considering the view of women as weaker, for them to claim to adopt any attitude but pity.

Just Deserts: Harassment as Woman's Fault

Some women and men felt that women provoked public harassment not only by the clothing that they wore but with a smile or eye contact (acts that might be taken as suggestive behavior) or simply by their attractiveness. Several women suggested that they were catcalled, pinched, or followed because they were prettier, sexier, more cheerful, or simply "nicer" than most other women. Some women said that women were to blame for their harassment, although the women criticized were customarily not of the same class or did not adhere to the informant's belief systems, and the informant seldom criticized herself. A typical remark condemned women who dress "to show off their bodies." Another typical remark suggested that men quite reasonably assumed from their experience that these women were "loose" or "sluts," and that such women appreciated public harassment of any type. Moreover, these women poisoned the well of public order for decent women like the speakers: Men could not be blamed for treating those they assumed to be sluts like sluts.

A few women, however, argued that the responsibility was their own and that harassment could be controlled by controlling women's appearance. This was also an argument of some politicized feminists who believe that if women moderate their attractiveness they will escape notice in public and hence the harassment that is the traditional woman's lot. Moreover, many women who otherwise resented exploitation, and roundly criticized the men who authored it, suggested that an element of their own attractiveness was the cause. Indeed, they suggested it was women's responsibility to dress and act "modestly" or to expect consequences. In fact, these women said that the consequences were a compliment, the result of the man looking for the most attractive target he could find.

Other women were less certain of how to interpret public harassment, but they still found cause in their own behavior, saying they may have looked too vulnerable or shy (it is difficult not to when you are in an environment that exacerbates your vulnerability and which is not crafted for you), seemed too polite (although part of what you learn is to be polite to strange men, in part because the dangerous ones may not attend to you if you are), dressed inappropriately (of course, you are not always dressing to please the diverse tastes of diverse strangers, nor is the street or shop always your final destination). Women who offer a self-blaming view of these incidents may be tempted to use this view if they are assaulted, molested, or raped. This interpretation of public harassment, then, sets a dangerous precedent in terms of the interpretation it encourages for incursions more violent and arguably more serious in nature.

THE POLITICIZATION OF THE PUBLIC ORDER: A DIFFERENT WAY OF ACCOUNTING FOR HARASSMENT

The hallmark of the politicized view of public harassment was to see it as comparable to sexual harassment in workplace and school and as evidence of men's power over women in other areas of society. Some women said that their first experience with sex discrimination in general was their childhood socialization for behavior in public places. A student recalled she had been socialized to smile: "That was probably the biggest thing, smile when you meet someone, that's supposed to be a sign of graciousness." This politicized view gave women a particular view of men; in public as elsewhere, concluded a young Asian-American woman, "young white males have an advantage over everybody everywhere."

Grand Claims

When women politicized public harassment, they sometimes gave it a noble cause, ratified the existence of other claims about the situation of women (or men, or African-Americans, or people with disabilities), and stimulated a sense of justice undermined or, when the target of the harassment took action, justice upheld. Women offered the following similes and metaphors for incidents of public harassment like ogling, following, pinching and grabbing, street remarks, and vitiations of expected public aid: women compared public harassment to, prominently, rape, prostitution, socialization to the "nice girl" model, women as entertaining visual objects, wife-beating, sexual and racial discrimination, sexual and racial harassment in workplace and school.

Mentioned less frequently were pornography, child abuse, the revictimization of victims, the Holocaust, Balkan genocide, crimes against women and girls, and the Rodney King and Reginald Denny beatings in the Los Angeles riots of 1992. Many women considered street remarks and exploitive touch on a continuum with rape, a possible "preamble to rape," "verbal rape," "a little rape," or connected to "sexual terrorism" in general.

When women implicitly or explicitly claim that their situation is comparable to situations that form a larger political issue, however modestly the claim is made, these women acquire the benefits of sympathetic popular opinion, and they also acquire the right to claim that they understand something of the point of view, experience, or trauma of those who have suffered in similar situations. (And so, of course, does anyone who invokes such metaphors for her or his own troubles.) For the moment, then, being pinched on a bus or being run through the gauntlet by a group of construction workers has the high gloss of a political cause. At the same time, indignation over the plight of others who are more obviously injured can fuel a woman's fear, anger, and resentment. A young white graduate student told of her experience of being painfully hit on the breast by a stranger, who then conveniently ran off into a crowd:

> [M]y feminist consciousness dates from that incident. It was so wrong. It made me furious, and then I knew that there was absolutely nothing I could do about it. It did something else: It made me understand how a rape survivor feels. I don't mean that I'm as bad off as a woman that's been raped, but the mechanics of the thing are the same. Now I find I really watch men carefully. Now I think, "You never know what they'll do." I feel I understand more what Blacks suffer in the society, too.

Not all women who cast public harassment in politicized terms went much beyond that label in suggesting it was offensive. A few spoke of public or sexual harassment, but only to trivialize offenses, either saying that they were something a woman should learn to manage or ignore or identifying only a few of the mildest sort of offenses as harassment and then concluding that these minor, verbal offenses were unremarkable. One college student said:

> Sure, women get sexually harassed in the street. Sure, they get terrified. But so what? Women just get yelled at, or they get goosed or grab-assed. Maybe sometimes hit, like I was. But nothing worse. Nobody gets killed. Women can handle it. So just forget about it. It's not a big deal. It's not important.
>
> [Are you aware that some of the offenses we've been talking about are against the law?]
>
> Well, they shouldn't be. All the guys do it. Get real.

Needless to say, to invoke a cause with a well-worked-out pattern of claimsmaking typically emphasized a woman's lack of responsibility for what happened to her (although the previous example neatly puts the responsibility back on the woman's shoulders). By and large, women who politicized public harassment said that they "accept no responsibility for being the victim of someone's vulgar remarks or actions," in the words of a lab technician in her forties from Indianapolis. Yet even women who were deeply offended were also often at a loss to know what to do when public harassment occurred.

ROMANCE OR POLITICS?

Both romanticizing and politicizing the public order are rhetorics that were typically expressed by women who espoused traditional gender roles and women who espoused a feminist perspective, respectively. Single accounts, however, were not always consistent: Sometimes a woman who termed herself "feminist" would relate that public harassment abuses were in fact the "fault" of women themselves—a self-blaming and appearance-evaluative stance that is more consistent with a romanticized rhetoric. There are practical problems for women with each articulation. If we keep them in mind as we read women's accounts of their public harassment experiences, we will be able to understand better why these limitations exist for both rhetorical articulations and, perhaps, something of the nature of the accounts themselves. The kind of practical social problems apparent in explanations of public harassment help us make sense of the problematic and disputed events that happen in our lives. What happens when the societal patterns of accounts themselves are absent or unsatisfactory, or when they present us with the stimulus for solving problems that are in fact so enormous that we cannot put our rhetoric into action? This is, I think, what happens with the rhetoric of public harassment.

Why did so many women who took care to identify themselves as feminists respond in traditional and self-blaming ways? Why did they mix these seemingly uncongenial articulations? I suggest that the reason is one inherent in the nature of our perception of the social problem of public harassment, namely that neither romanticized nor politicized articulation offers pragmatic strategies, although the romanticized rhetoric provides a more self-assured and more familiar grounding for the woman who wants to take action.

Finding Meaning

Public harassment can produce an atmosphere in which an individual experiences ill treatment in public places with a sense of *déjà vu*, which may be interpreted with wry and astute expectation or noted as proof of unreasonable paranoia: A social worker said she felt as if she was "just waiting to get yelled at by those boys. I knew the minute I saw them there [lounging against a building] what they were up to." Some women said that they spent a good part of their time in public places waiting to be harassed. When they were, their astuteness was not always credited. A young clerical worker was with her boyfriend in New York when she saw a "well-dressed white man walking toward us." She said, "I saw him look at me a little from far off," and she predicted to her boyfriend she would receive closer scrutiny. She was correct, for the strange man "almost looked straight down the front of my blouse. But Donny said, 'Oh, you're just imagining things.

Anyway, he probably just did that because he saw you whispering about him.'"

The speakers in these incidents existed somewhere in an uneasy twilight between feeling offended and trying to be convinced that they were imagining it all. In this atmosphere things will seem to be going well when there is no overt evidence that they are going badly—in other words, our normative belief about public places is that it should be a glass of water that is always half-full. Thus, when no harassment occurs, the individual can give way to a sense of disbelief or use the absence of harassment to make the point that not all members of an advantaged group are, after all, offenders. As an African-American health-care worker said, "not every time you go down the street, something awful happens." In this atmosphere intrusions that are minimal or ambiguous can be appreciated with a grotesque gratitude or even recast as civility, so that when a white secretary notes a group of men who "looked like lawyers on their lunch break . . . look me up-and-down," she finds herself "grateful" when they simply look away. "I just didn't want to be hassled that day," she went on to explain. "I was having a real bad day. I would say they were being real polite. That's because they were better quality men . . . younger, white, and professional men." Conversely, the man who does not harass signals to a woman that something is missing, typically from the man's quotient of heterosexual masculinity. Offenses are often tacitly taken as marks of a woman's satisfactory achievement of gender and proof of a man's satisfactory expression of his own gender. A woman may reason that their absence marks a flaw in her own or in the man's achievement of gender. One woman said she felt "creepy" when she was not noticed. Another woman related, "I saw a good-looking guy coming toward me, and I thought he was going to give me the eye, or say something—'Hey, baby, lookin' good,' or something. But he didn't. I guess he was a fag." She concluded that the man was gay rather than respectful or egalitarian. Men who decide to eschew public harassment of women and behave respectfully will not always meet women who appreciate their demeanor.

MEN: THE SITUATIONALLY ADVANTAGED INTERPRETATION OF PUBLIC HARASSMENT

Most men's interpretations made clear that they, without shame, took for granted their right to evaluate women. In the words of one of a group of young white men I observed shouting at a passing woman, men have the right to "put a price tag" on women they do not know. Such metaphors ran through men's accounts in abundance, especially in the accounts of white working- and middle-class men. These similes and metaphors were rarely present in women's accounts of men's action and, if present, they were criticized or laboriously rationalized.

There were many similarities between traditional women's and men's styles of accounting for public harassment. Most heterosexual men's accounts differed, however, from those of traditional women in several respects. Whereas women's accounts featured descriptions of the woman's own feelings and reactions *and* often included her estimate of a man's feelings or motives (sometimes quite sensitively, even overcharitably done), men's interpretations seldom mentioned a woman's reaction, either guessed at or observed.

Another difference was the prevalence, consistency, and firmness with which men used each rhetoric. Aspects of a romanticized rhetoric occasionally cropped up in the remarks of even the most outspoken politicized feminist: One woman expatiated even minor occurrences of public harassment as rendering women little better off than Blacks in South Africa, then worriedly asked my opinion of her own conservative style of dress as perhaps "causing" her to receive public harassment. I never heard this self-doubt expressed by any man I interviewed, nor did any interviewer on this project.

These general differences, along with others I will discuss in detail, originated because a man's perspective is that of the member of a group that is situationally advantaged in public places. Unless a man was also a member of a group that both experiences regular and demeaning public harassment himself *and* has no reason to support the heterosexually romanticized rhetoric, he was unlikely to have evolved insight into a politicized rhetoric. This, of course, explains why gay and bisexual men were prominent among men informants who adopted a politicized rhetoric as "enlightened oppressors," as I have called them.

Of course not all instances of communication between women and men strangers are wounding, terrifying, or physically painful. But—*of course* also—women have not yet had an opportunity to exist in an atmosphere without knowing that threats like these are possibilities. Until they do, women cannot be expected to appreciate encounters in public places as harmless, flattering, or good fun. That is, and will remain, men's privilege.

The Situationally Advantaged in Public Places

There are certain common features of the viewpoints of groups situationally advantaged in public places that deserve mentioning. My current research on public harassment across race, health status, sexual preference, and social class suggests in part that these are elements of a viewpoint that any situationally advantaged group member can adopt with relation to situationally disadvantaged group members. Thus, heterosexual women and men have these views toward homosexuals; ablebodied women and men have them in regard to women and men who are disabled; whites of both sexes have them with regard to people of color; younger people have them with regard to older people. Although membership in one group that is situationally disadvantaged in public places will certainly tend to increase the chances that an individual will gain insight into the experience other situationally disadvantaged groups—as gay and bisexual men tend to be more sensitive to women's plight—this identification depends somewhat on how revered or how despised the other group is.

Neatly demonstrating these gradations of sensitivity was a fifty-five-year-old gay white man, who spoke sympathetically about a white waitress he had seen harassed the previous week: "Finally, I just felt so bad for her. I knew what it was like, because that's what happens to queens [as he counts himself] especially. It's everything from sneering and mocking, to being raped and being beat up, or kicked. It's a power thing from men, straight men, for both of us." A hallmark of most situationally advantaged groups is the tendency of their members to define the troubles of the disadvantaged as being a flight of fancy of a whining minority.

Troubles as Rare or Trivial

Insisting that things as a whole are not really so dark is a hallmark of the situationally advantaged group member's account. As Stephen Gould wrote of those who complained of incivilities in public places, "nearly every encounter with another person is at least neutral and usually pleasant enough" (Gould 1988). In the same way, an African-American man who considered it hard for African-American men to meet African-American women to date, gave a very pragmatic reading of how an African-American woman should act:

> What do you [as an African-American woman] say when a brother or group of brothers say, "What's happening, baby?" or "You're looking good"? I've repeated those questions to sisters on the street where there was no one but us and over 90 to 100 percent of the time I don't even get a response. (Staples 1981)

One aspect of situationally advantaged members' understanding of public places is that they consider much of the face-to-face communication between strangers that occurs there to be insignificant—at least

when it is distasteful communication. Often, those advantaged in public places, especially those that are the most purely "public" like streets
and roads, consider them mere characterless transitways to other regions, not loci of interest in themselves; laws against loitering, lolling,
and vagrancy exist in part to insure that public places remain waysta-
tions, not goals. They are gone through, not gone to. When dysphoric
communication does occur, it can be ignored—or its targets can be advised to ignore it—with the argument that it is unimportant in the
light of more weighty items of communication in private places:

> It's funny, but just these kinds of happenings, of occurrences, have
> been a sore point, a point of discussion, between my lady and my-
> self. Not a week goes by but we don't argue about them. Last week
> we were walking to the Vogue [a music venue in a Yuppie area of
> Broad Ripple] to hear some music, and a crowd of teenagers, both
> Blacks and whites, from Broad Ripple High was lounging near the
> entrance. They started whistling and shouting at her—you know,
> "Hey, babe, c'mere, give us what you got!" and all that. It got
> raunchy, obscene, but so what? Nobody hurt her or anything—
> O.K., one boy threw M&Ms at her, they hit her. We stayed up all
> night arguing about that.
>
> [What did you think she should have done?]
>
> Just forget it. It was over. Nothing happened. I'm sure they were
> rude, yes, but they meant her no harm.

What *did* they mean if they meant her no harm?

Women who have experienced fairly extreme public harassment in
the streets are told that they should consider these snubs, starts, snarls,
and rejections to be unimportant or that they should, in some way, rise
above them. In fact, such discussions can become a staple in the life of
a couple or a group of friends.

Public Places as Romantic Frontiers

Men, although not women, have a long history of conceptualizing
their presence in public places as a masculine conquering of the fron-

tier, of open spaces, of the vagabond road. Indeed, as reflected in literature and poetry, every public place from the city street to the country road has been subsumed under this understanding of public places. Stevenson, for example, writes of public places as a home, where he "pass[es], a wilful stranger; / My mistress still the open road / And the bright eyes of danger" (Stevenson 1907). Lamb, with much the same ardor, rhapsodizes about what is available for the city dweller in London:

> Oh, her lamps of a night! her rich goldsmiths, print-shops, toy-shops, mercers, hardware-men, pastry-cooks, St. Paul's Churchyard, the Strand, Exeter Change, Charing Cross, with a man upon a black horse! These are thy gods, O London! (Lamb 1902)

This sense of adventure predominates in the interpretation of the public domain as a man's, not a woman's, pied-à-terre, where a man is not totally responsible for his actions and where, as a consequence, he may behave frivolously. This interpretation was especially evidenced by men who said that public places allowed them to behave sportively. Some women argued likewise.

The tradition of "girl-watching" also is considered by many to be a pleasant feature of some public spaces such as plazas. Thus, some analysts have suggested that girl-watching should be encouraged with other "delights" and marks of "sociability" such as lunching in the outdoors and the presence of buskers, mimes, musicians, and other street entertainers. Men's responses to girl-watching "acts" are "all machismo," since never has "a girl watcher picked up a girl, or attempted to" (Whyte 1980:16–18).

For situationally advantaged groups like men the metaphor of being in public places—anonymous, free of societal labeling, unrestrained—can be analyzed by men as a romantic foreign adventure, an anonymous drama, a mystery that holds who-knows-what-promise, an opportunity to appreciate the diversity of humanity: "I walk the fluent street," wrote one male poet (Robinson 1989). Sometimes such characteristics as "anonymity" are even cited by urban boosters to encourage people to move to a city (Hummon 1985). Certainly there are favorable aspects to the public atmosphere evident in many and the most complex of our public places nowadays. However, people who are habitually situationally disadvantaged and who know that there are severe, sometimes fatal consequences to being perceived as category members in public places can arrive at very different views. Recall, from the previous section, the catalog of metaphors that politicized feminist women used: A trip to Auschwitz, not a trip to the South of France, appeared in their imagery.

A man who sees a public place as a romantic frontier will probably choose an active role while in that place, either that of critical watcher (of women) and kin (of men), or that of competitor. A young white man, a college student, said that in general he preferred to "watch people instead of having people watch me." A white salesman in his late thirties noted he was effectively "glued to women" and fascinated by judging them, to the exclusion of attending to his own sex entirely. If, for instance, he "saw a man and a woman together and you asked me the next day if I remembered them or something on that order, I couldn't tell you anything about the man, [but] I could tell you everything about the woman, as far as physical characteristics."

Action—public harassment—on the romantic frontier was interpreted as playful or sportive competition. One man, when asked how he judged incidents of public harassment, noted that they made public places lively and enjoyable: "Are those incidents acceptable? Let me just put it this way: If they weren't, the world would be a very dull place." This frontier ethos sometimes resulted in showdowns with seeming competitors who passed in cars, while jogging, or while walking. A young white student noted that he would "get mildly offended when somebody passes me [in a car]," and another said that he "had at least one drag race a day with someone who thinks he can pass me—I don't *let* that happen." Some men simply noted that this frontier was, for them, home. Said one African-American engineer: "I'm at home anywhere in public, unafraid and unsure why anyone else would be afraid either." An Asian-American health-care professional said that "in public places I have a real feeling of well-being." And a white sales manager said that in public "I feel like I belong."

The Advantaged Are in Fact Disadvantaged

Men often argued that they, not women, were disadvantaged in public places. This disadvantage was sometimes described as a result of distrust: "Women don't trust us, and because of that they treat us badly," a young white manager said. An appliance service technician in his forties specified that women

> get waited on before men, by men. In some ways they are treated well, because men buy their drinks for them when they are out. Women bully other drivers—men and women—by being pushy, getting on each other's tails, and forcing their way into wherever they want to go.

Often women's ostensible status as a group deserving special etiquette and consideration from strangers was offered as proof of favored treatment in actuality.

Some men offered incidents of their own humiliation as a justification for public harassment that they or other men had committed. One man related that a group of women had laughed at him when his fly was open, causing him to feel "angry and pissed off, embarrassed." Other men recounted stories of women dealing competently with their public harassment, as when a pair of young women responded to a man who had "patted both their heinies" while he walked down the middle of a crowded mall. One woman stuck out her tongue, and the other kicked him. This man said he was "angry and deeply, thoroughly hurt" by the incident.

Romance, Flattery, and Heterosexual Masculinity

In the course of defending public harassment as complimentary, men often suggested that they were not simply helping attractive, desirable women, but had themselves "flattered" a woman who undeniably did not deserve it. This argument, of course, further supports the claim of gallantry and bolsters the romanticized rhetoric of public place harassment. For example, if the chance exists that a woman will receive a remark that ostensibly values her appearance or demeanor as less than the estimate she herself puts upon it, there is also the chance that the estimate she hears will be one that is higher than her own, which will bolster her confidence. With this understanding, a white businessman in his fifties was "just sort of following a woman in front of me, who had short shorts and a gauzy top, and I speeded up to get a look at her face. Uh-oh! She's gotta be about fifty! I do a double take and then I smile at her very graciously and tell her how terrific she looks, though she didn't." I asked what the effect of such an action would be. He thought for a moment, then said: "It's a compliment, I guess. I mean, who usually tells a woman that old she's good-looking?" Remarks in situations like this are often cited as proof that public harassment can indeed be complimentary, but without noting that the reasons one feels discomfort at appearing less than beautiful in public is partly because of male-governed standards of beauty—and that the reason one feels relief at being complimented is because one knows full well the insults a man could give and that, perhaps, one feels one deserves.

Part of what any "romantic" or "flattering" public harassment communicates, however, is a man's apparent heterosexual masculinity. Even the smallest act, such as a man opening a door for a strange woman simply because she is a woman, demonstrates this. One African-American/Native American salesman noted that men always tried to act courteous around women: "You don't go opening doors for a guy—you do, you're a queer, a faggot." Thus, part of the way heterosexual men felt they demonstrated heterosexuality to strangers was by treating women romantically and courteously and denying strange men the same measures of etiquette.

Men frequently suggested that public harassment often was honest and frank evaluation, an attempt to meet a woman or, failing that, to communicate admiration, or just a response to the calculated provocation of a woman's appearance. Thus both attempts at acquaintance and evaluation were foremost in men's accounts. A medical student "on a tight schedule" said tartly: "Of course I pass comments—at the malls, at the laundromat, at the grocery store, on my lunchbreak. With my schedule, how else am I going to meet women?" Such artless attempts to establish acquaintance with a woman can rarely be successful, since responding to a street remark with a bid for friendship or a date currently makes a woman seem too available. In any event, most of her responses will be used as fodder for further comment.

The argument that public harassment is in fact a sincere attempt at courtship is bolstered by men who note that they would commit these intrusions anytime, anywhere, to anyone *except* a woman escorted by a man. One man said that both nonselectivity in targets and using an escorted woman as a target constituted harassment: "If you constantly do it to everyone who walks down the street, then it ought to be considered as harassment or whatever. But as far as she's with her husband or boyfriend or male boyfriend, you know, you should have respect for him and her." A white salesman in his forties suggested that there was "nothing wrong with going up to a woman and complimenting her on her hair, unless she's sitting with her husband. That's just rude." In cases of women escorted by men, other men said, acts were "criminal," "bad manners," "disrespecting," or "crazy—why would you do it?" And harassers were also, it should be noted, likely to get retaliation from the escort.

Most men informants reported public harassment by women as flattering, a compliment, a proof of manhood, or a seal of approval on sexual attractiveness. One man said to be spoken to by a strange woman (he could not name an instance where it had happened) was "applause" for him, signifying that women appreciated him "as is." Such interpretations and feelings are in strong contrast to most of women's reactions, which were to question self, appearance, and behavior. No man reported that he had reacted in this way; of course, men experienced far fewer of these incidents than did women, and then only in relatively narrow circumstances and range. Some perceived women harassers—those who pinched, prodded, spoke, or gazed, since women reported little else more daring—as offering compliments of the same sort. Yet others perceived women harassers as "odd," since the behavior itself was "not something you'd expect from a decent woman"—although something, apparently, that one would expect from any decent man.

"ENLIGHTENED OPPRESSORS"

The phrase is that of George, a white insurance executive in his thirties with a sense of humor and "no sense of guilt—I change what I can, but I can't change it all." If this book dealt with men's strategies for "appearing innocent as well as being innocent," interviews with George would supply many examples.

Every majority group with opportunities to impose its judgments, definitions, and other powers contains some members who sincerely appreciate the situation of the "other" group or groups. So too with the two hundred men informants, of whom about a tenth were men who had, prior to the interview, given considerable thought to public harassment and formulated their own politicized opinions. Many, but not all, were gay or bisexual; almost all were white; almost all were middle- or upper-class. It is, of course, awkward to be an enlightened member of a group that exercises wrongful power: Common complaints expressed by these men were that they were scorned by some women and that they felt they were different from most men.

Many described the public realm as favoring and perpetuating men's (especially white men's) dominance, and those who took advantage of this were to be pitied as insecure bullies. A white manager in his fifties said men who bait and taunt "are missing the joy of living" and do so because they do not "feel good about who they are." A businessman in his fifties said, "As a white male, I have all the benefits. People treat white males like they know what they are doing."

Many of their insights were acute. One man, a real-estate developer in his forties, said that public harassment "runs covertly across all classes." In response to a query about gender-based harassment, he noted that at work "ninety percent of women" took the stairs in the parking garage instead of the elevator. He reported he had mostly managed to avoid becoming "a participant, but [I am] unsuccessful in that I have done nothing in the long run to change how people are treated. It's like a local anesthetic." Sometimes a disability or a different appearance could cause a man to speculate on how he, compared to other men, was treated in public, and sometimes the speculation enlightened him. This occurred for a white manager in his forties who had been treated "badly by strangers" because he was fat; nevertheless, he noted that, as badly as he had been treated, as a man in public he still feels the "strength of being a majority."

At stake in all public harassment is intrusion on privacy, the threat of an inability to maintain control. Some exploitations involve the production of physical pain, and in many exploitations, public places become precincts defined by heightened vulnerability and fear of intimidation. Public harassment abuses in general provide lessons in the fragility of public places and, more generally, in the fragility of the social web. It is clear that the individual's simple presence in a public place can prompt intrusion upon every part of the body by acts ranging from licking to slapping, and that every step and every path can be intruded upon. This stands as a general reminder of the vulnerability of the individual's presence and privacy; more to women it may stand as a reminder of their vulnerability not just in public places but in private and semipublic circumstances, too. In general, public harassment abuses accomplished without significant penalty send a symbolic message that male rights and control are predominant and omnipresent and can be communicated even in an arena where all citizens—but especially women—are most vulnerable.

Paradoxically, problematizing public harassment also reinforces the notion that women are delicate flowers, incapable of dealing with verbal obscenity, minor physical discomfort, and difficult situations. Traditional etiquette envisions women as incompetent and out of place in public, in need of others to intercede for her. Problematizing public harassment, including the enforcement of laws against infractions, substitutes the intervention of strategic behavior or of the law for the intervention of a protector.

CHAPTER SIX

Strategies

The fact that the construction workers seemed not to notice [middle-aged Kate] suddenly made her angry. She walked away out of sight, and there, took off her jacket—Maureen's—showing her fitting dark dress. She tied her hair dramatically with a scarf. Then she strolled back in front of the workmen, hips conscious of themselves. A storm of whistles, calls, invitations. Out of sight the other way, she made her small transformation and walked back again: the men glanced at her, did not see her. She was trembling with rage: it was a rage, it seemed to her, that she had been suppressing for a lifetime. And it was a front for worse, a misery that she did not want to answer, for it was saying again and again: This is what you have been doing for years and years and years. . . . Kate arrived again beside Maureen and said, "And that's what it's all worth."

Doris Lessing, The Summer before the Dark *(1974)*

The reactions of Kate, a middle-aged fictional character on the brink of self-discovery, is a relatively active response, as responses to public harassment go. Kate indicates her mastery over public harassment by willfully manipulating men's responses. This reaction is not confined to literature, although the informants in my study rarely reported it. The very existence of this reaction clearly demonstrates that women *can* critically and creatively mount strategies for dealing with incidents of public harassment. Moreover, my informants were more than fictional constructions for literary effect. But, although a typology of strategies shows that women can cope with, can manage, and can negotiate solutions for public harassment abuses, the same typology also shows women's dissatisfaction with the strategies available and with the fact that it seems to be the obligation of women to handle problems instigated by men.

In discussing their general fear of public places, women sometimes claimed that they were "too stupid to be afraid" while, with the next breath, they discussed the depths of their fears. A woman who noted the times when she did feel afraid added: "I'm too stupid to be afraid. It's a public place. I have as much right there as anyone else and I have the right to do my own thing, so I don't worry about it."

Every way in which women managed their interaction in public places was in contrast to men's and women's stated verbal romanticized rhetoric of the public order, as discussed in the previous chapter. These reactions to the "troubles" offered by public places can be analyzed as strategies by which a woman attempts to manage the abuse that she knows or suspects she will receive. However, the vocabulary of "management," "strategies," and "negotiation," although extensively used in discussing social interaction, has some limitations. This vocabulary presumes such a great deal of free and conscious will that the analyst is left with little choice but to conclude that, despite the subject's difficulties, she or he is indeed making do, or at least coping or trying to cope—conclusions that appeal to us in general as proof of an adult's ability to accept responsibility. Although I believe that it is a useful model and although women undoubtedly have raised their consciousnesses with regard to public places, this chapter should be read with one caveat: In this discussion of managing and strategies, as in most, the reader needs to recall the other-initiated background of troubles against which strategies are (sometimes painfully and not always successfully) weighed, contemplated, and put into action.

Yes, women *do* strategize with regard to their behavior in public but, were the behavior of many men different, women would not need to spend so much time and energy doing so. In other words, to note and applaud women's strategies should not produce an apologia for the *status quo.* I discuss the resourcefulness of women, but the reader must remember that it is a resourcefulness that should not need to be employed at all. Moreover, the strategies described bear on current discussions of the "softening" definition of sexual harassment (Wolf 1993) and the search to evaluate pragmatics, avoiding "victim feminism." As the last chapter showed, most men have assumptions that are different from those of women about public places and stranger relations— namely, men often feel that public places are nonproblematic and that stranger relations are characterized by such trust that strangers can use them as sites to meet others for romantic adventure. Since women do not always share these convictions in full, women need strategies suited to their situation.

Do men also need to strategize with respect to public harassment? Of course they do, and they will sometimes choose strategies with the same deliberation that women do when they feel themselves in physical danger, but these deliberations are, for the most part, unclouded by tension between safety and romance, and they are arrived at with less fear. Representative were the words of a white factory worker in his fifties who, when asked whether he had ever felt afraid in public places, responded that he never did, no matter where he was: "I always felt I had no enemies and could take care of myself. I stay out of places that are known as dangerous—and nobody picks on white men. They don't need to be afraid; they get respect. White men usually treat all other groups badly." Some men mentioned their physical size or prowess in explaining why they were unafraid. Of 213 men interviewed, 42 mentioned that they sometimes or habitually carried a weapon. Although this did not mean that a passerby would note the weapon—a knife or gun is not a sword, after all—it nevertheless gave men a feeling of inviolability. One white man in his fifties said, in detailing his strategizing, that the "easiest way for me is to ignore these types of negative behavior." He continued, "If you let them affect you, you have to deal with them. Normally, because of my size and because I am armed most of the time, no one really bothers me. So I would like to emphasize that most situations can be avoided by ignoring it." Assuming the men who claimed to be armed in fact were, it raises an important point for women, who only rarely mentioned carrying a weapon, even after being assaulted, stalked, or raped by a stranger. Not only do women experience public harassment and sexual violence from strange men, but they do so from men who are armed, and men arm themselves far more frequently than do women. It also colors any claims of equality between a woman's and a man's situation in public. Women sometimes harass, but they apparently do not often have knives and guns with which to back up their assertiveness or to retaliate.

REACTING TO PUBLIC HARASSMENT

Women's reactions were varied, but *every* women reported that she had practiced at least one of a group of strategies. Each strategy is practiced by members of all situationally disadvantaged groups in public; these strategies are chosen because of their suitability in the public realm.

Absence and Avoidance

The most popular reactions were sometimes formalized into a conscious strategy to avoid a place or situation where harassment was feared to occur or to avoid (or try to avoid) people the informant considered likely to cause it. Women also constructed, sometimes quite explicitly, their own personal geography of public space, especially urban public space. This geography, based on their experiences, comprised safety zones, danger zones, and zones where a woman would not dare go unless accompanied. Some women believed that certain areas would "give rise to" harassment. All women consolidated these personal beliefs with the received popular wisdom on crime prevention by women in public places. A young white woman with a laissez-faire philosophy noted, "You can avoid things by looking and staying busy and going out of your way to stay out of trouble. You can always play dumb or be in a hurry. To make things easier requires patience where men are concerned. Men don't realize sometimes they are obnoxious." She added that she felt her strategies were "successful if you can play dumb enough to be left alone and stay out of everything entirely."

Part of a woman's concern may not be to avoid acts of public harassment themselves so much as to avoid the type of site where she believes that others would believe she should not feel secure. Women avoid certain areas or situations not because they themselves might be targets of harassment or because they think they might receive them, but because they think others will believe them the sort of "loose" women to whom such insults mean nothing. In this way, Indianapolis women avoided being in public at times of the day and night when, as one said, "only a whore would be on the streets"—which was, for this young white health professional, past 11:00 P.M. in the downtown area.

Women solidified their typologies of categories of men—young or old, African-American or white, rich or poor—classifying those from whom they "expect" harassment and hence go out of their way to avoid. Women also said they avoided particular types of activities in which they suspected they would receive public harassment, including taking walks for pleasure or exercise, going on errands, delivering a child to school, bike riding, jogging, walking the dog or the baby—in short, nearly any activity at all. I did not examine the relationship between fear of public places in general and the burgeoning of mail-order and television-shopping channels; I do know that 43 women spontaneously mentioned that these services helped them avoid public places.

For 57 women in the study—3 African-American, 1 Asian/African American, and 53 white women—avoidance stemming from a particular instance or instances of public harassment persisted for periods ranging from a month, to years, to "forever." These women were roughly equally divided between those who identified themselves as feminists and those who considered themselves as traditional. Typically, a "bad experience" was the cause for long avoidance, as in the following cases. A white woman in her thirties, who lived in a flat next to a popular restaurant, had not been to the restaurant since she was in her teens because her first visit featured a waiter and a busboy who were "spectacularly suggestive." She continued, "The waiter had asked me my name, and I was hoping he'd leave me alone if I told him, so I told him that my name is Candy, and a lot of the conversation was, like, 'Hey, let's eat some Candy!' or 'What's your favorite flavor of Candy, the breasts?'" An Asian/African-American woman went to the Indianapolis Museum of Art to see an exhibit on Asian art. A young "goofy-looking" white man followed her while she determinedly toured the entire exhibit, "saying things to me about what race was I or how a Hindu sculpture looked like me." As a result she did not go back for three years. Lesbians were especially frequent among those who avoided places for long periods.

Sixty-five women informants said they had made a notable life decision on the basis of suspected or actual harassment in a public place. These 65 women were evenly distributed between women of color and white women. I defined a notable life decision as: moving from a neighborhood or from a city or state; moving in with someone; quitting a job or changing jobs within a workplace; quitting school or changing schools, majors, or classes; deciding to become engaged or married; buying protection, such as a dog, a gun or other lethal weapon, home burglar gates, or a car perceived as safer and more impervious. Extreme avoidance strategies included moving, altering one's occupation, changing a night job for what was hoped to be a safer daytime job, changing the branch of a company where one worked, and deciding to take time off and "work in the home." Women sometimes mentioned that their occupations put them at particular risk for following or for men who waited for them. In the case of a single young white woman who had worked as a bartender, men who waited for her after work became yet another occupational hazard, and she changed careers: "Too bad," she noted, "because in lots of ways [tending bar] was really 'me,' and I enjoyed the nightlife and being with people."

Tom Wolfe's *Bonfire of the Vanities* documents the means of insulation that the very wealthy have available to them that allow them to avoid possible harm or importunities in public places or simply to take up more luxurious transitways through the public realm; the book is also intended as a lesson in how frangible these means of insulation are for even the most privileged. Women who alter their lives by absenting themselves from public places remind us that members of at least their social category routinely use less costly measures.

A Public Appearance

Both women and men put high reliability on the fidelity of appearance when in public and expressed belief in faithful signals as well as insincere or misleading ones. Women said they especially used this strategy to avoid public harassment, to avoid notice that they thought would give rise to public harassment or, failing these, to provide defense against public harassment or to screen or mask their own reactions, which they feared would be avidly enjoyed by men. Some women reported donning sunglasses or floppy hats, or pulling up coat collars so that men had less access to their reactions. Some adopted what they felt were "tough" or "businesslike" walks and demeanor or, conversely, walks that were "pleasantly feminine" and therefore would help them escape further notice. Some avoided what they thought was either "provocative" or too casual dress. Some refrained from smiling, maintaining a serious, even "grim," facial expression; others wore a steady public half-smile in readiness to agree with whatever happened. When a woman noted that a certain prop such as a large package or condition such as a cold could prompt harassment, especially street remarks, she sometimes added that she lessened the chance of this happening by having the package delivered to her home or by staying in the house when she had a detectable cold or a sprained arm. A young white secretary said: "My fear is drawing attention to myself. It makes me nervous to wear form-fitting clothes, makeup, do my hair, etcetera, because of comments men can make and actions they can take. It makes me doubt my self-image, makes me worry about my attitudes." For these women, to be in public meant that they expected to be always ready for interaction.

One feminist argument urges women to effect ugliness in order to make their existence in public places less traumatic (Williamson 1971: 10–11). By this line of reasoning, clothes provoke disrespect from and ill-treatment by men. It is an enforced sociability that is at the root of what women are supposed to present by their grooming: Clothing suggests our social orientation, yet, since we must dress, it is a sociability we cannot decide *not* to communicate (Wax 1965). Thus, women must argue by their clothing that they are accessible to some men, but certainly not to all men, and that, even if no man can immediately be seen to be the target of the accomplishment of beauty, the woman's orientation is nevertheless to gather the admiration of the men who are present.

"My Boyfriend's Back (or He Will Be)": The Adoption or Simulation of Strategic Protectors

To need a companion indicates the need for protection by, implicitly, someone who is incompetent to protect him- or herself, such as children of tender years who should not go into public places without a parent or other elder. Women informants frequently mentioned that one strategy was to appear in public places with what was conceived to be a protective companion—often a man for heterosexual women. When unaccompanied, some women attempted to suggest the presence of a man elsewhere or stated that she could produce such a companion if need be. Invoking an absent protector or producing an actual one also had the possible effect of convincing the aspirant public harasser that a woman's reaction suggested neither rejection of him nor rejection of his gender.

Tacitly, then, any tactic that invoked a male protector falls into the romantic heterosexual template of the public order. A single young African-American secretary who was visiting Indiana from Chicago reported her philosophy of copresence, both apparent and real. She had neither husband nor boyfriend, and she summarized her philosophy as "if you're not with one man, you're a candidate for all the others, and that's a fact." Introducing or inventing a husband or boyfriend, then, can protect a woman; of course, a woman might also realize that she depends on a man rather than stands on her own.

A man need not specifically ask a woman if she is married to have a husband thrust in his face: A woman will sometimes assume that a stranger's romantic intentions will eventually become evident and will seek to obviate problems; a man's approach is enough to signal to most women that heterosexual romance is in his mind. In an ice cream shop I once watched a confident African-American man approach an equally confident African-American woman. Before he opened his mouth, she waggled the fingers of her left hand, tapped her wedding ring with her thumb, and shook her head ruefully—a gesture so smoothly performed I suspected she had used it before. The man inhaled sharply in mock shock, looked comically crushed, bowed deeply, then withdrew, and left them both laughing.

Women respondents realized that they could, perhaps should, employ the men they knew as protectors and knights-errant ("guard dogs," more than one woman said) for public places; sometimes unattached women said they were thinking of men they knew when they, alone in public and approached, claimed they were "taken." Symbolic use of a man as a "guard dog" depersonalizes and degrades him. To reduce a man one actually knows to a verbal ghost is also a depersonalization—although one might say that for a woman to objectify her male acquaintances is an apt response: She herself has been rendered an interchangeable member of an abuse-worthy class by men strangers.

Men were usually, but not always, the protective companions of choice. Sometimes women used any companion, calculating that mere accompaniment would discourage harassment. Significantly, some women said they preferred to go outside accompanied by a child, who would act as proof of virtue and save them the trouble of enlisting a male companion or dealing with one once out; still others touted the merits of the company of dogs, some small, most large—and some large dogs had been purchased just for public company. Three married women, 2 upper-middle-class whites and 1 upper-middle-class African-American, preferred to shop and, indeed, go anywhere accompanied by their mothers; and 10 women of varying sexual orientations noted that, by choice, they preferred the public company of a woman friend or lover.

Ignoring, Blocking, and Repressing: The Pretense that "Nothing Is Happening"

There is a single set of strategies that incorporates repression, that is, a woman's effort to ignore an incident of street harassment. Some women mentioned these in language that suggested psychiatric dissociation, remarking that "something takes over and I can't even hear what I know is being said," "I try not to think about it and sometimes I find I can't remember what they did to me," "I just repress it," or, "I block it out." For others, the same blocking had a more purposeful air: These women considered it to be a management strategy of some power, allowing them to feel that nothing was happening even when experiencing something as momentous as being called a slut, having the arm of store clerk creep over one's hand, or being tripped or hit to the raucous laughter of a group of men. This was especially so, women said, when they felt that part of the payoff for male street harassers was a woman's shock or hurt. These women could not erase what happened; they could, however, deny a man the satisfaction of that particular payoff, often by playing dumb. A variation was to adopt a placating stance—typically by dressing in a way that would please men or by assuming a friendly smile. A white upper-class homemaker in her forties was aware that she sometimes tried to "get quiet and try to melt into the woodwork." These methods are adopted to sooth potentially rufflable male feathers, much as members of one race seek to appear harmless to another.[1]

Although comfortable with her response to an individual incident, a woman occasionally remarked that she realized that "ignoring it" simultaneously depoliticized the incident of public harassment. Having pretended she did not hear a strange man who followed her for blocks gleefully yelling "Whore-bitch!" as she walked her young son to nursery school, an African-American/white librarian said she felt that, since she had acted as if nothing had happened, she then could not turn around and attempt to educate the man about the error of his ways, nor could she plausibly (she felt) go to a corner police officer. (This woman's statement implied a latent function of women who *do* competently handle their own troubles in public places: They relieve official institutions and agencies from the burden of preventing public harassment.) Some women ignored public harassment quite purposefully, foreseeing that conflict would ruin other pursuits.

Somewhere between these two extremes of women—those who said that they had a management strategy that eliminated public harassment and those who assumed iron exteriors that suggested that they could ignore or did not admit what went on—was a third group. These women said they used purposeful distractions, like "looking in shop windows," engaging in some minimal, often rhythmic motor activity like "clench[ing] my fist again and again," "tapping my fingers against my purse if he can't see it" (since, if he could, that might be fuel for another remark or attack), or talismanically "clutch[ing] my worry beads in my pocket" or subtly "cross[ing] my fingers."

Almost every one of the women informants mentioned the strategy

1. In my study-in-progress of many kinds of public harassment, young African-American men report that they approach white strangers whom the men fear will fear them, then deliberately greet the white person in hopes of signaling civility.

of ignoring, showing that no matter a woman's race, class, or how she conceptualized the differences and duties of the genders, women dealt with some public harassment by forcing it out of awareness—either actually, or apparently to onlookers. Of course, the usual method of strategizing public harassment is one of denial. Miss Manners is a sophisticated egalitarian with regard to lesbian and gay partnerships, yet she routinely advocates that women—presumably some of whom would be lesbian or bisexual—grin and ignore public harassment (Martin 1982).

Some women said they were inhibited from speaking to an offender, much less from retaliating, because they felt weak, insecure, or unprotected as women. Other women said they were inhibited from acting because of some feature of the interaction that disadvantaged them—for example, because the man had already made a getaway or had vanished into a crowd. In other instances, the man had assumed a blank or blasé expression that helped suggest that nothing, in fact, had happened. In order to reinterpret the situation as offensive, these women would have had to muster courage and radically redefine the situation.

The characteristic disadvantageous structure of public harassment for the target can discourage a previously determined woman from taking strong action and lead her to "repress" the abuse. Or a woman may consciously try different tactics and reactions, then despair of finding anything worth adopting and make what she feels is the best of a bad bargain by "blocking." If a woman takes up ignoring or repressing for this reason, she becomes caught in public harassment dilemmas.

Faced with situations that seem ambiguous, women react in various ways. Some of these reactions are involuntary and external, allowing the observer to note them. Women who receive public harassment sometimes visibly increase muscle tension, even start or flinch; they may adopt a fixed stare or direct their eyes to any target but the man who has spoken. Women may inhale, sniff, or cough, exhibit displace-

ment behaviors like preening and appearance checks, or suddenly initiate an activity like smoking. Other physical responses are interior
and hence more difficult to witness, as when women report that they
"stop breathing," become mentally or physically "numb" or "can't feel,"
become dizzy or nauseous or experience "jelly legs" or "rubber legs,"
or feel their "throat close up." They may start to tremble or hear their
blood pound, feel a sudden and atypical facial tic or muscle spasm, or
note the bile rise in their throat. They may involuntarily cover the part
of the body that has been touched or stared at, or they may find that
they have tugged a skirt lower to better cover their legs or pulled a coat
closed to cover their bosom. Significantly, many of these symptoms—
especially shaking, tremors, pounding heart, queasiness, and shaky
legs—are characteristic of agoraphobic women (Gardner 1983).

One danger of purposeful repression is that the repression is realized for what it is, and the act of repression can remain a painful, awkward, and unadmitted memory in the mind of the harassed. In contrast, some women said that, when they blocked or repressed public
harassment, or when they reacted with shame or terror, they could not
reliably recall an incident at all. Paradoxically, this selective amnesia
or dissociation can make it difficult for women to report what they say
are the worst cases of public harassment.

Politicized women, along with women who strongly believe in
men's obligation to behave as "gentlemen" at all times, often regarded
the obligation to act "as if nothing is happening" as fraudulent and an
imposition. It is certainly a strategy that can require a good deal of
psychic energy and presentational control—an obligation toward "au-
tism," in one woman's words (Damrosch 1975).

Staged Compliance

By terming compliance as a strategy, I mean to denote that some
women self-consciously—one might say cynically—indicate to the harasser that they accept his redefinition of the situation and act to

decrease the amount of retribution and anger that might be forthcoming (they hope). Women who reported that they complied took care to communicate that the interactional line a public harasser had taken was one she would willingly adopt by, for example, smiling and nodding a "thank you" to the man who uttered a street remark or, as one woman said adorably, "shaking my finger like I was pretending to rebuke" the man who had just pinched her buttocks. In such cases, the sincere complier said that she truly did appreciate what she saw as flattery, whereas the more strategically inclined complier adhered to what she saw as the reaction expected of her in order to minimize her victimization—that is, she cynically acceded to the man's imposed definition in order, she hoped, to escape further harassment. The pragmatics here are a problem: Although a woman may find her actions effective in preventing further harassment, she will know that whether her efforts are effective or ineffective, they are insincere. She has supported public harassment by her strategic unwillingness to confront the man who does it.

Understandably, the first type of complier usually counted herself as more satisfied with her strategy, since it enabled these traditional women to match philosophy to strategy. Cynical—and, as they commonly were, politicized—compliers were much less likely to be satisfied: although they might feel they had put something over on a man, the obligation to do so rankled. Politicized women sometimes included with compliance tactics "faked" reactions—startled surprise at being grabbed, for example. These, they hoped, would give the man what he wanted so that he would leave them alone.

Even when women sincerely complied and said they were satisfied with this strategy—for instance, when they directly supported and ratified public harassment by smiling, grinning, or gratefully acknowledging harassment—this apparent compliance was often fearfully or manipulatively done. When a woman identified herself as traditional and said she purposely complied, for example, she also often said that she chose this strategy because she was afraid *not* to smile or thank a man, for fear of what might happen: A man could use nonresponse to accuse a woman of cold humorlessness or vain inaccessibility; he could batter her; he could follow her home and rape her. Sometimes he did.

Politicized feminists had a heavier burden: all but 4 of these women said they too had used compliance, but they also noted that added to their fear was the knowledge that they were making an insincere presentation of self. The most self-aware of these women said that the tack of compliance removed a woman target from possible danger and might even sometimes be enjoyed as a modest prank played on an unsuspecting man (who, if her part was played correctly, would not appreciate his own, more minor victimization). However, these same women noted that to seem to comply persuasively to the man was also to seem to comply with expectations for public behavior condemned by society. In effect, then, they supported standards and values that misrepresented their feelings.

This misrepresentation tended to be experienced more vividly in cases where a woman felt her "true" self was already in jeopardy in public—that, for example, she already supported norms or suggested a character or identification that she knew was not hers just by appearing as a well-comported member of the public realm. Thus, lesbian and bisexual women were prominent among those who complied from prudence or terror but said that they despaired at having to misrepresent themselves in order to do so. Not every woman who said she staged compliance but resented the necessary misrepresentation was lesbian or bisexual, of course. In semipublic settings, like workplaces, insincere compliance flourished since a woman could reasonably fear that she might lose her job if she dealt more sincerely with an offender.

Answering Back, Acting Back

This is a diverse class of reactions that, in varying degrees, imply that public harassment is indeed an offense; with them the victim seeks to verbally or gesturally signify this directly to the harasser.

One element of answering or acting back is what some members of situationally disadvantaged groups term "educating the public"; these women sought to explain how offended they were or sought to correct their harassers on mistaken assumptions, which is a rationalized and politicized version of educating the public. "Shock turnabouts" were employed by some women, such as the woman who, harassed by construction workers, wheeled, removed her upper plate, and waved the dentures at the workers, effectively silencing them. Other women had evolved set strategies to express their displeasure with public harassment that were mainly verbal and were intended to communicate displeasure with harassment; some had developed nonverbal equivalents. In answering back to an offender, women chose styles ranging from the determinedly reasonable to vitriolic or vulgar. In fact, experts have recommended practicing smart verbal responses for public harassment, like thinking up "good" comebacks for various street remarks, which women are to practice until they are comfortable with saying them—an article in *Glamour* magazine (1984) is assertively titled "Verbal Abuse on the Street: How to Talk Back." But one significant barrier to effective answering back was the difficulty reported by many women in simply actuating themselves to turn or alter their gaze to look at an offending man. Establishing or maintaining eye contact with a harasser was difficult, and to do so also sometimes gained a woman the penalty of scrutiny.

Most women who said they attempted to answer back chose what they felt was a brief, simple, and mild response, as in this case of a young Asian-American student who spoke of her strategies for both sexist and racist harassment in the same breath: "If I do say anything, it is something like, 'Grow up!' Nothing vulgar."

A rape survivor classified street remarks with rape, as uninvited intimacies that women must suffer. This Asian-American medical student in her thirties recalled the time she was shouted at by a racially mixed group of offenders as she walked her college campus at night:

> The rape made me unwilling to feel afraid any more. When I heard them yelling, I turned around, and they looked like perfectly clean and decent young college men from IUB and I couldn't believe it. I

yelled back: "Will you just leave me alone! I don't want to have to stay home at night in order to feel safe! I don't want to have some strange guy yell at me! What did I ever do to you?"

I didn't expect them to do anything but go after me some more, but I was surprised: They all looked at each other, then I saw them talking, then one of them came over and very sincerely apologized to me.

I couldn't believe it. It worked.

Other women had been satisfied with giving a nonverbal response, often one meant for the perpetrator to catch but calibrated so as to not be offensive enough to spark further harassment. A woman might give a man a hard stare or "mean look." Some women purposefully screamed so loudly that a harasser might be embarrassed—a few offenders had even retreated in horror.

A few women who said they had tried to reason with a man noted that there was one particular weak spot in their strategizing: It depended on the man's willingness to listen, as well as on his continuing physical presence. Thus, one woman of mixed racial background began to explain to a white man how his following her made her feel when the man suddenly walked away with apparent nonchalance. At other times women's words were ignored or mocked by harassers.

Another set of strategies did not accept the redefinition that the man attempted to impose. Instead, these strategies used tactics that enabled a woman to gain distance, even shelter, from an unpleasant encounter by redefining a situation already redefined by the man. Examples of such strategies were: other types of talking back, such as making a humorous response (and seeking to redefine the situation as not nearly so important as the offender implied it might be); blithely ignoring the incident and changing the topic (also implying that the incident was too trivial to be noticed and signifying that the woman was not so intimidated that she could not converse with the stranger); educating the public (which sought to inform the man about the "true" significance of his actions); effecting a turnabout (seeking, by committing the same offense on a man that he had committed on her, to redefine their respective roles, he now the harassed and she the harasser); and theatricizing (seeking to redefine the incident by overdramatizing her response or misleading other members of the public as to what had occurred).

Women's physical reactions ranged from slapping the harasser's face to throwing a drink in his lap, with many variations in between. Despite their fear, many women managed what they felt to be active and often successful reactions to the offenses. Some of these were also, many women implied, on the *lex talionis* model—that is, purposefully insulting or embarrassing, and sometimes physical, retaliations that were meant to achieve a level of rudeness that matched the offender's. Other reactions, women felt, were so much beyond their control as to be virtual reactions to stimuli rather than strategic maneuvers under the woman's control. Examples I observed were: giving a direct or indirect physical response, such as slapping a man's face or pouring a drink over an offender's head (I watched one woman borrow a full stein of beer from another woman, a stranger that the man had also harassed, and pour it slowly over his head in front of a large appreciative mall audience while the second woman slowly clapped); verbally threatening an offender with retaliation by herself or by someone who (she hoped) could more plausibly intimidate him; and even threatening a man with a weapon, such as by pulling a knife.

Tricks and Turnabouts:
Redefining an Already Redefined Situation

Some women noted that they practiced a trick or turnabout (role reversal) on the harasser. In these situations the woman elaborately affected to be doing something other than what she was doing or reversed roles with the man, with the woman becoming the pincher or stalker, for example. In the least elaborate responses (and the ones less likely to subject the woman to further harassment) the woman affected to not notice harassment and approached the harasser with a disarming question. For instance, a man shouted "Whore!" at a passing woman, which momentarily redefined her as a prostitute. The woman raised her eyes to his and apparently trustingly asked him for directions to a place she knew well—as presumably no "whore" would do.

Tricks use specific maneuvers to defuse public harassment by transforming it into a different situation, one that is comparatively harmless. Typically, as in the preceding example, this meant that the woman needed to enact deliberate misunderstanding of the man's harassment; she must appear not to understand what the harasser has meant by a lewd remark, a whistle, a sly pat on the buttocks, or a persistent attempt to obtain her complete name, address, and home phone number—*and* she must further derail harassment by redefining the situation. The reported transformations always involved the pretense of helplessness or incompetence, which placed the offender in a vulnerable position of chivalry and called upon him to respond, out of his greater competence, with noblesse oblige.

Some women said they defused trouble before it began, for example, by assiduously greeting strange men, looking them in the eye "in a nonthreatening manner," or smiling a "minimal smile so a man will know he's someone I might like to know better but just not right now." Such strategies are undeniably friendly ones.

A rare type of turnabout was to do a study of public harassment, either informally and for one's own amazement, or for a class, or for reporting purposes. A few women had, for example, "kept a mental notebook of how many men said something to me and how and what they said," but those who did had their eyes opened. "I thought the situation was bad," said a woman in her thirties who did a "for-fun study" at a large mall. She then added, "By the end of the two hours I spent, I was scared." In fact, this is a general strategy that requires interactional acuity, but women do not always practice it with pride and confidence simply because it is a tactic practiced against someone they may fear. The strategy is also devalued because public harassment as a social problem is denied. The expertise is certain, but not all women who reported that they used this means of avoiding street remarks said that they felt confident. In fact, one woman said that as she found herself transforming the talk of a persistent admirer at a bar into a request for advice from a helpful fellow drinker, she felt as if she were having "an out-of-body experience." She said, "I was happy he left me alone after that, and he even told me I reminded him of his sister, and that made me feel safe. But after he finally left I felt exhausted." Women who use this tactic to defuse public harassment subject themselves to added conversational and emotional work they may regret. They may feel that their determinedly neutral stance is a less empowered, more obligingly submissive solution than is ideal. In this strategy, a woman presents herself as other than what she is. She misrepresents what she knows to be true about herself, and these are public and, almost invariably, vocal misrepresentations and are thus very significant ones. Of course, public harassment often puts the woman in the position of ignoring what purports to be a greeting, a request for help, or a summons; women who use these same dissembling tactics to defuse harassment can effectively turn the tables on men and place them in the very positions the women themselves fear.

Turnabouts are more involving and demanding than tricks, if only because they require the initiator to change the definition of a situation that has already been once changed—a woman subjects the man to the same (or somewhat the same) harassment that she had just received. Women reported that if they had decided to adopt a *lex talionis* of public harassment—to give a dirty look to the strange man who minutely examined her body—they often found it more difficult to execute than they had thought. Then, too, some apt retribution was too dangerous, women felt, to contemplate: One woman said she considered following a man home but concluded "that'd be a sure way to get killed." More rare was the turnabout practiced on men who had not specifically been observed harassing: only 17 of 293 women, most of whom strongly identified public places as "political," said they had practiced turnabouts. One woman, with a female friend, decided to sit on a bench downtown and thoughtfully comment on passing men; another, again accompanied by a female friend, heartily and, they hoped, painfully, pinched the buttocks of men they noted in crowds, so fed up were they with being "free meat" themselves. Although brave, these turnabouts did not always bring women the satisfaction for which they had hoped; typically, men took the woman or women's action as a romantic overture, using the attempt at retribution as an opening to ask for a date, for example, or for a telephone number.

"Scening" and Flaunting: Acting Up by Acting Out

Women who are habitually trailed, scrutinized, and approached can, of course, use the various elements of their pursuit strategically and for their own ends. An example would be the celebrity who flaunts, not hides, her or his identity in order to see how large a crowd of followers she or he can accumulate (as is reported of Marilyn Monroe in Pepitone and Stadiem 1979:211–212). Twelve women, none celebrities, reported they had done this, and I suspect that at least some of the women I observed did the same. Once followed, they deliberately encouraged the tracker with backward glances and smiles, "just to see if he'd follow me," as one young woman said.

Again, however, women who "flaunted" were typically young, typically white, and typically acted in groups. A standard scenario was one related by a twenty-one-year-old bank teller with vibrant red hair, a ready smile, some twenty or so pounds of extra weight, and a casually chic way of dressing that allowed her modest clothing to look more expensive than it was. When she and her "pack" of four girlfriends noted a man dogging their steps after a movie, they felt "a bit afraid, but not very. After all, there were four of us." They judged the man as respectable and probably wealthier than they, although not so socially adept: "Maybe a Bloomington student, maybe a pre-med," she said hopefully. The four friends led the man on a merry chase, "switching our butts and walking all over the place." The man at last seemed to give up the chase because "we probably scared him away—near the end we were saying 'Hey, come on—what's your problem?' and getting pretty raunchy, and one girl pulled up her T-shirt and showed him her tits!" Yet others made quite different scenes.

Official and Informal Complaints

A few women, 22 of the sample, had made or had attempted to make an official complaint. They did so by speaking to a boss or calling a workplace. Of the 22 who attempted to complain officially, 17 were women of color and all were relatively young (under thirty-five). Their satisfaction varied. Most often nothing at all came of their action, they felt; the best part of making the complaint lay in the act itself, together with communicating to the harasser that this was the woman's intention. Not all officials were sympathetic or helpful: in only 6 instances did a woman have a sense that "anyone would do anything to the man."

Then too, for most public harassment, the "official in charge" was the harasser himself. Unless public harassment occurred at a place of work or school, a woman was often in doubt as to whom she should complain. Two women chose to complain to police officers; one time, one of a pair of officers laughed, and the other time both officers asked the woman for her phone number. The message: a woman is freely available and approachable, unprotected, and any contact—even one that she hopes will guarantee her rights of passage—can be mined for sexuality and redefined by a man. These results are sad. They convey clearly that, as far as public harassment is concerned, women have a depressing lack of faith in officialdom—and, worse, that this lack of faith is well deserved.

Women who told someone—a woman or man friend, a parent, a spouse or child—were more often than not sadly disappointed. Such unofficial ears were little better than official resources. The sole reliable exception was for the 10 women who had made public harassment a topic for discussion in their women's group.

CLASSIFYING STRATEGIES

One way to typologize measures taken is by judging how "active," "assertive," or "aggressive" women felt they were being. Some women reported taking what they regarded as relatively active measures against public harassment, that is, answering back or taking physical retaliation or instituting some formal complaint procedure. Women labeled these measures as "active" ones: calmly explaining to ribald construction workers just why a woman would like to be let alone, not vulgarly assessed, when she walked into her office building; reporting the men observed following and verbally harassing another woman; rewarding a man—one who had pinched a woman's buttocks so painfully it left a large bruise "for weeks"—with a punch in his ribcage.

Of course the label "active" is a relative one; at best, these active measures typically express indignation at the immediate offense but typically do nothing to change the situation or subject the offender to more than temporary inconvenience. Strategies of reporting a man to his boss or enlisting a police officer rarely occurred to women and, when they did, were not always possible. Helping an unknown woman by going to her aid was the rarest measure of all.

There is another important axis along which to classify women's strategies—that of the degree to which a woman tried to redefine the situation of public harassment. Some of these strategies had some straightforward relationship to the offense that had occurred: The offender had redefined the situation from that of two unacquainted strangers to two persons engaged in the twilight zone of acquaintanceship, the bond that is forged by insult, and the woman's reaction ratified that redefinition. Such strategies were: avoiding all or some public places (here the defined situation is one the woman fears, not one to which she has immediately been subject); complying; some types of talking back; and physically retaliating.

Politicized feminist rhetoric and romanticized rhetoric both have several drawbacks for the task of finding a response to public harassment. For example, public harassment can occur at the hands of the most dangerous men, with whom it truly might not be wise to begin, let alone prolong, conversation. In this respect, the traditionally minded woman who, looking down from a moral pinnacle, decides that she can haughtily ignore the man who leers or rudely comments is less at risk and might come out of the immediate encounter less intimidated and with less chance of re-retaliation by the man. The disadvantage is that of the woman's support of public harassment: There are problems with even worse public harassment that cannot be avoided.

Therefore, in choosing whether to express a politicized feminist account, a woman can realize that to do so obligates her to be consistent: she may feel she should present, in short, a picture of herself as one who not only espouses, but puts into action, what she sees as the feminist paradigm. To choose an expressively active strategy, however, will require not only that a woman define or at least consider what retaliatory actions are feminist but also what implications these actions will have and what their likely sequelae will be. For example, one woman, who felt that public harassment was merely one of the many harassments women suffer, slapped the left cheek of a man who had stroked her back and buttocks while in line for a movie. He quickly slapped *her* left cheek "right back, and his nails tore my skin. I took some time to rethink my feminist orientation. Nowadays I'll think bad thoughts, but I've never done anything back since that happened." When a woman feels feminist rhetoric and action match, in other words, she could be in more danger than bargained for.

Although the match of traditional sex-role indignation and spunky response sometimes involved unwelcome, surprising, and painful retaliation from a man, retaliation was more likely to happen when feminists matched philosophy to action—perhaps because less was at stake in the traditional etiquette rhetoric than was at stake in espousing a feminist rhetoric. A woman who expected men to be gentlemen in public as elsewhere could, as one young white waitress said, "slap the gentlemen who pinch or say filthy things to me, and I say to them, 'I *don't* think that's a very gentlemanly way for you to behave,'" with perfect confidence that the breach was one for which the (presumably traditionalist) man was obligated to apologize. This woman reported that as a result of staying within the rhetoric of romance and traditional etiquette, the men who "insulted" her at work or on the street often shamefacedly apologized. For the traditionally based breach, a traditionally based accusation can (momentarily) succeed.

Reaction strategies comprise measures taken prior to appearing in public places and intended to deal with mistreatment and measures that category members will use when actually in public for the same purpose. Thus, members of disadvantaged groups must assemble a set of presentational skills and strategies, as well as situational necessities, that has a common thread. For purposes of situationally disadvantaged groups in public places, the presence of such a set argues that the individual is a trespasser in, not a rightful owner of, public places. He or she is in a performer's, not a director's role; criticism is to be willingly received, and is not to be given in return. I have discussed these elements in the chapters that form the body of this book. For now, it is important to reiterate that the effect of even a single instance of such treatment can be experienced as devastating.

Women who believe they are required to display confidence, bravado, or trust in public places to minimize harassment, *not* as accurate representations of their feelings, also sometimes feel that they must create public selves that vary widely from their real selves or the selves they present in other contexts and, further, that they must create these situated selves in trying conditions. Thus, a woman who has decided that her best strategy for minimizing harassment is what she really feels is craven compliance may also feel that this tactic renders her inauthentic in public. Women and men strangers who see her do not know and cannot conceive of the real person—and this real person follows this line only with reluctance and disgust.

Rarely, but occasionally, women reported a great deal of satisfaction, even enjoyment: One woman who decided to see how many "admirers" she could gather felt happy and confident about it; another woman who visited a turnabout on a man by returning his pinch was euphorically vindicated when he apologized to her. Yet another woman, urged to dissemble on the public streets, came to enjoy the act of dissembling and appreciated her own skills of impression management. Some women came to think of themselves as amateur small-time con artists and were fond of relating how gullible their marks were. Even then, however, these women alienated themselves from involvement with the concerns of many other citizens.

Taking up these typically momentary strategies—effective or not, humiliating or not—expends energy on an individual level that could well be put to use in formulating plans for reforming public places to make them better environments for women. It is not necessary to give men Staten Island and then take Manhattan. Given a general social understanding that decreasing the frequency and fear of rape and other crimes is, indeed, a desideratum, one can easily imagine architectural, legislative, economic, and interpersonal changes that could be adopted. Thus, buildings, plazas, and parks could be designed with regard to women's safety and concerns. We should not, for example, foster the belief that designing a plaza that encourages "girl-watching" is necessarily a good thing, nor allow the professionals who design public places to overlook the need for strategic police carrels or emergency phones. Additionally, presence in public places should be restricted to those who can be counted on to use them noncriminally, as one park analyst has already suggested for public parks that are sites of crime toward women and children (Perry 1983). Legislators must take ever more seriously stranger crimes toward women, and law-enforcement officers must respond to the regular menace of routine harassment as well as to more serious crime.

New services can be developed that can ameliorate current conditions. Women in some cities have started women-driver-only taxi companies in order to provide reliable transportation for women in public places (and, incidentally, relief from gender-based harassment from taxi drivers). Other women-run services offer escorts, either hired security or other workers, for women working late. Many women have networks of friends and family, and the support of therapists and advisors, to help them overcome the dangers of public places.

CHAPTER SEVEN

Conclusion

Touching the tour, I quite agree with you that you and Kate would
have been uncomfortable alone. It's a very fine theory, that of
women being able to get along without men as well as with them;
but, like other fine theories, it will be found troublesome by those
who first put it into practice. Gloved hands, petticoats, feminine soft-
ness, and the general homage paid to beauty, all stand in the way of
success. These things may perhaps someday be got rid of, and possibly with advantage; but while young ladies are still encumbered
with them, a male companion will always be found to be a comfort.

Anthony Trollope, in Can You Forgive Her?

The great problems are to be encountered in the streets.

Friedrich Nietzsche, Aphorism 127 from Daybreak

When a reference to my research appeared in *Newsweek,* I was briefly
inundated by media inquiries and requests for compact quotations
summarizing my work (or, more often, pithy quotations about men's
abuses). When I replied, I was always careful to say what no one
wanted to hear: Men *do* harass publicly, and so, unfortunately, do
women and even children. If there is yet another message I would like
to impart it is to be as cognizant of one's own behavior, of how one fits
into the value system implied by feminism, as one is of the behavior of
the "enemy" of the moment.

Discriminatory treatment in public places is for some social categories a fossilized discrimination: It can remain long after legal bars to employment and pay discrimination have been enacted, an uneasy reminder of society's discomfort with some social categories. A man might hesitate or scorn to harass in private or at work; perhaps he even feels contempt for those who do. In public places, a cloak of anonymity can allow him to express safely his contempt, hostility, or simply his feelings of entitlement to judge others by yelling an insult, by ogling, by slapping, goosing, or hitting, or by tracking a woman for blocks and excusing his action with the rationale that he is merely expressing his admiration. Public places offer citizens a site in which to practice discrimination that has been outlawed in other spheres and to practice it in circumstances that offer the highest probability of harming targets and escaping punishment.

Some situationally disadvantaged groups are easily discernible as "disadvantaged" in terms of their economic, occupational, and social status. Still other groups, like women, enjoy the possibility of high advantage in contexts apart from those of public spaces. In the introduction to this book, I drew on a disparate set of observations and interviews to suggest that as diverse as these groups were in terms of advantage in other areas of their lives, they all shared some elements of a public status as situationally disadvantaged.

Even the most privileged classes and groups may experience unpleasantness in public places and may certainly be the victims of the random violence and crime that is currently a feature of public places. There is also, to be sure, a role-reversal turnabout that is common when the lower orders observe the higher in public places, a nose-thumbing, as it were, when the have-nots observe the haves. When the member of a situationally advantaged group *does* experience the same common sort of harassment that situationally disadvantaged groups experience, many consider it a transitory rudeness. Public harassment is not received as a result of membership in any particular category—for example, as a woman or as an African-American. Thus, when a well-dressed white middle-class man walks past a group of poorly dressed African-American teenagers who make him the butt of their jokes or when a male college professor listens to college students compare his appearance to Clarabelle the Clown's, the disadvantage is no more than momentary: The well-dressed man's privileges are obviously numerous and the professor's can be reinstated as soon as he enters a classroom. Of course, harassment can have long-term consequences: the momentary butt of a prank can become a victim of violence, and the mere passerby can be snatched (in the manner of Reginald Denny) to become a convenient scapegoat.

Although public places are an important arena for reinforcing the second-class status of disadvantaged groups elsewhere in the society, they are not reliably and invariably so. However, the instances of momentary domination or threat by the normally disenfranchised toward the advantaged have a different weight, since they result from the disadvantaged's access to the other group that is only transient and thus must be maximized. The range of what is at stake in public harassment for every woman and every man is illustrated by the experiences of women who have multiple situational disadvantage.

MULTIPLE SITUATIONAL DISADVANTAGE IN PUBLIC

Lesbians, African-American women, and women with disabilities represent a useful variety of multiple situationally disadvantaged groups in terms of the spectrum from visibility to invisibility and in terms of likely consequences, violent or not, of public harassment. Additionally, there is something more involved in much of the public harassment of women who fall into a second situationally disadvantaged group. Something very different is ultimately at stake in the harassment of two lesbians holding hands in a family restaurant or a young woman in a wheelchair on her way across a busy downtown street: For the first, it is the sanctity of the family as an institution or heterosexuality as one of the bases of society; for the second, it is the presumed right of trespass of a group systematically denied trespass and access to public places until quite recently. My discussion is not only a brief but a general one, since I must ignore differences among these groups that may be pertinent to public harassment and that could level serious considerations such as life chances and opportunities. One caveat is that groups sometimes themselves have distinctive views and usages of public places that I do not incorporate in my discussion of their perceptions of harassment.

An individual's appreciation of membership in varied situationally disadvantaged groups can enable her or him to philosophize about the groups and society in general. When in public, individuals who are members of multiple situationally disadvantaged groups often balance and counterbalance the experiences that they associate with membership in each category. A lesbian African-American marketing executive in her forties, who said she took pride in maintaining both a fashionable and a professional appearance, said:

> Sometimes all this that happens in the streets makes me think: Is it worse to be black, or a dyke, or just to be a woman? And I've got to tell you, the being a woman doesn't bother me so much.
>
> Having the white people rag on me because I'm black doesn't scare me so bad either, though that's next.
>
> And then worst is being a dyke, because even if all that happens is just words or a look, you know, it has a very ugly feel to it when I can classify it as anti-lesbian, and it could get worse than words very fast, you know. Because lesbians *do* get attacked, sometimes killed, by strangers. *That* makes a wolf-whistle because you got a short skirt on look pretty harmless. Even though I don't like that either, you understand.

Of course, the individual's multiplicity of social characteristics is what will allow her or him to weigh and judge one social category versus the other, finding one beneficial, another neutral, and a third a clear disadvantage. In this regard, reception in public places can blind an individual to more general mistreatment and discrimination and can suggest that colleagues in a certain category complain too much, are in fact the authors of their own troubles, or are simply not experienced and sophisticated enough to view the relatively slight disadvantage attached to being a gay man in public places (for example, in the light of the disadvantage attached to being overweight). In this, individuals can mystify their own experience on the basis of their experience of public harassment, suggesting wrongly that having no problems in public connotes having no problems in private. These evaluations of multiple group membership may also lead the individual to splinter from one group with whom her or his interests more deeply lie and take up the cudgel for another group that is, in other spheres, relatively advantaged. Insofar as the individual is led to expect public harassment because of, for example, workplace harassment, the misuses of public order maintain and bolster discrimination in other spheres. When an individual, one who falls into two or more publicly harassed categories, becomes confused as to which characteristic is the source of any single incident of public harassment, the abuses of public order are obfuscated. Thus, just as elderly women might say they "missed these attentions" or resented the younger women with whom men spent time while ignoring the older women at counters or when they needed public aid, likewise women who garnered interest because of a disability, sexual preference, or race could say that they longed for compliments that were based on their appearance alone. One racially mixed woman said men queried her on her "exotic" hair, her skin color, and her "nationality" but treated her as a curiosity, and these "comments [got] a little old." A woman with leg braces was repeatedly approached by "men who seem[ed] to be fascinated by my calipers," while she wanted to hear "what a great-looking suit I've got on."

Although all of the groups I named as situationally disadvantaged—women, people with disabilities, racial minorities, people taken to be lesbian or gay—experience similar types of harassment, in part simply because communication in public places leaves certain avenues open to all, each group also has distinctive aspects that mark its members for particular troubles and leave them particular escapes. Through these avenues the situationally disadvantaged can sometimes turn the tables on those they perceive as their harassers.

I will discuss multiple situational disadvantage and how situationally disadvantaged groups are distinctively different, then note strategies for management that members of these groups reported as having relevance to their multiple disadvantage.

Lesbian and Bisexual Women

Women in general and gay men can share fear of being in public places. Although, as I pointed out earlier, women express much fear of public places, it is gay men, who express far less fear, who are the regular and reliable victims of violent crimes in public places.

I have typified the public harassment of women in general by dealing extensively with men's evaluative street remarks, various exploitations of presence, and underminings of public aid. Using a heterosexually romanticized vocabulary of interest and admiration, harassers suggested that they were ineluctably led by their targets to look, flatter, touch, and follow them. These women received ostensible compliments from their harassers. This is not so when public harassers classify a woman as lesbian. Lesbians receive from heterosexuals almost no ostensible compliments that acknowledge that the recipient is homosexual. Unlike most street remarks directed to women categorized as heterosexual, lesbian-baiting is characterized by abusive name-calling and the commencement of incidents that can and do easily escalate into violence.

Lesbians share with other women difficulties in obtaining and in proposing public aid: They are subject to refusals in both attempts, and they connect this with their category membership. Companionship does not invariably aid the lesbian as it often does heterosexual women, especially if the companion is "identifiably" another lesbian. In such cases, both women can be targets for harassment. Lesbian presence in public places is commonly said to place some ultimate threat on the family as a social institution: The harasser who sees a lesbian (or a gay man) can become incensed that the "family life" of America is assailed (Workman 1991).

Lesbians also share with other women the demonstrable need to be concerned with crime prevention, but lesbians lack an extensive specialized literature. Although one's identity as a lesbian can certainly be suggested by visual clues, lesbian category membership apparently can also be concealed. The visual clues that suggest category membership may not be present, so that a lesbian who types herself as "straight-appearing" noted that she had to wear a pink triangle pin or other insignia in order to feel she fit in at lesbian events. This woman was usually allowed to pass in heterosexual public order, for passersby focused on her "straight appearance" rather than correctly decoding her jewelry or T-shirt.

In addition to the lesbians and bisexual women who so identified themselves, some 10 other women said they had been harassed as lesbian although they were in fact heterosexual. This possibility extends the treatment that lesbians receive to every woman, and may make heterosexual women change their behavior in public so as to appear prudently straight. Being harassed as lesbian can make a heterosexual woman realize that lesbians and gays are badly treated: As one such straight woman said, "I now know how much people hate gay men and women. I now also know how fragile my acceptance by men is. I just cut my hair very short, and those [three] men ran after me and called me 'dyke.'" Only 2 of the 10 women felt they had been enlightened by these experiences; for the other 8 heterosexual women, being taken as lesbian was felt as a deep insult to their femininity. It called into question the choices they had made about their appearance, the choices they had made about dress style, and the choice they had made to appear in public unaccompanied by a man who would, as one woman said, "orient" possible harassers to the fact that "I'm connected to a boy, a boy who'll protect me."

African-American Women

Along with women in general, African-American citizens can easily be identified as members of their publicly disadvantaged group in most cases. African-Americans also experience the imposition of morally impugning stereotypes in public, as do women in general. Thus, one African-American woman noted that whites of both sexes avoided her either because of her race or because of the habits whites associated with her race: "They act like I'm going to steal something, or maybe I've got a big Black buck hidden up my sleeve, a man who's going to rape them or steal their wallets. Just an avoidance—they keep clear of men a lot."

In common with all women, African-Americans experienced difficulties in giving and receiving public aid and were more frequently victims of crime in public places, although no widespread literature counsels them to take up the elaborate strategies that are suggested with just women in mind. And African-Americans do not share a concern with access information in general on the basis of race, although it is the province of any truly determined harasser to make this a concern for all groups.

African-Americans have experienced a prohibition or segregation of presence and use of facilities in public places. They share this experience with women in general, but their experience is far more extensive. In addition, for African-American women there is no gloss of alleged compliments because of their race. Many African-American women did report a condescending set of race-based compliments from whites of both sexes and all ages that responded to certain physical features associated with their race, which prompted amazement or ostensible admiration from whites. One woman repeatedly had strange white women, men, and children comment on her hair;

another said a white man "patted me on my nappy head and said how much my head felt like SOS"; still another said one white woman had exclaimed over her "pink palms, as if she didn't know we had them." Most women to whom this happened interpreted these comments as patronizing. Women to whom it had happened many times noted that intrusions like these "get old after the hundredth one"—they were as predictable as they were gratuitous. Women felt they occurred because of whites' general racism (which demonstrably extended to even small children), of whites' privileged status in public, or of whites' desire to demonstrate unfamiliarity with African-American racial features.

There are, of course, other races that experience distinct situational disadvantage. Asian-American women told me stories similar to those of African-American women; as African-American women related discrimination by Asian-Americans, so did Asian-American women relate discrimination by African-Americans. Asian-American women too considered these harassments galling, since they felt that they shared the impact of American racism with African-Americans.

Women who identified themselves as "racially mixed" also experienced the same sort of public harassment. However, they were often even more at doubt about the cause: harassment might be prompted by race or gender. In this way, women who were "foreign-looking" or "dark-complected" sometimes reported public harassment that was clearly of the same stripe as other gender-based harassment. They also reported a particular set of troubles from white citizens, who sometimes "simply stared," "gave . . . an appraising look," or "a flat look of appraisal that said I don't belong here."

Women with Disabilities

One of the most frequently mentioned forms of harassment by women with disabilities was scrutiny. As a woman with facial burn scars noted, these experiences could be extreme:

People stared a lot. One time I was sitting in a car outside Sears waiting for [her husband] Bill, and two couples came out, and one woman noticed me sitting in my "ski mask." The other three kept on going—but she crossed the parking lot and brought the three others back to look at me. They all stared into the car at me. Finally, one of the men walked over to a store and acted like he was looking in a store window—but there was no display in that store window. (Ton 1991)

A concern with mere presence in public places distinguishes people with disabilities as a group from all other groups. Crucial, of course, is how reliably or accurately a disability can be judged and supported. Some informants with disabilities expressed fear of becoming the stereotyped person with a disability who is locked away at home or abandoned in a nursing home, never being allowed to venture out of confinement (this is perhaps equivalent to an agoraphobic woman's fear). A visually impaired woman suggested that "Americans understand that public places are for everyone, they're for all strangers. But then you discover some are stranger than others. I've been told to 'Go home. Keep away!'" A woman with cerebral palsy noted that people with disabilities had been told "they didn't belong in public" and that people with disabilities were "locked away in cellars and attics before, and being poorly received in public is equal to trying to relegate us to the cellar or attic again."

It is not simply a matter of exclusionary practices that affect women (and men) with disabilities, it is also different evaluative practices. A first difference is that a woman with disability that is regarded as disfiguring can regularly be faulted on her appearance by men evaluators. The woman with extensive burn scars quoted above said she had not received many street remarks "as a woman, because I was neither very beautiful or very ugly, before my accident." Once she had been burned, however, her life in public places changed. Among other bald evaluations, she had had a man frankly tell her, "Lady, you look like you been hit by a Mack truck" (Ton 1991). A woman whose face had undergone reconstructive surgery and was still asymmetrical heard men tell her she looked like a cartoon or heard them address her as "Funny Face" or "Lumpy" (Roe 1991).

To women who have had these experiences, the usual etiquette and crime advice offered to women seem cynically given. One of a group of Indianapolis women with impaired mobility who meet regularly to share their concerns spoke of "an article from *Mademoiselle* that told you how to meet guys: Don't go out of the house unless you look gorgeous, talk to guys in the grocery store and the laundromat, be friendly to strange men, etcetera." When a friend read it to the group they "couldn't stop laughing. If ordinary women have these problems, what do you think we go through?" Because of evaluative practices that insult these women for having disabilities, they sometimes said that ostensibly complimentary street remarks and mild exploitations of presence were not offensive. Instead, these women said that mild public harassment could welcome them to a gender club, membership in which they were often denied: at the same time they were being publicly harassed, the man who harassed them was ignoring their disability. A woman with a disability might even cherish each event:

> I remember every single thing that's been said to me. Every whistle and "Pretty lady!" I can almost remember the day and place and time of each one. Once I even got pinched on my rear end—very tough to do, if the lady's wearing calipers.

Comments from men can be perplexing, however. Like the able-bodied woman, the woman with a disability can be shaken when she hears vulgarity, as was a woman walking on crutches, who was pleased when "a hunk smiled at me," but "frightened when he said, 'Nice jugs!' then grabbed at one breast." Or a man's comment will scrupulously ignore or deny a woman's disability in such a way as to make her feel a successful woman at the price of denying disability: "A man who told me, 'You're so pretty, you don't need that wheelchair,' showed me how far healthy people are from understanding what disability is.

I can be pretty *and* need a wheelchair. That's me: I *am* my disability, too."

Women with disabilities mentioned another difference: their public harassers customarily included able-bodied women and children as well as men harassers. As men's public harassment perpetuates men's right to define the situation in other areas and demonstrates men's ability to impose strength and evaluate appearance, so too does women's public harassment of women with disabilities often cast women harassers as religious advisers or enthused nurturers.

People with disabilities cannot always disguise their disabilities, of course. When they cannot, they are arguably different from the gay man who says he can, with will, seek to disguise his gestures, alter his voice, and display an "acceptable" wardrobe for the area in which he lives. At stake in the disguises of some people with disabilities is also a concern for experiencing oversolicitous aid they do not need; this is not a reported concern for lesbians or African-Americans except rarely, when it is apparently done from a desire to demonstrate how liberal the other person is. Although these three groups differ from women as situationally disadvantaged groups, all share use of some of the common tactics for managing troubles experienced in public places.

STRATEGIZING FOR THE FUTURE

Although I have discussed women's present strategies from the point of view of their possible effect on the woman's sense of self and the modifications she makes to her life, my analysis is not meant to suggest that there *are* alternate strategies now possible for women that would leave women in public places both safe and self-possessed. Indeed, the concern of many of the women I interviewed—as well, presumably, as many of the women who read the popular literature on crime prevention—was to avoid the chance of rape and subsequent murder at the hands of unknown men who would assault them in public or follow them from public places to their homes. To analyze the character of the situated selves that these women are told and believe they must present in public in order to prevent crime is by no means to denigrate those beliefs and that advice, it merely notes that along with those beliefs and advice comes what women themselves have sometimes noted to be sadly necessary measures: the effect of successfully eluding a rapist would of course be far better for a woman than the cost of any humiliation might be.

But very few of the strategies mentioned in chapter 6 are permanent ones, aiming to effect change within men—who are the primary architects of women's fear in public places. Women's own romanticization of public harassment plays an undeniable role in this process; even women who most resent public harassment sometimes do so because they expect compliments that they find are not forthcoming, or concentrate upon the appearance of the men they come in contact with, or blame other women for men's harassment. Women's romanticization of public harassment—their selection of high-status, attractive men from whom they say they do not resent harassment, their scorn for those who do not meet these standards—is more than a coping device, however. Since it effectively removes the sting from man-to-woman harassment, it also serves to neutralize the seriousness of whatever public harassment a woman herself commits. Thus, in the end, romanticization and rationales for the public harassment of women support, justify, and maintain the public harassment of lesbians and gays, the public harassment of races, and the scorn that can be heaped on the awkward. In short, rationalizing the public harassment of women shores up the incivility and danger we now see in our cities.

For change to come about, basic changes must be made in interpersonal relationships between women and men, as well as in the use we make of the core character of public-place interaction and communication. As presently constituted, we use this interaction and communication to allow and encourage men to invade every nook and cranny of women's presence.

Radford has suggested that the sum of the message of the public order is to suggest that a woman who is not seen to be controlled by one specific man can at will be controlled by any man who so wants (Radford 1987:43). This informal social control results in a wide scope of beliefs and actions by women, in response to the similarly wide band of behavior by men in public places, that Radford (1987:passim) has referred to as a continuum of sexual violence. Absorption in these crime-preventive strategies—even by women who evaluate them negatively or cynically—can be understood as a woman taking responsibility to ensure her own safety and captain her own fate. At the same time, these are all measures that implicitly enjoin the prospective victim to experience blameworthiness for any harm that does come her way, despite the clear-cut finding that there is nothing the rape victim does that is as significant as the rapist's interpretation of what she does (Amir 1971). Researchers have, of course, commonly written of women's responsibility for their own victimization (see Edwards 1987, for example), and criminologists have pointed out the varieties of and prevalence of victim typologies in both popular and social scientific belief systems. Here, as elsewhere, it can be argued that the folklore and media advice to women on the avoidance of victimization could detract attention from more widespread causes of crime, as well as from the true culpability of those who perpetrate crimes or add to women's terror. Particularistic preventive strategies for victims can blind individuals—victims included—to the attention that needs to be given to larger sociocultural preventive strategies that would block the occurrence of crime in the first place (Ledray 1986:218–219).

Feminist researchers especially have documented the aftereffects of rape (Burgess and Holmstrom 1974; Neiderbach 1985); we should now continue to expand our examination of the effects of the fear of rape more thoroughly. Certainly an overwhelming bolster for women's sense of vulnerability in public places is the fear of rape and related violence: It is impossible to state too strongly how constant the theme of fear was in interviews with women from every part of the country and from every social class, race, age, sexual preference, and occupational group. There was no topic of inquiry—from scrutinizing gaze to "flattering" street remarks—that did not actuate women's ultimate fear of rape and violence. In considering the vastly different ways in which women and men experience public places, fear of rape and related violence is central. This fear must be taught to and understood by men if public harassment of women is to change.

These effects are more specific than just saying that women commonly have an abiding fear of rape. They suggest that the fear is nurtured by the various advice systems women receive and that these advice systems, in turn, remove the responsibility for that fear from the men who threaten women not only with bodily harm, but with everyday "minor" terrorisms. Likewise, women's own romanticized interpretations of street remarks and exploitations of presence, as seen in the previous chapters, work to help women internalize responsibility for affecting and controlling men's general public harassment of women. A central aim of violent aggression is to influence the victim's behavior, and the fear of street harassment and crime fulfills this aim satisfactorily. Although these strategies may well serve to reduce crime and thus protect women in some cases, they also perpetuate the suggestion that women in public are quintessential subjects of harassment and can be seen as pawns for street commentary, targets of gaze, subjects of touch, lures for trailing and stalking, dupes of foolmaking—and victims of rape and violent crime. The character of the belief, etiquette and behavior norms, and advice is often to further deny that it is men who are the general vectors of public harassment. This denial is also perpetuated by the belief that street remarks are high-spirited compliments or duly deserved insults or the belief that trailing a woman is a tribute to her beauty or a result of her unwisely displayed allure. Yet women's stated beliefs about men's public harassment are often unambiguous and outraged; there is, in fact, little doubt that it is now men's place to discover for themselves how they can stifle and end their public harassment of women.

REFERENCES

Abramson, Joan. 1993. *Old Boys—New Women: Sexual Harassment in the Workplace*. New York: Praeger.

Abu-Lughod, Janet. 1971. *Cairo: 1001 Years of the City Victorious*. Princeton: Princeton University Press.

Abu-Lughod, Lila. 1979. "A Community of Secrets: The Separate World of Bedouin Women." *Signs* 10, 4:637–657.

———. 1986. *Veiled Sentiments: Honor and Poetry in a Bedouin Society*. Berkeley: University of California Press.

Abu Saud, Abeer. 1984. *Qatari Women: Past and Present*. New York: Longman.

Allen, Anita L. 1988. *Uneasy Access: Privacy for Women in a Free Society*. Totowa, N.J.: Rowman & Littlefield.

American Psychiatric Association. 1987. *Diagnostic and Statistical Manual of Mental Disorders*. 3d ed., rev. Washington, D.C.: American Psychiatric Association.

Amir, Menachem. 1971. *Patterns in Forcible Rape*. Chicago: University of Chicago Press.

Aresty, Esther. 1970. *The Best Behavior*. New York: Simon & Schuster.

Balkin, Stephen. 1979. "Victimization Rate, Safety, and Fear of Crime." *Social Problems* 26:343–358.

Barnes, Albert. 1971. *Fighting Crime!* Omaha: Published by the author.

Bart, Pauline, and Patricia H. O'Brien. 1984. "Stopping Rape: Successful Avoidance Strategies." *Signs* 10:83–101.

————. 1985. *Stopping Rape: Successful Survival Strategies.* New York: Pergamon.

Barthol, Robert G. 1979. *Protect Yourself.* Englewood Cliffs. N.J.: Prentice-Hall.

Bell, Derrick. 1993. *Faces at the Bottom of the Well.* New York: Basic Books.

Berger, Gilda. 1986. *Women, Work, and Wages.* New York: Franklin Watts.

Berman, Clifford. 1980. "Crime: How Not to Be a Victim." *Good Housekeeping,* September, 247.

Berne, Suzanne. 1993. "Traveling Close, Very Close, to Home: Adventure Is Less a Matter of Distance than a State of Mind." *The New York Times,* 4 July, 19.

Bertram, Camille. 1975. "Protection: How, When, Where, and What to Do." *Harper's Bazaar,* March, 83, 131.

Blauner, Bob. 1989. *Black Lives, White Lives: Three Decades of Race Relations in America.* Berkeley: University of California Press.

Bowlby, S. R. 1984. "Planning for Women to Shop in Postwar Britain." *Environment and Planning* 2:179–199.

Brownmiller, Susan. 1974. *Against Our Will: Men, Women, and Rape.* New York: Simon & Schuster.

Brunvand, Jan Harold. 1981. *The Vanishing Hitchhiker: American Urban Legends and Their Meanings.* New York: Norton.

Burg, Kathleen Keefe. 1979. *The Womanly Art of Self-Defense.* New York: A&W Visual Library.

Burgess, Ann W., and Lynda Lytle Holstrom. 1974. "Rape Trauma Syndrome." *American Journal of Psychiatry* 131:981–985.

"Censor." c. 1899. *Don't; or, Directions for Avoiding Improprieties in Conduct and Common Errors of Speech.* London: Walter Scott.

Chernin, Kim. 1981. *The Obsession: Reflections on the Tyranny of Slenderness.* New York: Harper & Row.

Cherry, Mike. 1974. *On High Steel.* New York: Ballantine.

Clemente, Frank, and Michael B. Kleiman. 1977. "Fear of Crime in the United States." *Social Forces* 56:520–522.

Cohen, Bernard. 1980. *Deviant Street Networks: Prostitution in New York City.* Lexington, Mass.: Heath.

Compton, Thomas. 1989. "Discovering Disability as a Historical Phenomenon." Paper presented at annual meeting of Society for Disability Studies, June 21–24, Denver.

Corinth, Kay, and Mary Sargent. 1970. *Male Manners.* New York: David McKay.

Coser, Lewis A. 1988. *A Handful of Thistles: Collected Papers in Moral Conviction.* New Brunswick, N.J.: Transaction Books.

Cullen, Tom A. 1965. *When London Walked in Terror.* Boston: Houghton Mifflin.

Cummins, Cynthia. 1987. "Fight, Not Flight: Throw a Few Punches of Your Own." *Women's Sports & Fitness,* December, 30.

Dale, Daphne. 1891. *Our Manners and Social Customs.* Philadelphia: Elliot & Beezley.

Damrosch, Barbara. 1975. "The Sex Ray." *The Village Voice,* 7 April, 77.

Davenport, Gwen. 1959. *The Tall Girls' Handbook.* Garden City, N.Y.: Doubleday.

Davis, Angela. 1974. *Angela Davis: An Autobiography.* New York: Random House.

Davis, Larry E. 1993. *Black and Single: Meeting and Choosing a Partner Who's Right for You.* Chicago: Noble Press.

Davis, Phillip W. 1991. "Stranger Intervention into Child Punishment in Public Places." *Social Problems* 38, 2 (May):227–246.

Deegan, Mary Jo. 1987. "The Female Pedestrian: The Dramaturgy of Structural and Experiential Barriers in the Street." *Man-Environment Systems,* 17, 3–4 (May–June):79–86.

Dobell, Elizabeth R. 1977. "Self-Defense." *Seventeen,* April, 194–195, 216–217.

"Doe, Jane." 1991. Unpublished student paper.

"Doe, Mary." 1992. Unpublished student paper.

Dormen, Lesley. 1990. "The Highs of Being Without a Man." *Mademoiselle,* March, 155.

Dorsky, Susan. 1986. *Women of 'Amran: A Middle Eastern Ethnographic Study.* Salt Lake City: University of Utah Press.

Doyle, Bertram Wilbur. 1971. *The Etiquette of Race Relations in the South.* New York: Schocken.

Drake, St. Clair, and Horace Cayton. 1945. *Black Metropolis.* New York: Harcourt, Brace.

Duckett, Joy. 1982. "Rape Prevention." *Essence,* September, 68.

Earle, Alice Morse. 1969. *Curious Punishments of Bygone Days.* Montclair, N.J.: Patterson Smith.

Edwards, Susan. 1987. "'Provoking Her Own Demise.'" In Jalna Hamner and Mary Maynard, eds., *Women, Violence, and Social Control*. Atlantic Highlands, N.J.: Humanities.

Ellis, Albert, and Albert Abarbanel. 1973. *The Encyclopedia of Sexual Behavior*. New York: J. Aronson.

Enjeu, C., and E. Save. 1974. "The City: Off Limits to Women." *Liberation*, July/August, 9–13.

Farrar, Mrs. John. 1849. *The Young Lady's Friend*. New York: Samuel S. & William Wood.

Farrell, James T. 1965 [1935]. *Studs Lonigan*. New York: New American Library.

Feagin, Joe R. 1991. "The Continuing Significance of Race: Anti-Black Discrimination in Public Places." *American Sociological Review* 56:101–116.

Feagin, Joe R., and Clairece Booher Feagin. 1978. *Discrimination American Style: Institutional Racism and Sexism*. Englewood Cliffs, N.J.: Prentice-Hall.

Feigelbaum, William. 1974. "Peeping: The Pattern of Voyeurism Among Construction Workers." *Urban Culture* 3 (April):35–44.

Feminist Intervention Group. 1974. *So You Want to Date a Feminist: A Complete Guide*. New York: Feminist Intervention Group.

Ferree, Almia Jo. 1991. Unpublished student paper.

Field, Jill Nevel. 1980. "Playing It Safe: At Home, on the Street, in Your Car, on the Bus or Subway." *Mademoiselle*, September, 112, 120.

Ford, Charlotte. 1988. *Etiquette: Charlotte Ford's Guide to Modern Manners*. New York: Clarkson Potter.

Fox, M. B. 1985. "Access to Workplaces for Women." *Ekistics* 52:69–76.

Francis, Mark. 1989. "Control as a Dimension of Public-Space Quality." In Irwin Altman and Ervin Zube, eds., *Public Places and Spaces*. New York: Plenum.

Franck, Karen A. 1985. "Social Construction of the Physical Environment." *Sociological Focus* 18:143–170.

Francoeur, Robert T. 1991. *A Descriptive Dictionary and Atlas of Sexology*. New York: Greenwood.

Fry, Jane. 1974. *Being Different: The Autobiography of Jane Fry*. Collected by Robert Bogdan. New York: Wiley.

Gallatin, Martin V. 1987. *Lover Shopping for Men and Women: How to Be Married One Year from Today*. New York: Shapolsky.

Garber, Marjorie. 1993. *Vested Interests: Cross-Dressing and Cultural Anxiety.* New York: Routledge.

Gardner, Carol Brooks. 1980. "Passing By: Street Remarks, Address Rights, and Urban Woman." *Sociological Inquiry* 50, 3–4:328–356.

———. 1983. "Aspects of Gender Behavior in Public Places in a Small Southwestern City." Ph.D. dissertation, University of Pennsylvania.

———. 1986. "Public Aid." *Urban Life* 15, 2:286–301.

———. 1988. "Access Information." *Social Problems* 35, 3 (October):384–397.

———. 1992. "Kinship Claims: Affiliation and the Disclosure of Stigma in Public Places." *Perspectives on Social Problems* 4:203–228.

———. 1994. "Public Harassment." Unpublished manuscript.

Gebhard, Paul H. 1965. *Sex Offenders: An Analysis of Types.* New York: Harper & Row.

Geng, Veronica. 1979. "Scorn Not the Street Compliment!" In Helen Gurley Brown, ed., *Cosmopolitan's New Etiquette Guide.* North Hollywood, Calif.: Wilshire.

Glamour. 1969. "Do You Act Like a Beauty?" January, 138–139.

———. 1984. "Verbal Abuse on the Street: How to Talk Back." February, 118–119, 123.

Glanz, Larry, and Robert H. Phillips. 1994. *How to Start a Romantic Encounter: Where to Go to Find Love and What to Say When You Find It.* Garden City Park, N.Y.: Avery Publishing Group.

Goffman, Erving. 1959. *The Presentation of Self in Everyday Life.* Garden City, N.Y.: Doubleday.

———. 1963. *Behavior in Public Places.* Glencoe, Ill.: Free Press.

———. 1971. *Relations in Public.* New York: Basic Books.

Goldman, Marion S. 1981. *Gold Diggers and Silver Miners: Prostitution and Social Life on the Comstock Lode.* Ann Arbor: University of Michigan Press.

Gould, Stephen Jay. 1988. "Editorial." *Natural History,* December, 12–14, 16–17.

Gove, Walter, et al. 1980. "Playing Dumb: A Form of Impression Management with Undesirable Side Effects." *Social Psychology Quarterly* 43, 1:89–102.

Grahame, Kamini Maraj. 1985. "Sexual Harassment." In Connie Guberman and Margie Wolfe, eds., *No Safe Place.* Toronto: Women's Press.

Grayson, Betty, and Morris I. Stein. 1981. "Attracting Assault: Victim's Non-verbal Cues." *Journal of Communication* 31, 1 (Winter):68–75.

Gregory, Susan. 1970. *Hey, White Girl!* New York: Norton.

Grenfell, Joyce. 1976. *Joyce Grenfell Requests the Pleasure.* London: Futura.

Griffith, Liddon R. 1978. *Mugging: You Can Protect Yourself.* Englewood Cliffs, N.J.: Prentice-Hall.

Hair, Robert A., and Samm Sinclair Baker. 1970. *How to Protect Yourself.* New York: Stein & Day.

Hall, Captain Basil. 1827–1828. *Travels in North America,* vol. 2. Austria: Akademische Druck- u. Verlaganstalt.

Hanson, Dian. 1982. "34 Ways to Approach a New Man." *New Woman,* October, 56–57, 59–60, 62–63.

Harding, Susan. 1975. "Women and Words in a Spanish Village." In Rayna R. Reiter, ed., *Toward an Anthropology of Women.* New York: Monthly Review Press.

Harper's Bazaar. 1985. "Lock Yourself Up." April, 80, 84.

Hartley, Florence. 1860. *The Ladies' Book of Etiquette, and Manual of Politeness.* Philadelphia: G. G. Evans.

Hartmann, H. 1981. "The Family as Locus of Gender, Family, and Political Structure." *Signs* 6:366–394.

Hayden, Dolores. 1981. *The Grand Domestic Revolution: A History of Feminist Designs for American Homes, Neighborhoods, and Cities.* Cambridge, Mass.: MIT Press.

Heath, Linda. 1984. "Impact of Newspaper Crime Reports on Fear of Crime." *Journal of Personality and Social Psychology* 47:263–274.

Henley, Nancy. 1975. "Power, Sex, and Nonverbal Communication." In Barrie Thorne and Nancy Henley, eds., *Language and Sex.* Rowley, Mass.: Newbury House.

Higgins, Paul C. 1980. *Outsiders in a Hearing World: A Sociology of Deafness.* Beverly Hills: Sage.

Hill, Doug, and Jeff Weingrad. 1987. *Saturday Night: A Backstage History of Saturday Night Live.* New York: Beech Tree Books.

Hochschild, Arlie. 1991. "Gender Codes in Women's Advice Books." In Stephen H. Riggins, ed., *Beyond Goffman: Studies on Communication, Institution, and Social Interaction.* New York: Mouton de Gruyter.

Hummon, David. 1985. "Urban Ideology as a Cultural System." *Journal of Cultural Geography* 5, 2:1–15.

Israel, Richard J. 1985. "Jewish Haute Cuisine." *Hadassah,* January, 38–39.

Jay, Martin. 1993. *Downcast Eyes: The Denigration of Vision in Twentieth-Century French Thought.* Berkeley: University of California Press.

Kane, Paula. 1974. *Sex Objects in the Sky.* Chicago: Follett.

Kaye, Elizabeth. 1985. "Your Complete Guide to Self-Defense: Preventing Rape and Robbery." *Harper's Bazaar,* April, 72, 74.

Kazin, Alfred. 1978. *New York Jew.* New York: Knopf.

Krupp, Charla. 1978. "Solving Your Problem: 84 Ways to Feel Safer." *Mademoiselle,* October, 142–143, 146, 152.

Lamb, Charles. 1902. *Charles Lamb: Selections from His Essays, Letters, and Verses.* New York: Doubleday and McClure.

Lancaster, R. N. 1980. "Subject Honor and Object Shame: The Construction of Male Homosexuality and Stigma in Nicaragua." *Ethnology* 27:111–125.

Lapin, Lee. 1983. *How to Get Anything on Anybody.* Port Townsend, Wash.: Loompanics Unlimited.

Ledray, Linda. 1986. *Recovering from Rape.* New York: Henry Holt.

Lee, J. A. 1977. "Going Public: A Study in the Sociology of Homosexual Liberation." *Journal of Homosexuality* 3:49–78.

Lesbian Feminist Liberation. 1974. "Media: Of Ogling and TV News." *Majority Report,* 3 October, 7.

Lessing, Doris. 1974. *The Summer before the Dark.* New York: Knopf.

Lofland, Lyn H. 1973. *A World of Strangers: Order and Action in Urban Public Settings.* New York: Basic Books.

———. 1984. "Women and Urban Public Space." *Women and Environments* 6:12–14.

Lomack, Craig. 1966. *How to Protect Yourself with Karate.* New York: Pocket.

MacKenzie, S. 1985. "No One Seems to Go to Work Anymore." *Canadian Women's Studies* 5:5–8.

MacKinnon, Catharine. 1979. *Sexual Harassment of Working Women: A Case of Sex Discrimination.* New Haven: Yale University Press.

———. 1993. *Only Words.* Cambridge, Mass.: Harvard University Press.

MacLean, Judy. 1993. "A Not So Modest Proposal for Safer Streets." *Funny Times,* March, 1, 5.

Manning, Mrs. c. 1880. *Modern Manners.* Boston: n.p.

Marks, Isaac M., and E. R. Herst. 1970. "A Survey of 1,200 Agoraphobics in Britain." *Social Psychiatry* 5, 1:16–24.

Martin, Judith. 1982. *Miss Manners' Guide to Excruciatingly Correct Behavior.* New York: Warner.

McCall's. 1982. "Makeup on the Run." February, 22.

McLaurin, Melton A. 1987. *Separate Pasts: Growing Up White in the Segregated South.* Athens: University of Georgia Press.

Mehlman, Peter, 1987. "Male Guilt." *Glamour,* April, 332.

Mernissi, Fatima. 1987. *Beyond the Veil: Male-Female Dynamics in Modern Muslim Society.* Bloomington: Indiana University Press.

Millman, Marcia. 1980. *Such a Pretty Face.* New York: Norton.

Minai, Naila. 1981. *Women in Islam: Tradition and Transition in the Middle East.* New York: Seaview.

Mohsenzadeh, Stephanie. 1991. Unpublished student paper.

Monkerud, Donald, and Mary Heiny. 1980. *Self-Defense for Women.* Dubuque: William C. Brown.

Mosedale, Susan. 1986. "A Crime-Stopping Scent for Women?" *Glamour,* January, 105.

Murray, Frederick Pemberton. 1980. *A Stutterer's Story.* Danville, Ill.: Interstate.

Navarro, Mireya. 1990. "For Busy Storeowner, Nearby Protests Have Raised Fear of Misunderstanding." *The New York Times,* 17 May, A-10.

Neiderbach, Shelley. 1985. *Invisible Wounds: Crime Victims Speak.* New York: Haworth Press.

New York Times, The. 1991. "Women in Penn Station Stung by Pin Wielder." 15 February, A-16.

Nietzsche, Friedrich. 1982. *Daybreak: Thoughts on the Prejudices of Morality.* New York: Cambridge University Press.

Oates, Joyce Carol. 1973. *Do With Me What You Will.* New York: Vanguard.

O'Connor, Margaret, and Jane Silverman. 1989. *Finding Love: Creative Strategies for Finding Your Ideal Mate.* New York: Crown.

Office of the Inspector General, Department of Defense. 1993. *The Tailhook Report: The Official Inquiry into the Events of Tailhook '91.* New York: St. Martin's.

Otis, Leah L. 1985. *Prostitution in Medieval Society: The History of an Urban Institution in Languedoc.* Chicago: University of Chicago Press.

Packer, Jacklyn. 1986. "Sex Differences in the Perception of Street Harassment." *Women and Therapy* 7:331–338.

Peck, Arlene G. 1978. "The Southern Jewish American Princess in the

Fabulous Fifties." In Edith Blicksilver, ed., *The Ethnic American Woman: Problems, Protests, Lifestyle.* Dubuque: Kendall/Hunt.

Pepitone, Lena, and William Stadiem. 1979. *Marilyn Monroe Confidential.* New York: Simon & Schuster.

Perry, Michael. 1983. "Strategies for Combatting Crime in the Parks." *Parks and Recreation,* September, 49–51, 67.

Pickering, Michael C. V. 1983. *A Manual for Women's Self-Defense.* North Palm Beach, Fla.: The Athletic Institute.

Pickup, L. 1984. "Women's Gender Role and Its Influence on Travel Behavior." *Built Environment* 10:61–68.

Pizan, Christine de. 1983 [1405]. *The City of Women.* Harmondsworth, England: Penguin.

Plath, Sylvia. 1982. *The Journals of Sylvia Plath.* New York: Dial.

Porath, Ellen. 1982. "Fight Rude Remarks . . . But Don't Smile." *Contemporary Magazine* (supplement to *The Denver Post*), 26 October, 41.

Post, Elizabeth. 1969. *Emily Post's Etiquette.* New York: Funk & Wagnalls.

Pred, Allan R. 1990. *Making Histories and Constructing Human Geographies.* Boulder: Westview.

Pynchon, Thomas. 1973. *V.* New York: Bantam.

Radford, Jill. 1987. "Policing Male Violence—Policing Women." In Jalna Hamner and Mary Maynard, eds., *Women, Violence, and Social Control.* Atlantic Highlands, N.J.: Humanities.

Redfield, Robert. 1953. *The Primitive World and Its Transformations.* Ithaca: Cornell University Press.

Reich, Charles. 1966. "Police Questioning of Law-Abiding Citizens." *Yale Law Journal* 75, 7 (June):1162–1163.

Reiter, Rayna R. 1975. "Men and Women in the South of France: Public and Private Domains." In Rayna R. Reiter, ed., *Toward an Anthropology of Women.* New York: Monthly Review Press.

Rickey, Carrie. 1986. "The Errand Outfit: What to Wear to the Corner Store." *Mademoiselle,* March, 74.

Riemer, Jeffrey W. 1979. *Hard Hats.* Beverly Hills: Sage.

Riger, Stephanie, and Margaret T. Gordon. 1981. "The Fear of Rape: A Study in Social Control." *Journal of Social Issues* 37:71–92.

Robboy, Howard, and E. Eames. 1980. "British Midlands and Its Punjabi Migrants." In P. Saran and E. Eames, eds., *New Ethnics: Asian Indians in the United States.* New York: Praeger.

———. 1981. "Not Welcome: British Ethnocentrism and Punjabi Migrants." *International Journal of Contemporary Sociology* 1–2 (January and April): 97–101.

Robinson, Jeffrey C. 1989. *The Walk: Notes on a Romantic Image.* Norman: University of Oklahoma Press.

Rockwood, Marcia, and Mary Thom. 1979. "Making Your Block, Office, Parking Lot, Community Rape-Proof." *Ms.,* March, 79–82.

Roe, Mary. 1991. Unpublished student paper.

Rule, Ann. 1986. *The Stranger Beside Me.* New York: Norton.

Russ, Lavinia. 1972. *A High Old Time.* New York: Saturday Review Press.

Sacks, Harvey. 1972. "Membership Categorization Devices." In David Sudnow, ed., *Studies in Social Interaction.* New York: Free Press.

Scharff, Virginia. 1991. *Taking the Wheel: Women and the Coming of the Motor Age.* New York: Free Press.

Schefer, Dorothy. 1985. "An Interview with Lisa Sliwa." *Vogue,* March, 496.

Schraub, Susan. 1979. "*Bazaar*'s Anti-Rape Handbook." *Harper's Bazaar,* March, 152–153, 169.

Scribner, Marilyn. 1988. *Free to Fight Back.* Wheaton, Ill.: Harold Shaw.

Sillitoe, Alan. 1959. *The Loneliness of the Long-Distance Runner.* New York: Knopf.

Sims, Calvin. 1990. "Black Shoppers Call Korean Merchants Hostile and Unfair." *The New York Times,* 17 May, A-10.

Smith, Dorothy. 1991. *The Everyday World as Problematic.* Boston: Northeastern University Press.

Sommerfield, Diana. 1986. *Single, Straight Men: 106 Guaranteed Places to Find Them.* New York: St. Martin's.

Spradley, James, and Brenda Mann. 1975. *The Cocktail Waitress: Woman's Work in a Man's World.* New York: Wiley.

Stanko, Elizabeth. 1985. *Intimate Intrusions: Women's Experience of Male Violence.* London: Routledge & Kegan Paul.

———. 1990. *Everyday Violence: How Women and Men Experience Sexual and Physical Danger.* London: Pandora.

Stanley, Liz, and Sue Wise. 1987. *Georgie Porgie: Sexual Harassment in Everyday Life.* London: Pandora.

Stansell, Christine. 1986. *City of Women: Sex and Class in New York, 1789–1860.* New York: Knopf.

Staples, Robert. 1981. *The World of Black Singles: Changing Patterns of Male/ Female Relations.* Westport, Conn.: Greenwood.

Starr, Joyce, and Donald E. Carns. 1972. "Singles in the City." *Trans-Action* 9:43–48.

Stevenson, Robert Louis. 1907. *Songs of Travel.* Score by Ralph Vaughan Williams. London: Boosey and Hawkes.

Stewart, Marjabelle Young. 1987. *The New Etiquette: Real Manners for Real People in Real Situations—An A-to-Z Guide.* New York: St. Martin's.

Stimpson, Catherine R., E. Dixler, M. J. Nelson, and K. B. Yatrakis, eds. 1981. *Women and the American City.* Chicago: University of Chicago Press.

Suttles, Gerald D. 1968. *The Social Order of the Slum.* Chicago: University of Chicago Press.

Talamini, J. T. "Transvestitism: Expression of a Second Self." *Free Inquiry in Creative Sociology* 9:147–160.

Taub, Diane E. 1982. "Public Sociability of College-Aged Homosexuals: The Gay Bar and the Cruise Block." *Sociological Spectrum* 2:291–305.

Tegner, Bruce. 1965. *Bruce Tegner's Complete Book of Self-Defense.* New York: Bantam.

Thomas, Laurence. 1990. "Next Life, I'll Be White." *The New York Times,* 13 August, A-15.

Thompson, Sandra. 1979. "Children Welcome—If They're Neither Seen Nor Heard." *Ms.,* November, 122.

Ton, Mary Ellen. 1991. Unpublished student paper.

Trollope, Anthony. 1991 [1864–1865]. *Can You Forgive Her?* New York: Oxford University Press.

Trollope, Mrs. 1832. *Domestic Manners of the Americans.* 2 vols. London: Whittaker, Treacher.

Tuan, Yi-Fu. 1982. *Segmented Worlds and Self: Group Life and Individual Consciousness.* Minneapolis: University of Minnesota Press.

Vanderbilt, Amy. 1972. *Amy Vanderbilt's Etiquette.* Garden City, N.Y.: Doubleday.

Van Der Meer, Antonia. 1990. "You *Are* Somebody When Nobody Loves You." *Mademoiselle,* March, 155–156.

Verta Mae. 1972. *Thursdays and Every Other Sunday Off.* Garden City, N.Y.: Doubleday.

Wachs, Eleanor. 1988. *Crime-Victim Stories: New York City's Urban Folklore.* Bloomington: Indiana University Press.

Walum, Laurel Richardson. 1974. "The Changing Door Ceremony." *Urban Life* 3:17–36.

Warnock, Kathleen. 1987. "I Want to Be as Large as Life." *Ms.,* September, 6.

Warr, Mark. 1985. "Fear of Rape Among Urban Women." *Social Problems* 32, 3:239–250.

Wax, Murray. 1965. "Themes in Cosmetics and Grooming." In Mary Ellen Roach and Joanne B. Eichler, eds., *Dress, Adornment, and the Social Order.* New York: Wiley.

Westerman, Marty. 1992. *How to Flirt.* Los Angeles: Price, Stern.

Whyte, William H. 1980. *The Social Life of Small Urban Places.* Washington, D.C.: Conservation Foundation.

Williamson, Nancy. 1971. "The Case for Studied Ugliness." *Second Wave* 1:10–11.

Wilson, Julie. 1977. "How to Protect Yourself." *Harper's Bazaar,* March, 93, 151.

Wolf, Naomi. 1993. *Fire with Fire.* New York: Random House.

Wolfe, Tom. 1987. *The Bonfire of the Vanities.* New York: Farrar, Straus.

Woodward, C. Vann. 1955. *The Strange Career of Jim Crow.* New York: Oxford University Press.

Workman, Diane. 1991. Unpublished student paper.

Wylie, Laurence. 1975. *Village in the Vaucluse.* Cambridge, Mass.: Harvard University Press.

Young, John H. 1882. *Our Deportment; or, The Manners, Conduct, and Dress of the Most Refined Society.* Detroit: F. B. Dickerson.

Zauberman, Renee. 1982. "La Peur du crime et la recherche." *Annee sociologique* 32:415–438.

INDEX

Designer: U.C. Press Staff
Compositor: Prestige Typography
Text: 11/15 Granjon
Display: Granjon
Printer: Braun-Brumfield, Inc.
Binder: Braun-Brumfield, Inc.